Jewish Schizophrenia in the Land of Israel

David J. Forman

gefen נפן
publishing house בית הוצאה לאור
JERUSALEM ◆ NEW YORK

Copyright © Gefen Publishing House
Jerusalem 2000/5760

Typesetting: Marzel A.S. – Jerusalem
Cover Design: Studio Paz, Jerusalem

1 3 5 7 9 8 6 4 2

Gefen Publishing House   Gefen Books
POB 36004, Jerusalem 91360, Israel   12 New Street Hewlett, NY 11557, USA
972-2-538-0247 • isragefe@netvision.net.il   516-295-2805 • gefenbooks@compuserve.com
www.israelbooks.com
Printed in Israel   *Send for our free catalogue*

ISBN 965-229-261-3

Library of Congress Cataloging-in-Publication Data
Forman, David J., 1944-
Jewish Schizophrenia in the Land of Israel / David J. Forman
Includes bibliographical references
1. National characteristics, Israeli. 2. Israel—Social conditions. 3. Israel—Politics and
government. I Title
DS11.3.F67 2000 • 956.9405'4—dc21 • CIP Number: 00-062273

For my Family

My wife,
Judith

My children,
Tamar & Michael
Liat & Eran
Shira
Orly

"Without Family, No Nation Can Be Made"
Zionist Philosopher, A.D. Gordon (1856-1922)

Also by David J. Forman

Israel on Broadway, America: Off-Broadway — Jews in the New Millennium
The Israel-Lebanon War: Reflections of a Participant
Finding a Religious Peace in Jerusalem
Diary of a Mad Seminarian

CONTENTS

PART TWO: THE MICRO or "You say Potato, I say Pot*ah*to"

ACKNOWLEDGMENTS

For me, the experience of writing a book serves as a constant reminder of how fortunate I am to have had teachers, friends and family from whom I have learned so much. Their influence on my life has played itself out in a myriad of ways that I could never fully articulate or fully acknowledge. So it is with genuine appreciation that I pay tribute to some of the people who have helped me in the writing of this book.

Wally (Ben) Smoke is one of my oldest and dearest friends whose creative and inventive poetry and prose warrant a book of their own. He painstakingly read through the manuscript in its developmental stages. He served a dual role. As a writer himself, he was able to help me fine-tune much of the book's text, and as the director of a social-work department in a mental health hospital, he was able to give me insights into understanding the complex world of schizophrenia. I am truly grateful to him.

Avi Levine, Shaul Feinberg and Lee Diamond each perused sections of the book prior to its completion. Their comments, along with the encouragement of Larry Jackofsky and Richie Address, were vital to my writing of this volume. Stanley and Marlene Ringler and Joshua and Maxine Haberman may recognize themselves in the book, as I included the experiences they encountered upon moving to Israel. I thank Hank Skirball for his contribution to the introduction.

I also want to thank my copy editor, Ms. Esther Herskovics. Her keen professional insights can be felt throughout this work. I am particularly grateful to Ilan and Dror Greenfield, the publishers of Gefen Publishing House. As with my first book, they have served as enthusiastic supporters. My thanks not only extend to them, but also to the entire staff at Gefen. Their blend of the personal and the professional accords a writer an environment that helps to serve his or her creative energies.

I wrote this book as a follow-up to a previous one, *Israel on Broadway;*

America: Off-Broadway — Jews in the New Millennium (Gefen Publishing House, Jerusalem-New York, 1998). From the moment I finished writing that book, the idea for a second installment was born. The question was how to find the time for such a demanding venture, as I would not enjoy the luxury of a sabbatical, which provided me the leisure to write the first book.

When I was engaged in that undertaking, my family would often complain that I spent too much time locked away in my study, ignoring family responsibilities. Therefore, the idea that I would embark on another literary journey, without being on sabbatical, but rather fully employed, did not necessarily excite everyone in my home. Yet, as with the first book, as soon as my wife and children saw me sitting at the computer, eagerly and happily jotting down notes, looking up quotes and writing new chapters, they enthusiastically encouraged me.

And so it is to them that I dedicate this book, not only for their continued support, but also because of their subjective pride in virtually anything I try to accomplish. No husband or father could ask for more.

May, 2000 — Iyar, 5760
Jerusalem

PART ONE
THE MACRO

or

"You say tomato,
I say tom*ah*to"

INTRODUCTION

Comedian Woody Allen claimed: "I was expelled from university for cheating on my metaphysics exam. I was caught looking into the soul of the person sitting next to me."[1] If one looked into the soul of an Israeli, one would find it broken down into a thousand and one different particles. The thesis of this book is that Israelis live among paradoxes. They are not just split down the middle, they can be dissected into a multitude of divisions. While at times a myriad of approaches to issues in Israeli life may bring about a creative tension, for the most part the complexties of the Israeli personality hamper any decision making process. The words of the great Jewish medieval philosopher Maimonides[2] ring true: "The soul has health and sickness just as the body." In order to guarantee that the soul does not become subject to the same illness that the body can suffer, "one must rule over the soul, and hand it to the intellect" (*Shmuel Hanagid*[3]).

Israelis are always doing battle with themselves. Body and soul, mind and matter, intellect and emotion seem to work at cross purposes. Israelis are forever struggling to harmonize the poles that exist within them — with little success. Viennese pyschiatrist, Victor Frankl, in his book, *The Unconscious God*, developed a theory, which recognizes the possibility of God having access to us through our conscience. He wrote: "Conscience would be ineffective if it is only me speaking to myself. Conscience is experienced as a dialogue, and not as a monologue." Anyone who has experienced "pangs of conscience" knows the tension of conflict, with the ego contesting and resisting the pull of a commanding sense of "what I ought to do" with what, in fact, "I actually should do." There is an "I" within me that wants the opposite of another "I" within me; the two cannot be identical.

---

1. From one of his rare live performances at Mr. Kelly's, Chicago, 1964.
2. Moses Ben Maimon, also known as the Rambam (1138-1204), was a codifier, philosopher, and physician — the outstanding Jewish personality of the Middle Ages.
3. Shmuel Ben Yosef HaLevi HaNagid (993-1056) was one of the great Jewish poets of Spain.

Herein lies the source of what this author has described as "Israel's schizophrenia." One "I" pulls in one direction while another "I" pulls in the opposite direction and then a third and fourth "I" pull in yet other directions. When this happens, all hell can break loose. Is this stretching the point? Are internal and perpetual contradictions the stuff of a "schizophrenic" personality?

Schizophrenia is a serious and debilitating illness that afflicts approximately one percent of the world's population. It is currently understood as a brain disease, which manifests serious psychotic symptoms. The causes of this illness may include everything from a possible chemical imbalance to bad parenting. It is a mental disorder marked by internal contradictions resulting in "split or even multiple" personalities. Fantasies and delusions govern the personality so that behavior can be out of keeping with reality — oftentimes resulting in unpredictable and irrational thoughts and actions.

The author wishes to emphasize that the **clinical use of the word schizophrenia is not employed in this book**. Despite the technical definition of schizophrenia, the term schizophrenic is mostly used colloquially. In common usage, the schizophrenic person is considered one who is obsessed with internal (and eternal) conflicts, forever contradicting him or herself. **It is the colloquial usage of the term schizophrenia to which this book will refer.** "Schizophrenia in the Land of Israel" should be understood strictly as a metaphor for a social psychology that the author has drawn from Jewish life in Israel. It is more accurate to speak of schizophrenic tendencies that occur with seeming regularity in the Land of Israel. Therefore to help the reader, from this point on, when the word "schizophrenia" or "schizophrenic" appears as a noun, it will be surrounded with quotation marks. Such will not be the case when referring to its colloquial use as an adjective, as in one's schizophrenic tendencies or leanings or approach, or as in the schizophrenic mind.

Socially, "schizophrenia" carries a great stigma for the individual afflicted, and for his or her family. The furthering of this stigma is the furthest thing from the author's mind. And so, throughout the book, the author points to certain similarities that Jewish social existence has with what psychiatry calls "neurotic features." This sometimes includes difficulties in distinguishing between the real and the unreal, as well as displaying contradictory kinds of thinking, grandiose thinking, sometimes aggressive behavior, sometimes withdrawn behavior and sometimes, simply, incomprehensible behavior. It includes being sometimes hopelessly confused and oftentimes off-balance as one "I" squares off against another "I." All these manifestations of "schizophrenia" should be understood on the broadest social plane, and not necessarily from the standpoint of each individual. Ultimately, they should be understood as a hint of a national character rather than a definitive statement of a particular personality.

Yet, in spite of the contradictions of Jewish life in the Land of Israel (or because of them), let there be no mistake: one's feelings for Israel and the Jewish people engender great pride, because Israel and the Jewish people have a long history of some of the bravest and most sane behavior in an otherwise often insane world.

The Jewish people have always been faced with inherent contradictions. The reason that schizophrenic tendencies have plagued the Jewish people from their earliest stages of growth is rooted in the ultimate theological question: What is God's role in the historical development of the Jews? Taking into account the colloquial understanding of "schizophrenia," for the Jew, this theological question, which is indeed eternal, produces powerful internal conflicts that often result in contradictions, inconsistencies and incongruities.

Jews have been taught that God is intimately involved in their history — from their allegorical (or factual) beginnings as defined in the creation stories to the appearance of their patriarchal ancestors (as recounted three times a day in their daily prayers), through their historical "coming-of-age" as a people somewhere in the Sinaitic wilderness, to the monarchies of David and Solomon (each of whom was a most contradictory personality in and of himself), and, some would say, until the "miraculous" reestablishment of the sovereign Jewish state of Israel in 1948 after almost two thousand years of dispersion.

Regarding Creation, as would befit a "schizophrenic," even here there are two conflicting versions of the birth of man and woman: 1) "And God said: Let us make man in our image, in our likeness... So God created man in His image — in the image of God did He create him, male and female did He create them" (*Genesis* 1:26-28) and 2) "And God formed man from the dust of the earth and blew into his nostrils the breath of life and man became a living soul... Then the Lord God caused a heavy sleep to overcome man, and as he slept God took one of his ribs and then closed up his flesh. And the Lord God fashioned the rib that He took from man into a woman..." (*Genesis* 2:7, 21-22). With this sort of bifurcated beginning, is it any wonder that a Jew (or anyone who believes in the Creation) should be confused?

So the real theological contradiction for a Jew manifests itself in the role God plays in the history of the Jewish people. Either a Jew believes God is intimately involved in the history of the Jewish people or does not. The accounts of Creation, as contradictory as they might be, indicate that God is indeed intimately involved in our lives. What could be more intimate than being the One who gave birth to us?

On the strength of the Creation narrative itself, God has become the object of worship. Since the entire Old Testament is a record of God's "guiding hand" in the onward march of the Jews throughout the biblical era — thus setting the stage for the Almighty's continual involvement with the Jewish people — the two-fold question as to whether God is or is not intimately involved in the lives of the Jewish people must now be sharply (perhaps dramatically) posed. If God is the object of worship, and is intimately involved in the history of the Jewish people, how can a Jew pray to a God who wantonly inflicts cruelty (or allows cruelty to be inflicted) upon the Jewish people — as the death of six million Jews in the Holocaust would suggest; and on the other hand, if God is not intimately involved in the history of the Jewish people, why pray to a Divine Being?

There is no facile way by which a Jew can answer these questions. Blind faith in a God whose mysterious ways mortals cannot possibly understand will not do for the modern Jew. Jews are too rational to be satisfied with such a seemingly easy solution. While a middle path may be sought between these two extremes and a myriad of explanations may be posited for God's involvement in the lives of the Jewish people, or the lack thereof, personally and collectively, these two competing theological world-views are always tugging at the Jewish soul. And so Jews live with a theological split personality that filters down into their every day life.

The modern state of Israel, which possesses the only self-contained Jewish community in the world that is ultimately responsible for its own political, social, economic, religious and moral decisions, sees this theological tension continually play itself out in the most contradictory ways imaginable. For many believing Jews (and non-Jews), Israel represents the biblical promise of a Divine redemption that will usher in a Messiah. In Israel, two very different theologies crowd the believing (Orthodox) mind. One claims that Israel can only be redeemed with the advent of the Messiah, while the other holds that the Messiah will arrive only after Israel redeems itself. In the Israeli reality, such a multi-dimensional approach has produced the "cranial Jew." The left side of Israel's brain is dominated by a "Jewish state," while the right side reveals "a state of Jews."

In Israel, this metaphysical "schizophrenia" has turned into a real physical duality, where Jews seem to live out their daily lives in perpetual conflict with themselves. Religious and secular, right and left, veteran and immigrant, *Ashkenazi*[1] and *Sephardi*,[2] urban and rural — all internalize this Jewish spiritual dilemma. This explains the age-old Jewish adage: "Ask one Jew and you will get two opinions!" Or when two Jews give contradictory answers to the same question, invariably the response from the third party is: "You're right… and you're right!"

Therefore, in Israel, this schizophrenic approach to life's ultimate questions affects the most mundane issues to the same degree (and with the same passion) as it affects the most critical issues. Jews in Israel seem incapable of

---

1. Term applied to Jews of Germany and their descendants, but widely accepted to include Jews from a European background. The Ashkenazi tradition developed in the Rhineland and spread through France under the influence of the 11th century biblical and rabbinic commentator Rashi (Rabbi Shlomo Ben Yitzhak). Ashkenazim developed customs and rituals, including an everyday language, Yiddish, derived from a combination of Hebrew and German.
2. Descendants of Jews who lived in Spain and Portugal until the expulsions in the late 15th century. After the expulsions, most Sephardim moved to Mediterranean lands. They brought with them their own customs and rituals, including a different everyday language, Ladino, derived from a combination of Hebrew and Spanish.

distinguishing between matters of personal concern and events of national and/or collective importance. This is probably quite natural if one considers that "schizophrenia" can forge a bizarre and delusional reaction to people and events. Lucidity and irrationality go hand in hand.

To bolster these schizophrenic tendencies, Israelis (and Jews in general) have given new meaning to the role that guilt plays in their everyday lives. They possess too much of it and too little of it at the same time. Such a dialectic is usually resolved by a synthesis of just the right amount of healthy and justified conscious guilt. It may seem strange to hear of a Jewish approach to non-neurotic guilt, but as Stan Greenberg wrote in his book, *How to be a Jewish Mother*: "Let your child hear you sigh every day; if you don't know what he's done to make you suffer, he will."

Jews have had a long history of suffering and have often walked the fine line between feeling guilty for what has happened to them and feeling totally absolved of any responsibility. A perfect example of divergent attitudes toward guilt and responsibility is the reaction of the Israeli populace to the *Intifada*.[1] Many Israelis understood the need for firm action, but felt incredible guilt when viewing Israeli soldiers' harsh responses to stone-throwing Palestinians. While absolving themselves of any blame for the outbreak of the Intifada, they blamed themselves for not foreseeing its advent.

Such a conflicting reaction makes perfect sense, for contradictory feelings of guilt and innocence have their roots in the Bible, and therefore are invested with a Divine thrust, making an everlasting impact upon the Jew. A classic example finds God upbraiding the Israelites for rejoicing after the drowning of the Egyptians in the Red Sea.[2] After all, here the guiding hand of the Divine Presence was most definitively felt as God provided for the escape from Egyptian slavery by splitting the Sea, only to close it once the Egyptians were in the middle of its cleavage (*Exodus* 14:1-15:20). Castigating someone else for what he or she has wrought serves as an excellent example of transferring guilt.

---

1. Palestinian uprising against Israel's occupation of the West Bank and the Gaza Strip that began December 9, 1987 and lasted until September 13, 1993 when Israel and the Palestinian Liberation Organization agreed to mutual recognition.
2. "Are these people not part of My Creation? Are you to rejoice at the suffering of others" (*Babylonian Talmud, Sanhedrin* 39b).

Jacob and Esau are forever battling in the Jewish womb. Even after birth, the struggle wages on, as later Jacob and Israel become one and the same person.[1]

Throughout Jewish history, a virtual-reality war has been waged between the prophet and the priest, the Pharisee[2] and the Sadducee,[3] the Hasid[4] and the Mitnaged,[5] the Revisionist[6] and the Labor Zionist,[7] the Palmach[8] warrior and the Lehi[9] fighter, the secular and the observant. A middle path seems to elude the Jewish people. Israel is that singular Jewish community where this historical polarity most glaringly exists; and if anything can capture the ambivalent nature of life in Israel, it is this continued battle between cool logic and creative insanity. The convergence of fact and fantasy, reality and illusion may just be the right prescription for Israel's seemingly incurable issues. Given the Jewish ability to survive throughout its simultaneously torturous and glorious history, the complex machinations of the Jewish mind may be seen as a positive personality trait.

Many attempts have been made to achieve a consensus that would bridge the gap between the contending forces within the Jewish people. To reconcile such paired opposites as Cain and Abel, Jacob and Esau, Samson and Delilah,

1. In *Genesis* 32:29, the story is told of Jacob's dream in which an angel wrestles with him, and changes his name to Israel because "you have struggled with God and with others and prevailed." Jacob did battle with his conscience and matured from a deceptive individual to a responsible and honest person as Israel. According to Rashi (see footnote 1), the name Israel is based on the Hebrew root word "struggle" (legitimate striving) and the name Jacob is based on the Hebrew root word "cunning." In the earliest stages of Jacob's life he was deceptive, having, as a result, to serve his uncle Laban as little more than a slave for twenty-one years, and only later, through an honest confrontation with himself, did he achieve any sort of wholeness. Yet, throughout his life, Jacob contended with these internal competing forces of deceit and honesty.
2. Ancient Jewish sect at the time of the turn of the Common Era, described as having been very skilled in interpreting the Torah and in its adherence to the Oral Law. The influence of the Pharisees is felt throughout rabbinic Judaism.
3. Small religious sect that flourished during the time of the Second Temple. Mostly politically oriented, less so religiously, and said to have followed the priestly caste.
4. A member of a religious movement founded by the Baal Shem Tov in Volhynia and Ponolia in the 18th century. It was primarily an Eastern European religious ecstatic movement, and has spread to nearly all parts of the Jewish world, best exemplified by the Lubavitch movement. The word Hasid means pious one.
5. An opponent of the Hasidic movement. Elijah, the Gaon of Vilna in 1772 gave rise to the movement that was more serious in its approach to Jewish learning. The Mitnagdim rejected Hasidic prayer customs that resulted in ecstatic singing and dancing.
6. Movement founded by Vladimir Jabotinsky in 1925 that advocated the establishment of a Jewish state on both sides of the Jordan, criticizing official Zionist policies as being too timid.
7. Believed in the reestablishment of a Jewish state in Israel based on the principles of socialism.
8. The elite fighting force of the Hagana, the underground Jewish paramilitary organization in Palestine during the British Mandate.
9. "Fighters for Israel Freedom," it was the underground revolutionary organization fighting the British in Palestine. Far more aggressive than the more dominant Hagana, Lehi's members numbered only about 300.

Jeroboam I[1] and Rehoboam,[2] is no easy task. Even the formidable twosome of Shammai[3] and Hillel,[4] who were virtually "joined at the hip," instead of reaching any level of compatibility in their interpretation of Jewish traditions, eventually founded competing schools of thought. Maimonides felt obliged to develop a *"shvil hazahav"* (a golden mean or middle road), but to little avail.

Jewish History has witnessed the rise and fall of the Jewish people over and over again. From the time of the destruction of the Second Temple in 70 CE,[5] a Jewish Diaspora repeatedly emerged, only to be submerged at a later date. With the establishment of the modern state of Israel, one might have hoped that a certain stability would ensue. Instead, from its earliest stages, tension has been Israel's hallmark. Surrounded by so many enemies, it has had to expend enormous energy on its very survival. One would expect that a country as threatened as Israel would find its citizens united in a common cause — to fend off the enemy. This is generally true, particularly when Israel is actually in the throes of war. But even here, the emotional pendulum swings from one extreme to another. Fear and confidence, pride and shame, hope and despair, joy and sadness vie for the same human space in an almost momentary span. The struggle for dominance of one emotion over the other wreaks havoc with the Israeli psyche.

Further, once the immediate threat caused by war subsides, Israel's multifaceted personality returns to the fore, and the seemingly most innocuous issue occupies a place of grandiose significance. The fleeting topic of the day becomes so blown out of proportion that one would think that life or death hangs in the balance; and issues of life and death are almost always accompanied by contradictory inner emotions.

---

1. Jeroboam I served as king of Israel (928-907 BCE).
2. Rehoboam served as king of Judah (928-911 BCE).
3. A Palestinian rabbi (50BCE-30CE); he and Hillel were the last of the "zugot" (couples). He was vice-president of the Sanhedrin (the Assembly of 71 Elders, which served as the supreme political, religious and judicial body). He established a school, Beit Shammai, known for its stringent interpretations of the law.
4. Rabbinic authority and Pharasaic leader (1st century BCE). Born in Babylonia, he settled in Palestine and became paired with Shammai. He established a school in his name, Beit Hillel. Hillel's legal decisions were noted for their leniency. The disputes between the schools of Shammai and Hillel were continued long after their deaths.
5. CE refers to Common Era and BCE refers to Before the Common Era.

The Chinese curse, "may you live in interesting times," is more applicable to those who live in Israel than in all of Asia. Boredom is simply not part of the Israeli scene. "Schizophrenia" may be a psychological disorder that is difficult to deal with, but it does provide for surprise and creativity, excitement and tension. The "schizophrenic individual" can, at one rare moment, display an inventive genius, and, at the next moment, a disabled irrationality. A strong dose of medication is one way to stabilize the "schizophrenic." Yet Israelis have never been particularly good at swallowing a dose of anything. Too often, they seem determined not to learn from their own contradictory errors. It is as if the Jewish people's long history has little to say to the modern Israeli.

Even as "schizophrenia" dwells within one individual, so too can it find a natural habitat in one state as well. **In Israel's case (as with the Jewish people), an understanding of "schizophrenia" might best be defined as "a divided people with a common identity."**

This book explores the schizophrenic nature of Israeli society. The psychological reasons behind this confused reality are manifold, and affect all aspects of Israeli life. For example, most Israeli politicians have made an art form out of "speaking out of both sides of their mouths." Minister Natan Sharansky helped to fashion the Wye River Memorandum[1] between Israel and the Palestinian Authority, only to later vote against it. Jerusalem Mayor Ehud Olmert claimed that Shimon Peres, if he were elected Prime Minister, would <u>and</u> would not divide Jerusalem. Yossi Sarid, Israel's minister of education, wants the Knesset[2] cafeteria to be both kosher <u>and</u> non-kosher! Orthodox rabbis recoil at any alternative sexual orientation, but publicly pronounce that an Israeli transsexual can be counted as part of a *minyan*.[3] There are literally countless examples of such contradictory views existing within the Israeli mind.

This book has no pretensions of providing a full psycho-social history of the

1. An interim accord reached at the Middle East summit in Wye Mills, MD, on October 23, 1998, that included an agreement for Israel's return of 13% of the West Bank to the Palestinian Authority (PA), release of Palestinian prisoners held in Israeli jails, and a Palestinian crack down on terrorist activities.
2. Israel's parliament
3. A quorum of ten people (men, in the Orthodox world) over the age of thirteen required for communal prayer.

challenges that modern Israel faces. Traditional practices for mending an individual who suffers from some psychological disorder, whereby a diagnosis and treatment plan can lead to a cure, are not employed. However, throughout the book, there is a clear attempt to understand the Israeli mind and why it is so conflicted. After outlining a particularly troubling issue, often suggestions for solutions are presented. One should keep in mind that not all conflicts can be resolved, but the manner in which one lives with such irresolution is critically important in determining the mental health of an individual.

While never having been diagnosed as "schizophrenic," or even as psychologically unbalanced, this author admits that he too suffers from many of the neurotic tendencies he attributes to his fellow Jews and Israelis. Therefore, the reader need look no further than the author to supply him or herself with sufficient evidence of contradictory thoughts and ambiguous behavior.

Because of the relative complexity of these conflicting internal struggles within the contemporary Israeli scene, each chapter is divided into topics. Among the subjects discussed are: the Palestinians and the West Bank, Jerusalem, war and peace, Jewish holidays, religious life, the Holocaust, political leaders, democratic institutions, minorities, immigration, the judicial system, Diaspora-Israel relations, educational and cultural life.

In addition, observations of ordinary events in the daily life of an Israeli — from the way Israeli drivers express themselves on the road to the public reaction to former prime minister Benjamin Netanyahu's admission of an extra-marital affair — will strengthen the notion that right and wrong, good and bad, sanity and insanity can abide each other in one happy (or sad) discordant harmony.

Finally, this book will definitively demonstrate that **Jewish "schizophrenia" is alive and well in the Land of Israel.**

CHAPTER 1

AN OCCUPATIONAL HAZARD

Delusions of Grandeur

The "schizophrenic personality" is often possessed with "delusions of grandeur." This definition of "schizophrenia" perhaps fits the modern state of Israel more accurately than any other. Israel is the size of the state of New Jersey. It has a population of 6,300,000 people, of which eighteen percent are not Jewish. Its natural resources are few. Oil, and perhaps even water, must be imported. It no longer can compete in the international markets in the area of agriculture, once one of its prominent sources of income. Limiting entry into Israel of the Palestinian population because of security concerns and the needs of an emerging Palestinian state, Israel has had to turn to foreign workers to fulfill the agricultural, service and building needs of the economy.

Israel is surrounded by numerous Arab nations, many of whom still do not recognize its very existence. Even its peace treaties with Egypt and Jordan are uneasy ones, continually on the verge of some new crisis. Israelis are out-numbered by Arabs by a ratio of almost one hundred to one. Surrounded by monarchies, military dictatorships and feudal fiefdoms, Israel is the only democracy in the Middle East.

When Great Britain withdrew its mandatory control over Palestine on May 14, 1948, Israel declared its independence the same day. Shortly thereafter, eight Arab nations began their war of destruction. Against all odds, Israel prevailed. As it has throughout history, the Jewish people survived, securing a third Jewish Commonwealth after nearly two thousand years of dispersion, thus proving itself to be the architect of the longest liberation movement in human history.

From that point on, Israel has been in a continual battle mode, warding off its enemies in order to guarantee its perpetuity as a sovereign nation in an alien region. The very fact of its existence is a testimony to the Yiddish proverb: "A Jew cannot live without miracles."

Along their way to establishing a Jewish state in the modern era, the Jewish people have withstood a Babylonian exile, a Roman exile, a Holy Crusade, a Spanish Inquisition, Cossack raiders, Czarist pogroms, Nazi death camps, wars of destruction and terrorist murderers. This would be enough to discourage any people, causing them to ask themselves if such suffering is worthwhile. If the Jew experiences bouts of paranoia, it is understandable. One would think that Israel would be overwhelmed by an inferiority complex.

Somehow, the opposite has happened. Ensconced in his and her own land, the modern Israeli has established an image of a self-assured and indestructible individual, capable of challenging one and all — friend and foe alike. The former United States secretary of state, Henry Kissinger, once said of Israel: "You could offer Israel the use of the US Navy's entire sixth fleet, and if Israel accepted, it is as if it was doing you a favor!" Israelis are convinced that their turbulent history should accord them a place of privilege among the nations of the world. In truth, it would be difficult to argue otherwise after the mass extermination of the Jews by the Nazi regime of Adolf Hitler, with the complicit silence of too much of the free world.

How ironic, that after all that has plagued the Jewish people from the precursor stages of their existence as a semi-nomadic tribe somewhere in the Near East, they should assume a national posture of self-aggrandizement and an almost universal character trait of invincibility. One might expect just the opposite, where humility occupies a position of central self-definition. But true to the definition of "schizophrenia," an analytical and/or logical Israeli reading of history does not necessarily lend itself to a coherent Jewish understanding of the past... unless the interpretation of Jewish history is determined by that one definitive theological moment when the Jews were born as a people in the Sinaitic wilderness after their miraculous escape from Egypt.

As the nascent stages of Jewish history unfold, we read in the book of *Exodus* how Jewish national identity was forged on the anvil of the Egyptian experience of slavery. It was against this background of collective suffering and disenfranchisement that the Jews became a people, and charged with becoming a "kingdom of priests." It was at that dramatic moment when the biblical texts tell us: "Now therefore, if you will listen to My voice and keep My commandments, then you will be My **treasure** among all the peoples... (*Exodus* 19.5); "For you are a holy people unto the Lord, your God, and the Lord has **chosen** you to be His **treasure** out of all the peoples on the face of the earth" (*Deuteronomy* 14.2).

The concept of "choseness," a subject of perennial controversy among non-Jews (as well as Jews), is understood to mean that Israel has been selected for a particular purpose or mission — to bring to the world the Divine message of a decent humanity. This concept is interpreted by most modern Jewish thinkers as an obligation to implement God's demand of fulfilling moral and ritual commandments rather than an attempt to ascribe superiority of any sort to the Jews.

Any way one interprets the meaning of "the chosen people," the very nomenclature itself would prompt one to have "delusions of grandeur." Given the perpetual traumas that have accompanied the Jewish people throughout their dramatic history, perhaps they owe their very survival to a chauvinistic and possessive notion of "chosenness." As vulnerable and insecure as the Jews have been throughout history, they could always be bolstered by recalling their heroic past. The Jewish people's very survival is a supreme statement of their invincibility. So an exaggerated view of one's self, along with this sense of invincibility, has been an essential ingredient in defending against the enemies of the Jewish people. Incredibly, the Jews have proven themselves to be indestructible even in the face of all the Amaleks[1] who have sought to destroy them throughout every epoch in their history.

On the "macro" level, delusions of grandeur have served the Jewish people well, particularly the Jews who live in the modern state of Israel. This sense of invincibility, validated by Jewish history, was crucial at the beginning stages of the state, as Israel had to defend itself against eight invading Arab armies and absorb hundreds of thousand of immigrants from such disparate backgrounds as the ghettos of Casablanca and the ashes of the Holocaust. In the midst of such

---

1. The leader of the ancient nomadic people, the Amalekites, who lived in the Sinai Peninsula. They carried out a treacherous attack on the Israelites who were on their way to Mount Sinai to receive God's commandments. Since then the name Amalek has been used to describe any archenemy of the Jewish people, from Babylonia's Nebuchadnezzar to Adolf Hitler to Saddam Hussein.

turmoil, it had to set in motion political institutions that would secure its social, religious and economic base.

Often isolated, certainly in its own geographical region, it had to virtually institutionalize its "macho" image in order to survive continual wars — the Sinai Campaign of 1956, the Six-Day War of 1967, the War of Attrition of 1969-1970, the Yom Kippur War of 1973, as well as the scourge of terrorism within and without its borders. (Some would say that machismo was necessary to stave off the Intifada.) But the sense of a spiritual and physical capability that knows no limits, which served the country well in its incipient stages, may damage it as it moves beyond its fiftieth birthday and into the new millennium.

And so, it is on the "micro" level that today's Israel is no longer served well by a definition of "schizophrenia" that includes in it "delusions of grandeur." When devoid of power, conferred on a people by nationhood, a sense of self-importance is necessary in order to substantiate one's self-worth and to provide one with the will to survive against virtually all odds. Even in the developing stages of statehood, characteristics of strength, fortitude and impregnability are crucial. But unless these tendencies are held in check, when statehood is secured and power is well established, then all manner of behavior may cloud an understanding of "chosenness" that speaks of an obligation on the part of the Jews to be "a light unto the nations." Such tendencies can become allied with a chauvinistic ideology in which the national ego, fed by delusions of grandeur, is projected upon the self, unleashing behavior patterns that are morally unacceptable. They can also damage one's practical self-interests.

Israel's more than thirty-year occupation of the West Bank and the Gaza Strip, along with its eighteen year occupation of South Lebanon from June, 1982, to June, 2000, is a perfect example of grandiose plans gone awry. While the events leading up to the Six-Day War seemed to justify Israel's rule over the territories, the notion that one could hold onto the land and its almost two million Palestinian Arabs indefinitely was naive at best.

The invasion of Lebanon was a far more controversial issue. Indeed, Israel's withdrawal from that country indicated that the whole affair was mistaken, driven by the then minister of defense, Ariel Sharon, who is the paradigmatic patient to lie on a psychiatrist's couch. The attempt since 1967 to alter the demographic composition of the West Bank through an aggressive settlement policy and to invade Lebanon in the first place were fueled by delusions of grandeur.

If the United States of America could not maintain its hold on Vietnam, and Russia its hold on those regions that made up the former Soviet Union, as well as its satellite states in Eastern Europe, what could have possessed little Israel to think that it could subject hostile Arabs to its dominion? How much has Israel been influenced by its history of being an oppressed and persecuted minority? Has the motto "Never Again," which dates to the time of the battle at Massada[1] ("Massada will not fall again"[2]), distorted Israel's vision of itself as a morally upright and democratic state? Indeed the lesson of Massada should have taught Israel that it is impossible to suppress the national will of a people. The reawakening of Jewish national identity in the former Soviet Union after the Six-Day War is another example of such an impossibility.

Modern Zionism[3] defines itself as a national liberation movement. But what it would acknowledge as the most steadfast and durable characteristic of its own personality, it would deny to others. It is true that in the small tract of land that is Israel and "Palestine," there are two nationalities locked in deep conflict. But this should in no way obviate the need for the nation in a position of power, Israel, to accord the Palestinian people a state of their own, fulfilling their national aspirations. The Jews are a living testimony to this being realized, having thrown off the yoke of British rule in 1948. In this case, Israel's dual reading of its history and bipolar applicability to its present reality does not serve it well. What probably is needed best to tend to Israel's schizophrenic approach to Palestinian nationhood is not a palliating sedative, but a healthy dosage of LSD!

---

1. Situated near the Dead Sea, it is one of the last Jewish strongholds to remain under Roman rule. Rather than submit to foreign rule, the Jews at Massada committed mass suicide, bringing to an end a brief resistance in the year 73 CE.
2. The statement made by Eliezer Ben Yair, the leader of the Massada revolt.
3. An ideological/political movement whose goal is the return of the Jewish people to the land of Israel. Throughout Jewish history, Jews always prayed for a return to the biblical land of their ancestors. Modern Zionism was founded by Theodor Herzl, who established the World Zionist Organization (WZO) in Basle, Switzerland, in 1897.

A Moral Aphrodisiac

It is here that the practical elements of statehood and the ethical components of nationhood intersect. There is a direct connection between politics and morality. Politics, as the process that shapes the social order, is inclusive. Every political decision and social act necessarily has its moral equation and practical outcome. The policies of the Jewish state reflect upon the moral principles of those who make its policies. Once the practical side of politics is harmonized with clear ethical standards, then sanity can reign.

The occupation of the West Bank and the Gaza Strip that resulted from the Six-Day War has worked against Israel's self interest, both morally and practically. A pragmatic solution to the continued occupation that would see Israel relinquish its hold on Palestinian territories should result in moral benefits. Israel's rule over two million hostile Arabs not only physically endangered soldier and civilian alike, but also morally corrupted too much of Israeli society. In the course of time, Israel, once portrayed as the humble shepherd David of biblical history, was seen as the aggressive warrior Goliath. This image was reinforced by the Intifada.

It matters little that compared to other nations, Israel's handling of the occupation and response to the Intifada seem mild. After all, in 1970, the late King Hussein of Jordan killed 10,000 Palestinians whom he felt were threatening his regime in what has been described as "Black September." For Israel to use the lowest common denominator as a yardstick to measure and ultimately justify its behavior is an errant reading of the concept of "chosenness," which includes the lofty biblical (and Divine) ideal and command: "When strangers live with you in your land, you must not oppress them. The strangers who live with you shall be like citizens, and you shall love them as yourself, for you were strangers in the land of Egypt..." (*Leviticus* 19:33-34).

The late Moshe Dayan, defense minister during the Six-Day War, and the architect of the type of rule that would extend to the territories, promulgated the idea of peaceful coexistence. Basically he set in motion a public relations campaign that would portray Israel as a benevolent occupier. The euphoria of the early days after Israel's sweeping victory over Egypt, Syria and Jordan was not tempered by any practical long-term planning.

Understandably, Israel which saw itself on the brink of elimination on the eve of the war (a view shared by much of the world), saw only its own self-image in the mirror. It concerned itself with its own physical needs, primarily reflected in the field of security. But these needs were intensified by the spiritual high that even the most secular of Israelis felt when the "Holy Western Wall," the last remaining remnant of the Second Temple period, was liberated. The golden age of Jewish sovereignty was restored.

This ecstasy clouded all rational thought, and an elemental neuroticism took hold. The cool heads that engineered a brilliant military victory somehow got lost in the excitement. A fever invaded the Israeli body-politic, and Israel began to hallucinate. Anything seemed possible. And so, anything was possible, no matter what the consequences might be. Cause and effect, so carefully adhered to in the waging of the war, evaporated in the Israeli mind. Military intelligence, which played such a crucial role in the Six-Day War, in the wake of the war proved itself to be a "contradiction in terms!"

From the outset, Israel's occupation of the territories was never benign. It was always aggressive. If there was any long-term plan on the part of the Israeli government (of whatever coalition), it was to reduce the Palestinian entity to such a diminutive position that any hope of a viable independence would never come to fruition. The late prime minister, Golda Meir, declared: "There is no Palestinian people." Spurred on by delusions of grandeur, plentifully nourished by its astonishing victory, Israel sought to rule over a couple of million Arabs. So blurred was Israel's image of what should be, it developed what it considered a creative and progressive world-view whereby it would rule the land, but not the people. If Israel had applied this world-view to itself, then Turkish or British rule in this part of the world should not have been considered antithetical to Jewish nationalism.

Virtually from the moment that victory was proclaimed, Israel began to reorder the West Bank and the Gaza Strip. Not only did a secular quasi-left government begin to establish settlements in the territories, it helped to unleash a new religious movement, *"Gush Emunim"* (The Block of the Faithful), whose raison d'etre was the biblical promise by God to the Israelites to redeem the entire land. With God on their side, a holy mission was proclaimed: "No piece of land for a land of peace." This matched the three "no's" of the Arab nations after the Six-Day War: "No Negotiations, No Compromise, No Peace!" It was an "eye for an eye" and a "tooth for a tooth." What Israel did not realize was that such a policy would leave it blind and toothless!

Within Israel, one of the greatest threats to a peaceful accommodation with the Palestinians is the philosophy of "Messianism" that many of the religious settlers express. Messianism belies the possibility of any sort of compromise because it is based on a belief rooted in the Divinely immutable words of the Written[1] and Oral[2] Law. Therefore, the entire Land of Israel has been divinely promised to the Jews. More than any other philosophy or ideology in Jewish life, Messianism is driven by delusions of grandeur. Yet a messianic approach to the territories will not stand up to the pressures of reality. *Realpolitik* will eventually overwhelm the messianic mind.

Indeed, Israel has adopted a practical approach, realizing that it is in its self-interest to disengage from the territories. After years of occupation, the question remains: Will Israel gain any moral benefits once it rids itself of the territories? Has the occupation so eroded Israel's moral fiber that it will take years to regain its moral stature?

One must not approach this subject in a vacuum. The Palestinians have not necessarily proven themselves to be the most worthy partners to a peace treaty, even if the process is based on an unequal relationship. The excessive brutality that was (and still is) employed by the Palestinians against the Israeli population and Jews around the world, that saw, inter alia, twenty-one children gunned down in a school in the north of the country, eleven Israeli athletes murdered at the 1972 Olympic games in Munich, and hundreds of citizens blown to bits by exploding buses, has not stirred confidence among Israelis. Every liberation movement has its violent side to it, but the Palestinians, even when dealing with their own people, have set standards of extreme behavior that dwarf the actions of many other similar movements.

However, Palestinian brutality must not be matched by Israeli brutality. Israel's moral standards must not be determined by Palestinian moral

---

1. A reference to the Torah, the Five Books of Moses (or The Pentateuch).
2. A reference to the Talmud, the body of Jewish law that expounds on the commandments in the Torah.

standards, otherwise it will invite invidious comparisons (which already have been made). There are very legitimate reasons for Israelis to feel obligated to struggle with the questions of their own moral behavior, and to not feel equally able to deal with questions of how Arabs do or do not behave in terms of their ethical code of conduct and faith. While Israelis cannot guarantee the standards of others, they must be consistent in maintaining their own integrity. For an Israeli Jew, questions of acceptable moral behavior are of an ultimate kind. They are of such ultimacy that what hangs in the balance is the very idea of a Jewish **and** democratic state.

Transferring Blame

It was a Friday afternoon when Jerusalem is a hub of activity, as its residents do their last minute shopping for Sabbath. Jerusalem's central bus station turns into a virtual mob scene as soldiers return home for the weekend and religious Jews rush to get home before Sabbath descends on the country.[1] Newspaper stands, flower vendors, food concessions and kiosks are packed with pre-Sabbath buyers. With the Intifada in its eighth month (it was August, 1988), security at the bus station was extremely tight. All who entered or exited the area had their bags searched by a security guard, thus creating an atmosphere of short-tempered impatience among the crowds of people.

A fourteen-year-old girl had just arrived at the central bus station to meet a friend who was coming to spend the weekend with her family. She wore a T-shirt with the words in Hebrew, Arabic and English: "Freedom for the Press." As the events of the Intifada had unfolded, reaching an international audience thanks to the advent of Cable TV, many Israelis felt that the bad publicity Israel was receiving was because of press exposure. While many maintained the Intifada had to be addressed harshly, they were troubled by the TV film clips that entered their living rooms of Israeli soldiers beating Palestinian children. Some Israelis were genuinely upset by the excesses of the army, while others, who tended to the extreme right of the political spectrum, were nevertheless bothered by the

---

1. A religiously observant Jew is not permitted to ride on the Sabbath, which begins Friday at sundown.

image that Israel was receiving: the image of an oppressor nation. The Israeli personality was split down the middle. Contain the Intifada, but do so either gently, or don't show what is actually happening.

So the press, particularly the Israeli press, was blamed not just for the negative exposure in the world media, but for the Palestinian uprising itself. The press was held responsible for encouraging acts of violence. A bumper sticker appeared: "The People against a Hostile Press." To counteract what was perceived as an incendiary response to the facts on the ground and to what led to the Palestinian revolt against Israel's occupation, an opposing bumper sticker hit the streets: "Freedom for the Press."

That young girl who had gone to the bus station found herself suddenly surrounded by an angry mob. Slowly the crowd of about fifty people closed in on her, hurling all manner of verbal insults at her: "traitor, whore, self-hater." Some spat on her. When she attempted to break away, she was blocked by two national guardsmen sporting rifles. A policewoman appeared on the scene and, after an initial survey of the situation, declared that the girl was wearing an "illegal" T-shirt and ordered her to change it immediately. Just then her friend arrived and the two of them escaped briefly to the bathrooms, where the girl put on another T-shirt she borrowed from her friend. Emerging from the bathroom, she was shocked to see the crowd still gathered. The policewoman then confiscated the shirt, yelling that if she were to ever wear a similar shirt again she would be summarily arrested!

Upon returning home, the girl wept in her father's arms. The first words out of her mouth were: "Daddy, I now know what it must feel like to be a Palestinian." The moral erosion of being an occupying power had taken its toll on a fourteen-year-old child. (Not far from the central bus station, an Israeli women's protest vigil against the occupation was held in a city square. As drivers passed by, one could hear the catcalls emanate forth: "Arafat's whores" and "PLO[1] prostitutes." It seems that women who express their political views regarding Israel's treatment of Palestinians unite men to exert their virility by heaping sexual abuse upon them.)

Any sense of moral equilibrium seemed to get lost as the Intifada raged on,

---

1. The abbreviation for the Palestinian Liberation Organization, the forerunner of the Palestinian Authority.

and Israel's response became more severe. It reached a climax in the words of the late Yitzhak Rabin, Israel's defense minister at the time, in which he commanded Israeli soldiers to "break their bones." But violence directed outward eventually gets redirected inward. Too often Israeli disdain toward the Palestinians was matched by an equal contempt for other Israelis who expressed alternative ideological views.

Yitzhak Rabin, who later became prime minister, recognized this new reality. His death was a direct result of inciteful rhetoric reserved for the Palestinian enemy, now pointed at him. His "rapprochment" with the Palestinians and with their titular leader, Yasir Arafat, was prodded by a desire to preserve the delicate moral fabric of Israeli society, so severely damaged by so many years of the occupation. The delusions of grandeur that swept him up along with everyone else after the triumphant Six-Day War, at which time he was chief of staff, were pared down to a manageable size. Rabin's "therapy" was rooted in what he saw happening to his own people, which was a mirror image of what his people were doing to him: distributing a poster of him dressed in a SS uniform or wearing a keffiyah.[1]

I was invited to Oslo as part of the Israeli delegation to attend the Nobel Peace Prize Ceremony at which Yitzhak Rabin, Shimon Peres and Yasir Arafat were granted this most prestigious award. I was accompanied by an unofficial delegation of Israeli demonstrators who opposed the peace process. Democratic expressions of protest, from the left and the right, are legitimate — providing they do not go beyond the limits of decency.

Unfortunately in Oslo, the limits of decency were abused. Walking with the former chief rabbi of Syria, Avraham Hama, toward the Oslo City Hall where the ceremony was to take place, we were confronted with hateful epithets: "The blood of the Jewish people is on your head," and "Traitors." The barrage kept up as these Jewish protesters burnt a life-size doll of Yitzhak Rabin in effigy for all the world to see.

An image had been created in the public eye that these demonstrators spoke in the name of all those who were victims of Arab terror or wars. No one group of people has a monopoly on Jewish suffering. Inside the hall was Yitzhak Frankenthal whose son was murdered by

---

1. Arab head dress, usually warn by observant Moslems.

terrorists. I had been wounded in the Lebanon War. On the way out of the ceremony, I walked with the then Speaker of the Knesset, Shevach Weiss, a Holocaust survivor.

At times it was frightening to see the demonstrators' venom being hurled upon the Jews in attendance. Weiss saw in the demonstrators an almost uncontrollable behavior that manifested itself in "a cynical exploitation of the victims of Arab terror."

This was all a precursor to further violent demonstrations that would stalk Rabin wherever he went, including at the entrance to his private home. No protest affected the late prime minister more than the theme of the demonstration in the center of Jerusalem, expressed on a placard that read: "The Rabin Government = Judenrat."[1] To this visual aid, political speakers at that anti-Rabin rally added an audio component, which made that poster seem an acceptable expression of protest. Opposition leader, Benjamin Netanyahu (later to become prime minister), shouted these inflammatory words: "Menachem Begin made peace with Egypt with a national consensus, represented by 90 Knesset members who voted for the agreement. We will not let Yitzhak Rabin sell the land of Israel based on the single vote of Abdul Darawshe!"[2]

The late Prime Minister Golda Meir blamed "Arab boys for making killers out of Jewish boys." Yitzhak Rabin hated the fact that he executed a policy of aggressive repression and so decided to reconcile these competing emotional and intellectual forces that were wreaking havoc with his psychological well-being, and to extend his hand to Yasir Arafat on the White House Lawn on September 13, 1993. He did not anticipate a reunion of the diverging personalities that swarmed around that fourteen-year-old girl that summer day in August five years earlier where all would suddenly be overcome by a sense of brotherly and sisterly love. He did hope that generosity to those outside the family would foster civility and decency to those within the family, despite his own penchant for intemperate statements directed at Jewish settlers.

---

1. The term that referred to Jews who were physically forced to work for the Nazis, often against their Jewish compatriots.
2. An Israeli Arab member of the Knesset.

While the rhetoric in Israel is still at a high volume, it is clear that it is now reduced, as the vast majority of Israelis accept withdrawal from the territories, not only as a given fact, but also as a necessary act. Even those in the religious camp have come to understand the practical and moral advantages of disengagement. More so, Israelis have come to see that disengagement is not enough, that Palestinian statehood is what is needed. In many respects, former right-wing prime minister, Benjamin Netanyahu, who once so bitterly attacked Rabin, deserves as much credit as Rabin. The moment that Netanyahu, a spiritual descendant of Vladimir Jabotinsky,[1] shook hands with the arch-enemy of the Jewish people, Yasir Arafat, a sea-change in Israeli society took place.

The left and right of the Israeli psyche, while not reconciled, have become more balanced. However, along the way, the strains of internal struggles have left their psychological scars. The schism in the Jewish state will only be healed when there is a fuller understanding of the role the occupation has played in the lives of Israelis. Behavioral disorders can best be resolved by recalling past events.

"A Bridge Over Troubled Waters"

Not far from the Knesset stood two tents, representing seemingly opposite sides of a heated political debate. One tent was populated by the victims of Arab terror while the other tent was filled by the families of Palestinian deportees.[2] A virtual no-man's land separated the two camps. To cross from one side to the other was to cross an imaginary mine-field.

If one were to examine the cause each side championed, there should have been no logical reason for a person from either side to feel any contradiction in visiting both tents. To deplore terrorism has no syllogistic link to the denial of due process for deported Palestinians. Furthermore, for those who cared (and

---

1. Writer and founder of Revisionist Zionism, he lived from 1880-1940. A member of the Zionist executive, after a falling out with Chaim Weizmann, Israel's first president, he founded the Revisionist movement in 1925 which believed in a program of activism to rid the Jewish people in mandatory Palestine of British rule. He became the supreme commander of the Irgun Tzva Leumi, a Jewish underground movement that operated outside the normative Zionist organizations.
2. In February of 1993, the late Prime Minister, Yitzhak Rabin, deported in a pre-dawn action 415 suspected Hamas terrorists from the West Bank and the Gaza Strip to South Lebanon, causing a world-wide protest.

still care) deeply about internal security, it could be forcefully argued that extreme measures taken against suspected terrorists, such as mass expulsion, could bring about an increase in terrorist activities — revenge and bitterness serving as a motivating factor. Here is yet another example of where a more practical decision rooted in the self-interest of physical security could have served the essential requirements of moral behavior.

There should be no misunderstanding. *Hamas*,[1] and what it stands for, is an anathema to Israel. Hamas is also a cancer within Palestinian society. The rhetoric and violence of its members are so vehement that they had led to suicide bombings, which claimed hundreds of Israeli lives as well as some of their own. During the period of the deportation, the Israeli government tried to reach a compromise by allowing one hundred of the deportees to return. Hamas' response was portrayed to the world as "all or nothing," as if to show that they were expressing unity and sacrifice for a noble cause. The Hamas claim that Israel must let them all go back, or none would go back, was a mere cover-up for a far more sinister reality. The initial one hundred deportees permitted to return refused to cross the border back to the West Bank because they feared other Hamas activists would kill them for "abandoning" their compatriots remaining in Lebanon — in the same way Hamas kills suspected prostitutes and drug traffickers, all under the guise of "collaboration killings."[2]

Hamas is a brutal terrorist organization. But the question is: Did any of the deportees actually kill any one of those victims of Arab terror? And if one of them did, does not the family of the victim have the right to know? The mass deportation denied both sides a democratic hearing.

To counter the public relations advantage that the deportees and their families were enjoying in the international media, Israeli government spokespersons belittled the plea of the deportees' children to see their banished fathers. They compared their wish to those of the Jewish children who would never be able to see their fathers again because they had been killed by terrorists. But the central point was missed. A Jewish child's bereavement over the death of a parent because of a terrorist act can never be ameliorated by an act

---

1. An Islamic fundamentalist movement that often rejects any peace overtures to Israel and frequently supports terrorist activities against the Jewish state.
2. Palestinians who were summarily killed for allegedly working or "collaborating" with the Israeli security forces.

of wholesale revenge against the parents of an Arab child. Does one want to see two tents filled with a child's bitterness?

Unfortunately, the media — local and foreign — portrayed the residents of the two tents as sworn rivals. In this media war, Israel was unfairly disadvantaged, as the Jewish victims of Arab terror were usually shown as an irrational and vengeful lot. The media never showcases people like former Israeli president, Ephraim Katzir, or former Knesset member Eliezer Granot, whose brother and wife respectively were victims of Arab terror. According to both men's public statements, they could have spoken with empathy to those in both tents.

In today's reality, dialogue does exist between the figurative inhabitants of those two tents. Palestinians and Israelis are presently talking to one another. But what takes place on a political level must filter down to the grass roots level. An Israeli should be able to cross back and forth over the field that divides the two camps. An Israeli must deplore Arab terror with a concomitant commitment to a judicial process. Israelis must depose themselves of the errant notion that, in order to defend their own rights, they must deny the rights of others. The dignity and rights of both Arab and Jew must be equally and vigorously pursued. As difficult as it may seem, an Israeli (and an Arab) should be capable of identifying with those who occupy either tent. There is nothing contradictory in such a stance.

The human mind functions in mysterious ways. Often it works at cross-purposes. Mind and matter must be balanced equally in order to guarantee the mental welfare of an individual. Intellectualism and emotionalism must play parallel roles in the human thought processes. Interaction, openness and dialogue are characteristics that lead one to be at peace with oneself. Feelings of severance, separation and closure can only provide for continual conflict.

At times it seems that a moral bankruptcy has seized those in Israel who profess to be "active" peace seekers. Successive Israeli governments have called for closure of and/or separation from the territories, those very ingredients that cause instability to an individual's personality. By nature a human being does not wish to be alone. This has its Divine precedent in the Garden of Eden, when God says: "It is not good for man to be alone..." (*Genesis* 2:18). If interaction, openness and dialogue are the characteristics that lead one to be at peace with oneself, then by logical extension, they should lead one to live in peace with others. Bridges, even over the most troubled waters, provide the only means to reconciliation.

While the murderous acts of Hamas always put a dent in the peace armor of Israelis, this should not lead them to abandon the tiring search for peace. The conflict between Israelis and Palestinians must not be resolved through total separation from the territories. Separation is a euphemism for closure, which is a progenitor of strangulation. All are a result of moral apathy.

The Israeli peace movement has too often cynically exploited Hamas violence in order to advance its political goal of establishing a Palestinian state. But the establishment of a Palestinian state must not be predicated on a total separation from Israel, and a closure of the borders of whatever type of Palestinian state will emerge. If Israel wants the Palestinian state to fail before it barely embarks on its independence, all it needs to do is cut off its economic viability.

Closure of the territories is collective punishment of an extreme kind. After years of exploiting cheap Arab labor, do Israelis now fire Palestinians who built Jewish settlements without according them the social benefits that are required for Israelis? Closure will condemn an entire population to live in dire poverty. If the left opts to support such a policy, then the right in Israel will have won the day. The stereotype that all Arabs, Israeli and Palestinian, are murderers will have taken hold. Next will come the Druse and the Bedouin. Jews must never succumb to the use of stereotypes. Their suffering as a people cries out against such action.

It is here that one sees a strange partnership between the Israeli left and right, with each side calling for closure. But those in the peace camp who advocate a position of closure should be forewarned: If you jump into the bed of those whose support for separation of Palestinians and Israelis is motivated by extreme nationalism, you cannot know where you will end up. One theory as to what will happen if Israel follows the line of closure is that there will be a ghettoization of the Palestinians.

Recent events on the Israeli scene helped to sweep the festering sores in the West Bank and Gaza Strip under the rug — the Persian Gulf War, the arrival of hundreds of thousands of Russian immigrants and, most significantly (and deceptively), the peace negotiations themselves. If Israel were to close the borders, it would conveniently shut its eyes to the injustices it has wrought upon the Palestinians since the occupation, which included administrative detentions, deportations, extended curfews and house demolitions (which still occur). To mend a damaged psyche, the past must not only be confronted, but must lend itself to curative measures.

The left's rush to use the all too real pent-up fear abounding in Israel to satisfy ideological goals that are diametrically opposed to those at the other end of the political spectrum, who have translated fear into hatred, should be unacceptable. This will only reinforce the uglier side of Israeli society. It will glaringly show that the moral erosion of serving in the position of occupier, no matter how that occupation came about (justifiably or not), is a problem too deep-rooted to be simply wished away. This is exactly what the act of closure would achieve. Neurosis, real or imagined, is not solved by a therapy of denial.

The pursuit of peace must not be based on expediency. "Justice, justice, you shall pursue, that you may live and inherit the land the Lord your God is giving you" (*Deuteronomy* 16:20). The ancient rabbis postulated that the reason the word justice was mentioned twice was to emphasize that the pursuit of justice must be carried out in a just manner. Unfortunately, in recent history we have plenty of examples of peace being pursued under the banner: "The end justifies the means!"

Dropping a hydrogen bomb on Hiroshima and Nagasaki was considered reasonable because it allegedly hastened the end of World War II. America's relentless bombing of Cambodia and Laos was acceptable because it supposedly brought the North Vietnamese to the negotiating table. That hundreds of thousands of Japanese were left to suffer from radioactive fall-out, and an equal number of Cambodians, Laotians and Vietnamese were left napalmed and homeless, did not figure in the long-term planning of America. And so the psychological traumas of both these events have yet to subside for those who lived through them.

By stating that the only way to ensure peace is to close off the territories, with all the human suffering that would be caused as a result, is a distorted view of the pursuance of peace. Unethical means to secure peace will return to haunt the one who employs them. Peace can only be achieved with a sense of moral equilibrium. Ends and means must be balanced. All this is necessary for a healthy persona.

It is unpopular to stand up for the other's rights. But in pursuing peace, popular appeal and expediency cannot become gods. One must keep in mind the best tactical approach to achieve one's goal, but the end must never justify the means. For ultimately, it is morality, not strategy, that the Palestinian-Israeli conflict is all about.

Yet certain peace strategies can bring about a moral reciprocity. Any peace agreement must provide for an ethical tit-for-tat that should include the following ingredients. For Israelis: 1) an end to all expulsions, 2) a stop to all house demolitions and house sealings, 3) permission to rebuild destroyed homes, 4) release of all administrative detainees and hardship cases among prisoners, 5) the granting of family reunion permits, 6) the elimination of quiet transfer from Jerusalem, 7) the return of a pre-determined number of Palestinian refugees and 8) the containment of settler violence perpetrated against the Palestinians. For Palestinians: 1) the cessation of all terrorist activities, 2) peaceful demonstrations as a substitute for armed parades of masked Palestinians, 3) the application of judicial processes for alleged collaborators with Israel, and 4) the prosecution of all Palestinians involved in hostile acts directed at Israelis.

If Israelis want to be part of the Middle East landscape, as they must be by right, then they must recognize that integration — not assimilation or acculturation — is necessary. If Palestinians expect to enjoy freedom and reap the benefits of independence, which is their right, then they must acknowledge the sovereignty of Israel, and the right of all its citizens to live free of fear and violence. No one expects Israelis and Palestinians to crawl into the same sleeping bag, but one would hope that they would be able to live under one tent.

"Cry Peace, Peace; where there is no Peace" (Jeremiah 6:14)

It is emotionally challenging to deal with the highs and lows of Israeli life. Just when one thinks that the prospect of a peaceful resolution to the Israeli-Arab conflict is at hand, the enemies of peace tear it asunder with bestial acts that seemingly condemn Israelis (and Palestinians) to a never-ending cycle of hostilities. Palestinians set off a bomb, killing fifteen Israelis in a crowded market in downtown Jerusalem, an Israeli enters a mosque and guns down twenty-nine Moslem worshippers. The people ask: "Where is peace?" It is right around the corner. The late Jordanian King Hussein and the late Israeli Prime Minister Yitzhak Rabin sign a peace treaty. The psychological pendulum is always swaying back and forth.

Almost the last remnant of Syrian Jewry is released from Syria, symbolized by the arrival in Israel of Damascus' chief rabbi. His welcome is thwarted by the murderous thunder of a bus explosion that claims eighteen Israeli lives. The juxtaposition of these events taxes the mind and strains the heart. How much longer can Israelis continue to rescue hostages at Entebbe[1] and one month later see Israelis gunned down at Ben Gurion National Airport? How much longer can Israelis walk out of sealed rooms[2] to welcome Ethiopian Jews? How much longer can Israelis pursue peace when war seems continually knocking at their front door? It is difficult to "cry peace, peace, where there is no peace" (Jeremiah 6:14).

My child studies in a high school next to Mahane Yehuda, the crowded open air market that has been a target of numerous terrorist attacks over the years. Am I frightened for her, for me? That is an understatement. But somehow reason must rule over my tendency to feed my fear. I cannot give in to irrational responses or emotional tirades. To do so would not only exacerbate the situation and affect my own sense of stability, but also would hand a victory to those whose sub-human acts are designed to undermine the passionate need of the Jewish people to live in peace.

---

1. The dramatic rescue by the Israeli army of over 200 Israeli and Jewish hostages flown to Entebbe, Uganda, by Palestinian and German terrorists.
2. A reference to the sealed rooms that Israelis stayed in to protect themselves against potential chemical bombings carried by scud missiles hurled against Israel during the Persian Gulf War.

It is often difficult to find positives when negotiating the Middle East quagmire. Yet given the harsh reality of Israeli life, it is surprising that there are not more terrorist atrocities. In view of Israel's long and often harsh occupation, one would expect more than a localized Intifada (confined to the territories). Even more satisfying is the lack of reprisals on the part of Israelis. Baruch Goldstein's[1] act was an aberration, as was the attempt to form a "Jewish underground."[2] Taking into account the fact that Israelis are armed to the teeth, with virtually every eighteen-year-old kid walking around with a weapon,[3] it is a tribute to Israel's sense of moral restraint that physical vengeance has not become a watchword of the population.

It is unfortunate that this sobriety on the part of the Israeli populace is not reflected in the behavior and rhetoric of its political leaders (for certain, this also applies to the Palestinian community). Before the bodies of Israelis killed in the bombings are buried, we hear political pontification that a particular government's policy is the cause of terrorist acts. It is as if the politicians are playing a child's game of baseball card trading, with each side of the political spectrum saying: "I'll trade you three stabbings for four hijack killings!" Maybe it is good that Israelis have short memories. But any sane look at the past reveals that terrorism crosses all political lines. Every Israeli government, whatever policy it pursued, witnessed the tragic murder of Israeli citizens. Hamas could not care less who is in political power.

Tragedy must not be politically exploited. If it is, it could trickle down to the general public, altering a sense of reason and response present even in the midst of emotional upheaval. In fact, Israel almost witnessed a worst case scenario. Shortly after a bombing was reported at an outdoor cafe in Tel Aviv, a soldier falsely claimed that he had been stabbed by a terrorist. Arabs were rounded up and word got out that the terrorist had been captured by an enraged mob. This unstable soldier had cynically exploited the tension of the moment to push Israelis toward a hysteria that could have resulted in shameful actions.[4] After

---

1. On February 25, 1994, Dr. Baruch Goldstein gunned down twenty-nine Moslem worshippers at the Cave of Machpelah in Hebron.
2. A group of religious Jews who plotted and executed attacks against Palestinians in the territories. Many were convicted of crimes, including the shooting death of Palestinians.
3. At the age of eighteen, most Israelis are conscripted into the army and given a rifle (M-16, *Uzi* or *Galil*) that they are required to carry with them at all times.
4. A policeman arrived on the scene and successfully pried the Arab from the midst of the crowd.

Baruch Goldstein killed those Moslem worshippers, Israel imposed an around the clock curfew on the Arab parts of Hebron, not the Jewish section from where Goldstein came. (It is not enough that Palestinians are placed under curfew when terrorism comes from their ranks. They are also confined to their homes when murderous attacks are carried out against them by Israelis.)

The pendulum will continue to swing if Israelis and Palestinians move from mourning to gleeful revenge. Any revenge would belie the aforementioned sense of moral restraint. After every terrorist act, there are calls for the institution of capital punishment. Even on practical grounds, anyone who believes that capital punishment would deter Palestinian fanatics from blowing themselves up along with dozens of Israelis in pursuit of a "holy mission" is naive at best. Instead, what will happen, should Israelis cast aside a sense of equilibrium, is the lynching of any Arab allegedly caught for stabbing a soldier.

As Israel moves toward accommodation with the Palestinians and its other neighbors, it can expect that more violent personal tragedies will occur. All these events will produce a host of ambivalent feelings, feelings which will sometimes border on extremist thoughts. Israel's collective personality will continue to elicit ambiguous responses. Given the climate in the Middle East, this is understandable. But today is no different from yesterday or the day before yesterday. This reality has been endemic to Israel's very existence.

What must not become eroded is Israel's adherence to a moral integrity that embraces a Jewish sense of balance and purpose. This balance and purpose must stand in sharp contrast to the vacillating aspects of Israelis' lives that play havoc with their emotional stability and mental well-being. Israel must not alter its quest for peace while guarding its need for personal safety — a quest and need that must be steady, just and sane. Peace cannot be served by any stretch of the "schizophrenic imagination."

CHAPTER 2

JERUSALEM OF GOLD
(AND OTHER COLORS)

Open Your Gates

Nothing highlights the inner conflict of the Israeli more than his or her attitude toward Jerusalem. It would seem that there is unanimous opinion regarding the political status of the holy city. Israelis seem of one mind: Jerusalem should always remain the united capital of Israel under its sovereign rule. But Israel's behavior regarding Jerusalem, while theoretically indicating a unity of thought, in practice suggests a duality when those thoughts are put into action.

From the establishment of the state of Israel in 1948 until the Six-Day War of 1967, Jerusalem was a divided city. Access to the Jewish holy places was denied, not only to Israelis, but also to all Jews. At no time did the world community call for opening up the city. There were no cries for the internationalization of the city, neither from the United Nations nor from the Vatican, both of which immediately lobbied for an open Jerusalem upon Israel's capture of the city in 1967. The entire West Bank, East Jerusalem included, was occupied by Jordan from 1948-1967, in blatant violation of international agreements.

Worse than the Jews not being able to visit their holy sites, many of their most sacred religious symbols were abused. Homes were built right up to the Western Wall. The graves on the sacred Mount of Olives Cemetery were desecrated, some of headstones being used as the concrete foundation for buildings in the eastern part of the city.

At the conclusion of the Six-Day War, with all of Jerusalem united once again, Israel announced to the world that from then on Jerusalem's holy places would be open to peoples of all religions. The walls of separation would be brought down.

It is over thirty years since Israel united the western and eastern parts of the Jerusalem, and since it instituted this "open door" policy. It is more than thirty years since Israel has perfected its public relations on this matter.

The one thing that is constant in the Moslem-Jewish dialogue groups in which I have participated is the tendency for both Israeli and Arab to carve out an apologetic stance that both justifies one's behavior and faults the other's actions. Yet sometimes, a claim is made by one side that is virtually impossible to refute. Such is the case with almost every interfaith conference I attend.

For example, at one such interfaith event in Japan, Dr. Younis Amar of Hebron University told the audience that it was "easier for him to secure a visa to go abroad than to receive a pass to Jerusalem." So too was the case with Mitri Raheb, a Lutheran minister from Bethlehem, and Sheikh Mohammed Al Jabari from Nablus. And these are Palestinian religious leaders who are moderate, believe in dialogue, condemn violence and support the peace process.

The arguments employed to deny Amar, Raheb and Al Jabari access to Jerusalem are reduced to a single justification — **security**. There is no evidence that these clergy have done or said anything to indicate they would threaten the Jewish state by visiting a particular mosque or praying in a certain church.

But they are not alone. Jerusalem is off limits to the majority of Arabs in the territories. Restrictions regarding Jerusalem that have been placed upon Palestinians are extremely stringent. While security issues are not to be belittled, they must not be used arbitrarily whereby an entire population is being collectively punished for the actions of a few. Further, closing off the territories not only does not solve the situation, but actually exacerbates it. Cutting off economic viability and/or spiritual fulfillment heightens the frustration level of a Palestinian population already suffering from deprivation. This is a classic example of where the practical application of a liberal policy would impact on the moral rectitude of an entire people (Israeli).

One can argue that Jews are not free to go wherever they want to in the territories. This sad reality is unforgivable. Yet this must not be used as an excuse to justify holding Jerusalem and its holy places hostage.

In the last Israeli elections, the "right" put forth the theme that the "left" would divide Jerusalem. Reality would have it that Jerusalem is already divided. Jews do not go to Wadi Joz, Abu Dis, Issawiya, Tzur Bahar or Batir.[1] These villages are virtually off limits to Israelis. The vast majority of Israelis also do not go into the Moslem or Christian quarter of the Old City. Most certainly, they avoid East Jerusalem.

In a public show of chauvinistic pugnacity, provocation and sheer "chutzpah," former defense and foreign minister, Ariel Sharon, bought a home in the Moslem quarter of the Old City. He wanted to prove that Jews could live anywhere. He was not followed to his new place of residence by a flock of Israelis clamoring to buy houses next to his. What about Palestinian Arabs? If Jerusalem is not divided, then why does one not see Faisal Husseini[2] purchasing a home near the Cardo?[3]

How often does Mr. Sharon stay in his Moslem Quarter home? When he is in Jerusalem tending to his business as a member of the Knesset, does he choose to stay in his Arab abode, or do the Israeli taxpayers pay the bill for him to stay in one of Jerusalem's hotels in the west side of the city? The answer is contained in the latter part of the question. Is it the city's division that keeps him from his home or the fact that he needs a police escort to go there? What of those Jews who are trying to prove that the city is not divided by living near the Holy Sepulchre[4] or in Silwan?[5] If the city is so open and unified, why do they need an around-the-clock military guard to protect them?

Jerusalem is a divided city, not de jure, but de facto, not in the eyes of a public relations gimmick, but in the eyes of a practical reality. Despite all the security issues that abound, a way must be found to let Christians and Moslems express their religious needs in the holy city. No one should be fooled into believing that since matters of peace are being handled on a political level, one

---

1. Suburban areas of Jerusalem populated by Arabs.
2. The Palestinian representative of Jerusalem in the Palestinian Authority.
3. A main area in the Jewish quarter of the Old City.
4. The holy church where Jesus Christ is said to have ascended to heaven.
5. A small Arab suburb outside the Old City walls of Jerusalem which is said to be the original ancient city of Jerusalem during King David's reign.

can close one's eyes to the continuing violations of human rights, including the prevention of Palestinians from the territories to travel freely to Jerusalem.

Allowing free access to the holy sites in Jerusalem for all peoples is a Jewish matter as much as it is an Arab Moslem or Christian issue. For all the years that world Jewry was so pained because of the inaccessibility of the Western Wall (*Kotel*) to Jews, Israel must not impose a similar hardship on others. As a people who have been so persecuted for their religious beliefs, it is incomprehensible that Israel would pursue a policy that would deny others their religious freedom. The collective historical experience of the Jewish people teaches the value of tolerance. This value must stand the test of even the most violent confrontation with the Jewish people's enemies.

Israelis need to reconcile their collective historical experiences as an emerging people, with a value system rooted in social justice and equality, with the present reality of a growing nation, and with a responsibility to apply that value system fairly. Israel's long-term memory needs to restrain its short-term initiatives. Eventually both poles of the memory span must work in sync with each other.

At the close of the most sacred historical and theological holidays in the Jewish calendar, Passover and Yom Kippur, Jews end their prayers with the supplication: "Next year in Jerusalem." This spiritual yearning does not mean to exclude others from access to Jerusalem. "Who prays in Jerusalem is as one praying before the Throne of Glory, for the Gate of Heaven is there" (*Pirke de Rabbi Eliezer*, 35). Heaven's gate should be open to everyone.

The Holy City of Three Faiths: A Prescription for Religious Harmony

In a discussion on the Middle East between former British Prime Minister Margaret Thatcher and the late Israeli Prime Minister Menachem Begin, Ms. Thatcher, apparently in a peak of frustration, turned to Mr. Begin and blurted out: "Why can't you Jews and Moslems make peace like good Christians?" Northern Ireland aside, the answer to that question is that

Jerusalem is a **holy city** to three monotheistic religions — Islam, Judaism and Christianity.[1]

These religions have shaped the history, geography, demography and theological bent of the city. The spiritual literature of each religion is filled with earthly and mystical musings about Jerusalem. Yet, Jerusalem is also a city of strife. Ethnic, political, social and ideological conflicts are constant elements in its history. Years of peace and prosperity have been rare. Division and war are the standard emblem of the city.

Today in the holy city, there are three religions coexisting within two nations, continually divided by deep conflict. As Jews, Christians and Moslems who have learned from their respective religious traditions the value of Jerusalem, the spiritual center of their religious home, they must know that the enemies of true dialogue are cynicism and despair. The cynic holds that the only real motivating factor in human life is self-interest, while the desperate person claims that all human discourse is useless. However, their religious faiths teach that genuine dialogue among people of differing views and backgrounds is not only possible, but also can bear positive fruit.

For too long religion's negative influences upon the peace of Jerusalem have stemmed from an interpretation of truth in an exclusive manner, rather than by an inclusive and positive approach. Nationalism and theology have been fused into one whole, and Divine blessings are seen to be bestowed upon one community above the other.

Unfortunately, this is a common phenomenon in human history. But in any protracted conflict, there is a temptation to enlist religion as another weapon in the national arsenal. Since "Holy Land" and "Holy City" are primary elements under dispute regarding Jerusalem — and since Scriptures link the holiness of the land and the city with the very nature of a Divine covenant — there is an inevitable theological tension between particular claims to Jerusalem and more

---

1. The passion of Judaism and Christianity for Jerusalem has produced the "Jerusalem Syndrome," a temporary psychiatric condition, which is characterized by patients believing that they have become biblical figures such as John the Baptist or Moses. Israeli Professor of Psychiatry, Eliezer Witztum, who has dealt with patients suffering from this temporary mental state, explains that many Christians view Jerusalem as the site of the Armageddon and the "Second Coming." When they visit Jerusalem, they may experience cognitive dissonance because of the conflict between their mental image of ancient Jerusalem and the reality of the modern city. Religious Jews with the "Syndrome" believe that the building of the "Third Temple" is imminent, that the ancient animal sacrifices will be restored and that their own Messiah will soon arrive. The "Syndrome" is not exclusively confined to those pilgrims coming to Israel who have suffered from previous mental illnesses. It effects seemingly normal individuals.

universal understandings of how Jerusalem is destined to be a means to fulfill transcendent ends.

The positive or redemptive potential of the three monotheistic religious traditions must not be eclipsed, even by the sometimes perverse attempts by religious extremists to paint the Almighty in their own narrow image. Judaism, Islam and Christianity emphasize values and principles that transcend the confines of national identifications by reminding one that we are all God's children, created in the Divine image. All human and national rights are predicated on this fundamental theological tenet; and religious leaders ought to be shouting this reminder daily, to counteract the tendency to adopt a partisan stance without any compassion for the suffering of the other side.

Each tradition offers role models for exemplary behavior in the personalities of such leaders as Abraham, Moses, Jesus and Mohammed. Abraham, the common ancestor of all three religions, could serve as an exemplary figure in his relations with his nephew Lot (offering territorial compromise) or with the Hittites (negotiating over the Cave of Machpelah in Hebron[1]). The praxis and discipline of faith in any one of the three monotheistic religious traditions ought to be presented as a practical path toward justice, righteousness and peace. A religious contribution to the peace of Jerusalem ought to be focused on translating prophetic ideals into everyday imperatives.

Father Thomas Michel of the Vatican, in a paper on Jerusalem, presented at an interfaith conference of Jews, Moslems and Christians from the Middle East, sponsored by the World Conference of Religion and Peace (Kyoto, Japan, 1993), held: "If Jerusalem is to serve as the paradigm for peaceful coexistence among Jews, Moslems and Christians, then all resistance to peace has to be broken down. Fear, anger and grief — the emotional investments that most Israelis and Palestinians have when contemplating Jerusalem — must be dispelled. In order to transform fear to trust, anger to forgiveness, and grief to compassion, spirituality has to have some therapeutic effect on these basic human responses to conflict. It is the conviction of the religious person that to sanctify God's name, there must be sacrifices that amount to earthly ego-renunciations, including the attachments that nurture fears, hostilities and grievances. These

---

1. The burial place of Abraham, ground considered holy to Jews and Moslems.

sacrifices are often harder to make than material ones, such as loss of land and fortune. Yet this is precisely where religion should be helping to transcend one's emotional investments and self-perceptions."

Michel continued: "Religious dialogue depends upon honesty and frankness, on a willingness to say things that may be painful for the other side to hear, but at the same time to listen with openness. In listening, one discovers the realization that the words of the other side have a history — years, decades and even centuries of painfully lived experiences. These historical experiences have produced personal and national aspirations and sufferings that color and shape the way that present realities appear, just as one's participation in history has molded a certain perception of reality."

All three faiths profess peace, a peace that must first be symbolized by an open Jerusalem. The peace that is proffered is like a unity, a theological unity that sees the people of the three faiths living together by overcoming enmities and moving beyond the wrongs of the past.

history

In the Middle East, the burden of history has often presented a formidable obstacle to peace. It seems impossible to gain a common reading of the history of Jerusalem. Facts, events and even statistics have been selected and manipulated to "build a case" or to support a predetermined position. Two courses on the Middle East taught by a pro-Israeli professor and a pro-Arab professor often diverge so sharply from each other that one wonders whether the same subject matter is being discussed.

According to Michel: "Selective readings of history, which appear to sustain contradictory judgments on the justice of one or another cause, are often too easily dismissed as propaganda, even if they contain elements of truth. An endeavor that would serve the cause of peace would be an effort by religious leaders to move to a common reading of history. One must be able to grant that another has bases in history with valid points, and areas of agreement which can provide a foundation for impartial judgments, even in a slanted presentation."

a jewish/israeli world view

For Israelis, Jewish history began in the Land of Israel four thousand years ago. Throughout those centuries there have always been Jews in the land. In exile and in dispersion, the Jews cherished Israel in their hearts and repeatedly sought to return. Jerusalem, as the Jewish people's first capital, became the single focal point of Jewish national and religious restoration. (For many believing Christians, Jewish return to Israel is a biblical fulfillment that will hasten the coming of the Messiah.)

During almost half of the biblical period, the land was wholly Jewish, under Jewish sovereignty or self-rule. After a period of tribal organization and government by Judges, a monarchy was established by Saul in 1025 BCE. His successor David consolidated the Kingdom and made Jerusalem its capital, with his son Solomon building the Holy Temple there. Around 930 BCE, after the death of David and Solomon, the Kingdom was divided into Judah in the south and Israel in the north.

The expansion of the Assyrian and Babylonian empires brought first Israel and later Judah under their sway, and many Jews were exiled to Babylon in 586 BCE, after the destruction of the First Temple. Repatriation in the days of Cyrus of Persia and the building of Jerusalem's Second Temple eighteen years later marked the beginning of a period of revival that witnessed the creation of the Second Jewish Commonwealth.

For four centuries the land of Israel enjoyed a large measure of self-rule under Persian and Hellenistic tutelage. When in 168 BCE Selucid Syria sought to interfere with the autonomy, the Jews rose in revolt under the Maccabees[1] and regained full independence, which lasted over two centuries in the Kingdom of the Hasmonean and Herodian dynasties.

Toward the close of this period, the Jews, in a series of uprisings and wars, defied Roman imperial might. Ultimately, in 70 CE, Rome subdued Judea and destroyed Jerusalem's Second Temple, whose remnant, the Western Wall, became a focus of pilgrimage.

After two generations, revolt flared up again and independence was briefly

---

1. The popular name of the priestly family, the Hasmoneans. Led by Judah Maccabee, they organized a revolt against the ancient Syrians which lead to the cleansing and rededication of the Holy Temple in Jerusalem. Their efforts are commemorated in the annual *Chanukah* festival.

restored in 132 CE under the leadership of Simeon Bar Kochba.[1] The Roman crushing of the Jewish independence did not dislodge the Jews from what they considered their homeland, and most certainly not from Jerusalem, their eternal capital. For centuries afterwards, the country continued to be predominantly Jewish. Even under Roman and Byzantine supremacy, the Jews maintained and developed their autonomous cultural and religious institutions.

Upheld and fortified in dispersion by a messianic vision of ultimate return, Jews never forsook their homeland nor forgot their spiritual links to Jerusalem. This tie was and is realized in the daily life of a religious Jew who, three times a day, faces Jerusalem and prays for a return to the holy city. A Jew closes every meal with a prayer for Jerusalem. On weekdays one says: "By the waters of Babylon, there we sat and wept as we remembered Zion" (*Psalms* 137:1) and during the Sabbath one recites: "When the Lord restores the fortunes of Zion, we will see it as a dream. Our mouths shall be filled with laughter and our tongues with songs of joy. Then shall they say among the nations, the Lord has done great things for them" (*Psalms* 126:1-2). At the conclusion of a Jewish wedding, the married couple says: "If I forget you Jerusalem, let my right hand wither, let my tongue cleave to the roof of my mouth, if I cease to think of you, if I do not keep Jerusalem in my memory at my happiest hour" (*Psalms* 137:5-6).

This brief panoramic view of the Jewish historical links to Israel, and to Jerusalem in particular, should in no way be interpreted as an attempt to deny the historical claims and spiritual attachments of Christians and Moslems to the holy city. Quite the opposite, because of the compelling historical claims that Jews can make upon Israel and Jerusalem, they must respect the claims of others. And here, historical claims must not necessarily take precedence over religious and/or spiritual arguments.

methodology

Related to any historical argument is the issue of methodology. For every person, some issues are more important than others. Whether speaking about relations between nations, labor negotiations or marriage counseling, one must

---

1. Leader of the Jewish revolt against Rome 132-135 CE.

admit that if not all, then at least some elements of a possible solution are desirable. The factory worker might like a longer summer vacation, but is ready to concede that he or she is much more concerned about wages and pension benefits, and so will be satisfied if these demands are met.

However, some issues so intimately touch on matters of self-identity, or on economic or political survival, religious or national concerns, that one would consider these matters intrinsic to any acceptable solution to the issue in question. Naturally, the larger the body of non-negotiable demands that each party brings to the conflict, the less likely it will be that any type of resolution can be reached. The danger then becomes that one might not achieve one's basic priorities.

It is human nature for people to confront one another like bargainers in the market place, slow to reveal the top price and concealing the bottom line at which the enterprise is no longer worth the effort: the point at which one is ready to walk out empty-handed. In human relations, people often act like card sharks, refusing to show their cards and always saving the aces in reserve.

In several spheres of human life, this principle holds sway: international diplomacy, stock takeovers and divorce proceedings. However, for the three monotheistic faiths which intersect in Jerusalem, their God, the common God of their common father Abraham, does not follow the method of the market place. God's speech is direct. As believers whose behavior is formed by the way God has revealed a Divine way of dealing with humankind, should not Christians, Jews and Moslems try to reverse the usual human process, revealing their hands at the beginning, stating the bottom line on which they believe a just peace can be founded?

Might it not be useful for each religion to try to articulate the barest minimum of non-negotiable truths without which they are convinced that there can be no justice and there will be no peace? In such statements of minimal acceptability, is it not possible the three faiths might discover areas on which there is agreement, which could then become the basis for exploring new issues and enlarging the field of accord? If peace and justice are to be more than platitudes, which are recited ritually to show good will, a methodology must be found which can enable Jews, Moslems and Christians to move in the direction to which people of faith should be committed.

It is clear that Israel will never again submit to a divided Jerusalem. It is equally clear that Palestinian Moslems and Christians will never accept Jewish sovereignty over their holy places. Why then not opt for religious self-rule over holy sites, **as well as** national self-rule over different regions in Jerusalem?

truth

Methodology alone does not solve a problem. One cannot deal with the devil. To the extent that propaganda can demonize another person or another people, whether it be by repeating half-truths, distorting national characteristics, reinforcing prejudices, generalizing specific wrongs or exaggerating actual weaknesses, demonization of the other gives a spurious validity to the refusal to cooperate in seeking solutions. Demonization reduces fellow human beings to an enemy who does not need to be listened to and against whom no action taken can be considered excessive.

Propaganda directed against others reduces the complexities of human life to a two-dimensional television drama where the "bad guys" exist in order to be destroyed by the "good guys." The danger of propaganda lies in its disregard for truth. It creates an unreal world where the forces of good take it upon themselves to use whatever means are necessary to oppose the demonic enemy. Those who convince themselves that they are on the "side of the angels" feel justified in whatever action they take against those they have dehumanized.

If Judaism, Islam and Christianity are to play any direct role in the construction of Jerusalem as a city of peace, then it must be in this area of combating hostile propaganda. The Hebrew Scriptures, the Koran and the New Testament all emphasize that God is Truth, God is 'Al-Haq' (Arabic), God is 'Emet' (Hebrew). The three communities of faith affirm that this God can never be served by disregarding the truth, no matter what the cause.

Jews, like their co-believers around the world, know how much they themselves have suffered and how many lives they have lost over the centuries as a result of hate propaganda. In recent decades, Moslems and Christians can point to countless instances of their being the victim of unjust defamation and their cause being subject to unfair distortion.

Each community must defend itself by exposing and correcting lies, half-truths and distortions directed against them. It is difficult to admit that on too many occasions government agencies, religious institutions and leaders have been disseminators of false information and hateful propaganda. Moreover, whenever a religious or ethnic group is victimized through a disregard for the truth, it constitutes an offense against all who believe in the God of Truth.

Therefore, it is a concrete step toward peace whenever a Moslem counteracts anti-Christian propaganda in his milieu, when a Christian defends a Jew against the calumnies committed by another Christian and when a Jew works to correct a slanderous image of a Moslem. More broadly, peace is served by the three religious faiths making common cause to oppose injustice and oppression, and defend the victim, no matter to which religious community he belongs.

violence

This leads to the whole question of violence. No doubt Jews, Christians and Moslems recognize those of their religious texts that seem to encourage violence. But these texts are overwhelmed by other religious texts that opt for peaceful resolutions. For example, in Judaism Amos the prophet of social justice and equality should take precedence over Joshua the conqueror, David the psalmist should touch one more than David the war hero, and the builders of the houses of study in Yavne[1] should impress one more than the heroic fighters at Massada. Religious leaders must call upon the more enlightened literature in their religious traditions to guide them. No more can their spiritual guardians come down to the right of "Attila the Hun."

equal rights

Another obstacle to peace is the matter of citizenship in a modern state. Second class citizenship, in whatever form it takes, is no longer acceptable in the international forum.

---

1. Rabbi Yochanan Ben Zakai established the Sanhedrin (Council of Jewish Sages) that would guide the people between the fall of the Second Temple in 70 CE and the revolt of Bar Kochva in 132 CE. The greatness of Yavne as a center of Jewish learning reached its heights during the time of Rabbi Gamliel between 95 and 115 CE.

All human beings are created in God's image. If so, the ancient rabbis of the Jewish tradition rhetorically ask: "Why was humankind created out of the dust of the earth? To affirm that none among us is made of superior stuff;" and they added: "Why was but a single man created? It was for the sake of peace, that none could say, 'my father is greater than your father'" (*Mishna Sanhedrin* 4:5). None can claim that his or her lineage is greater than yours. To be certain this was understood in terms of race as well, these same rabbis taught: "God formed Adam out of the dust from all corners of the world — yellow clay, white sand, black loam and red soil. Therefore the earth can declare to no race or color of human that you do not belong here, this soil is not your home" (*Yalkut Shimoni*, 1:3).

The peace the three religions must seek is one that does not ignore the demands of justice for all peoples concerned. Justice demands the implementation of the equality of God's creatures, which includes the right to be treated as equal citizens. This means the institution of the rights of assembly, free movement, free speech and press, the right to protection from attacks or harassment, the right to participate in government, the right to an open education, the right of economic viability.

conclusion and cure

In order to involve religious traditions in the service of establishing Jerusalem as the city of peace, the mere utterance of prophetic teachings will not be sufficient. Quoting from *Isaiah*, the *Sermon on the Mount*, or an inspiring *Sura* from the Koran will not create much headway in bringing peace to a polarized Jerusalem. What is demanded is positive religious intervention.

Judaism, Islam and Christianity must actively help each person of its faith-tradition to transcend narrow applications of religion in the search for peace. A commitment to historical objectivity, a methodology that incorporates the art of compromise, an adherence to truth, an end to violence and the equal application of full human, civil, political and national rights for both Israeli Jews and Arabs and Palestinian Moslems and Christians must all serve as the religious ingredients in the quest for the tranquility and peace of Jerusalem.

Ultimately, for the religious person this means undergoing repentance, '*teshuva*' (Hebrew), '*gwab*' (Arabic) and recognizing himself as both victor and victim, oppressor and oppressed, dominator and subject — and recognizing the other in similar terms. Only when this moral dualism is transformed into an acceptance of the Divine Image in the "enemy," will there be a foundation for genuine and lasting peace.

Jerusalem… Jerushalom… Jerusalaam
How similar — how different.
Are you capital
Or the center of three ways to
One God?

You were made by change
And you will grow through change.
Jerusalem, you were never property,
Only possession, as you were always lost
By the one who tried to claim you.

You are a paradox,
As one cannot prove you
Without proving oneself.

Jerusalem, you who mean peace,
Show us the way to your deepest destination.

Jerusalem, you who mean peace,
Help us
So we can fulfill the meaning of your name.

(Ernest Haas)

The War of the Jews

For the vast majority of Jews, Jerusalem is the most important historical and spiritual symbol of the Jewish people's unity and longevity. During religious services, when taking out the sacred Torah from the Ark, Jews recite: "From Zion the Torah goes forth, and from Jerusalem, the word of the Lord." That single statement expresses the centrality of Jerusalem to the Jewish people.

If one were to ask an Israeli what is the first place he or she would visit with a guest from abroad, the response would invariably be: "Jerusalem and the Kotel" (the Western Wall). The Wall is the last remaining physical evidence of the Jews' presence in Jerusalem after the destruction of the Second Temple and the expulsion of the Jewish people in 70 CE (see page 49). Most Israelis feel an historical attachment to the Wall. Yet there are many Israelis who see in the Wall a spiritual attachment.

the "holy wall" of jerusalem

Just behind the Wall is the holy mosque, the Dome of the Rock. The mosque is built on Mount Moriah (the mountain jettisons out in the middle of the mosque), the place at which Abraham almost sacrificed his son Isaac at God's command (*Genesis*, 22). It is here that Elijah the prophet is to lead the Messiah's return to Israel. The assumption is that the Messiah's first stop will be the Wall, prior to settling in Jerusalem.

When the Messiah does return, he (or she) will find a divided Wall. As a place of worship, since the Six-Day War, the rules that apply regarding prayer at the Wall are Orthodox ones — separation between the sexes. There is a relatively large men's section and a much smaller women's section. There is no historical basis for this division, for throughout Jewish history the Wall was always integrated. Yet, like on all matters of religious import, the Orthodox community has ultimate control.

I was lecturing a group of tourists at the Wall, male and female together. I was standing in the plaza, well away from the Wall itself where people pray. An Orthodox Jew began yelling at us: "You are degrading my Wall!" I responded: "Your Wall? It is my Wall." Whose Wall is it? In whose city is it? It is only on the rarest of occasions that I go to the Wall to pray. But every so often, I get the urge on Sabbath to walk to the Wall. Once there, I must confess, I am always drawn into its spiritual mystique. Standing before the most powerful symbol of my people's continuity always overwhelms me.

I looked around. While somewhat saddened that the Wall has become an Orthodox haven, exclusively ruled by their religious preferences, I still felt a comfort in seeing other people approaching the Wall with a certain awe. I felt a surge of Jewish history and Jewish peoplehood.

At the time I was at the Wall, there were a number of Bar Mitzvahs[1] taking place. While not knowing the families who were celebrating this Jewish "rite of passage," I was still moved by the fact that these young thirteen-year-olds were casting their lot in with the Jewish people through a public display of communal worship in front of this holy remnant of our people's long rich and varied collective experiences.

For that moment, I felt the Wall was mine. But is it mine? It can only be mine if I can share it equally with other Jews, and particularly with those who are closest to me, my family. But, I cannot. They can stand before the wall in reverential prayer like I did. They can absorb the historical and spiritual (and even political) significance of the Wall. But beyond that, they cannot express their feelings through traditional ritual manifestations. Why? Because my family includes four daughters![2]

That day I was at the Wall, I thought about my three older daughters who had already celebrated their Bat Mitzvahs in our local synagogue. But being at the Wall on this particular Sabbath, I felt this spiritual rush. I wanted to have my youngest daughter celebrate her Bat Mitzvah at the Wall. Why should she not be entitled to enter the community of our people at the Jewish people's most sacred place, the place that symbolizes that community? Why cannot I stand before these ancient stones and recite the priestly benediction over her (*Numbers*, 6:24-26)? Why must she be denied religious inclusion at the epicenter of religious expression?

I am not asking for an integrated Wall. I am not even asking that my daughter parade in front of the Wall in a *Tallit*[3] or *Tefillin*.[4] I am only asking that she be permitted, on a Sabbath, in

---

1. The occasion on which a boy (Bar Mitzvah) reaches the age of 13 and a girl (Bat Mitzvah) reaches the age of 12, and is officially ushered into the adult Jewish community, and is expected to assume full religious duties. The Bar/Bat Mitzvah is called to the Torah to read all or part of the biblical portion of the week, and a section from the prophetic writings. In the Orthodox tradition, only boys undergo this ceremony.
2. On May 22, 2000, Israel's Supreme Court ruled that women could read from the Torah at the Wall, separate from the men, while wearing prayer shawls.
3. Prayer shawl. A large four-cornered shawl-like garment with fringes on the corners, worn by men during morning religious services.
4. Hebrew for phylacteries. Tefillin are two black leather boxes containing a parchment with the biblical injunction for their use (*Deuteronomy*, 6:8), worn by adult males Jews at morning religious services (except the Sabbath and Festivals). One is worn on the forehead and the other on the arm, both affixed by black leather straps.

the women's section, to read from the Torah and be confirmed as a Bat Mitzvah. The Wall should belong to her. Sadly, this did not (and will not) happen. The Wall has been taken away from her and too many other Israelis.

The Wall's history, its glories and its tragedies — ancient and modern — has been usurped by one community from all others. This powerful symbol must not serve the parochial interests of one religious stream in Judaism. When paratroopers are inducted into the army, it is done at the Wall. The opening ceremony for Memorial Day of Fallen Soldiers is held at the Wall. As long as the Wall is used as a Jewish national symbol, not just a religious one, it is unjust that an Israeli soldier, who literally fought to defend the Wall in the Six-Day War as an act of commitment to the perpetuity of the Jewish people (perhaps even died in action), should later have his daughter denied the right to hold a Bat Mitzvah at the very place of her father's heroic sacrifice. Some sort of compromise must be found to accommodate varying religious attitudes and the need to express these attitudes at the most dramatic religious place of the Jewish people.

the "holy streets" of jerusalem

But what holds true for the Wall, holds true for other areas of Jerusalem.

It was 10 o'clock on Saturday evening and I was driving from the western part of the city to the eastern part. In order to do this I had to drive through an Orthodox neighborhood. As I approached the area, I had to dodge burning garbage cans. The road was wet from the water cannons used earlier to disperse ultra-Orthodox Jews who had protested the road being open to cars on the Sabbath. The slippery surface of the street caused the car in front of me to slide into one of those burning barrels of trash. Only a miracle saved the car and its occupants from exploding into flames. All the while crowds of ultra-Orthodox men were hurling insults at passing cars, despite the fact that the Sabbath had already ended.

Because of the historical and religious significance of Jerusalem for the Jew, the unholy alliance between religion and state has produced a theological chauvinism that can rip the city apart. All national symbols become exclusive religious expressions, expressions of one stream in Judaism — Orthodoxy.

A handful of "believers" feel that by waving the flag, placing a note between the stones of the Wall and invoking the name of the Almighty, they have a right to claim Jerusalem as their own. But the symbols, values and beliefs of the Jewish people — God, Flag, the Wall and Jerusalem — do not belong to only one segment of the population. A skull-cap does not give an individual the Divine right to the "one and only truth." Judaism emphasizes universal principles that transcend the confines of partisan identification, and indeed relativize those identifications by reminding us that we all are equally heir to them.

a treatment for jerusalem's split-personality

Jerusalem is always at center stage. While the voices of the "religious right," as personified by the Orthodox establishment, are extremely vocal in putting forth their views, they are not the only voices heard in Jerusalem. The "religious left" have also taken to the streets of the city to express their views.

Rabbis of the "right" use their bodies to block entry into Jerusalem. They stage prayer vigils at the Wall. Their protests are set in motion to reinforce their religious position, often a position that opposes any compromises on Jerusalem. They urge religiously observant soldiers not to obey orders that would have them remove settlers from any part of the land of Israel.

Rabbis of the "left" stand in front of Heichal Shlomo,[1] the spiritual "High Place" of Jerusalem. They hold an afternoon religious service with an opposite theme to that of the rabbis of the territories. They hand out leaflets to soldiers urging them to respond to their conscience, not to a *halachic*[2] dictate which comes from what they feel is a narrow interpretation of Jewish law.

In tying their protests to Jerusalem, the emotional center of the Jewish people, both sets of rabbis feel that public sympathy will come their way. What in effect happens is that both exploit Jerusalem, not for their own religious purposes, but for their ideological aspirations. Both are using theological positions to promulgate political world-views, not necessarily ethical imperatives.

---

1. The central synagogue in Jerusalem that houses the offices of Israel's chief rabbis.
2. The term used to refer to Jewish law. It denotes the legal portion of the Talmud (the full body of Jewish law that interprets biblical commandments) as well as the subsequent codifications of legal writings. The word literally means "the way."

In the 1960s, I was a rabbinic student in the United States. At one time I served as the chairman of the organization "Seminarians for Peace," the junior partner of the powerful "Clergy and Laity against the War in Vietnam." At that time some of the great religious leaders in America — Abraham Joshua Heschel, William Sloan Coffin Jr., the Berrigan brothers and, later, Martin Luther King Jr. — called upon American soldiers to refuse to serve in Vietnam.

During the war in Lebanon of 1982 and the first stages of the Intifada, some Israeli soldiers refused to honor mobilization orders to serve either in Lebanon or in the territories. While many political leaders on the ideological left did not call openly for such action, they tacitly supported these soldiers, and sympathized with those who honored the dictates of their conscience.

The religious right and left have failed the test of consistency, both posturing themselves on the moral high ground. Before their declarative call to religious soldiers to refuse to dismantle settlements in the West Bank and Gaza Strip, right-wing rabbis attacked in a vitriolic manner so great a religious luminary as Professor Yeshayahu Leibowitz,[1] who called on Israelis to resist service in the territories.

Yet those on the religious left do not act much better in matters of consistency. They have remained wedded to their political leanings, as opposed to being true to a progressive ideology. They hailed Leibowitz as a courageous religious spokesman while condemning those rabbis, who from their own religious perspective, were not behaving very differently. While rabbis of the left may disagree with the political stand of the rabbis of the territories, they must appreciate that the latters' protest is no less legitimate than their own.

The left and the right must not distinguish between religious beliefs and moral conscience. Often the two go hand in hand, and both should take precedence over national loyalty. Yet when each side uses Israel's capital as the staging ground for its ideological world-view, moral and religious arguments become dwarfed by nationalistic sentiments. The fusion of religion and nationalism is a sure recipe for a political explosion.

---

1. (1903-1994) A brilliant unorthodox Orthodox Jewish philosopher and religious thinker, considered by many to have been an iconoclast. His radical views on Israeli society, particularly regarding Israel's occupation of the West Bank and the Gaza Strip, based on his understanding of the Jewish tradition, turned him into an intellectual "guru" of the left.

Neither side of the religious spectrum (or political divide) can split Jerusalem in two. It is ironic that every Israeli government has spoken of a "united Jerusalem." Of course this is in reference to Israel's sovereign rule over the Arab sections of the city. But too few Israelis have given enough consideration to the fact that the warring factions within the Jewish people are casting a schizophrenic pall over the city, whereby it might eventually be ruled, not by two nations, Palestinian and Israeli, but by two minds — a Jewishly open one and Jewishly closed one.

If this were to happen, a psychological trauma would ensue similar to that which occurred during the days of divided kingdom at the turn of the Common Era. According to Jewish tradition, the Second Temple was destroyed and the Jewish people driven into exile because of *"Sinat Chinam"* (baseless hatred from within). It took close to two millennia, with the eventual establishment of the modern state of Israel, for the Jewish people to be "healed."

The realization that a split Jerusalem could lead to another extended exile should justify drastic treatment. Shock therapy may be called for. When religious leaders of the left or the right demonstrate in Jerusalem, they not only confuse the issues, they inflame the situation. Israel cannot allow itself to reach a point where religious divisions become the basis for an ideological and/or theological civil war. Surrounded by those who would wish to destroy them, Israelis cannot afford to pit themselves against each other. Jews simply must reach the therapeutic point where they can comfortably counsel moderation. For sanity to reign, the Israeli mind cannot be a loose-leaf folder, clogged with an overabundance of polar or extremist ideas. It must be an advocate for equilibrium. The Israeli mind must keep its best interests at heart.

CHAPTER 3

POLITICAL CONTRADICTIONS

Double-speak

"It was the best of times. It was the worst of times" (*A Tale of Two Cities*, Charles Dickens).

"It was the best of times." Prime Minister Benjamin Netanyahu announced from the Knesset rostrum that Israel had reached an agreement to return to the Palestinian Authority one of the holiest cities in Jewish tradition, Hebron, which was an essential element of the Oslo Accords.[1] Netanyahu's statement reflected the vast majority of opinion of the Israeli populace, as indicated in the 87-17 Knesset vote in favor of the agreement. With the exception of a small, albeit vocal, minority, Benjamin Netanyahu could record with pride that he stood before a united nation.

"It was the worst of times." No sooner did the prime minister make his dramatic announcement, when he mounted a bitter assault against the opposition for placing before him a "horrid" agreement that had required him to toil hours in order to make it palatable. Within minutes of placing before the elected legislative body of the people of Israel an agreement that represented an incredible harmony of thought among most segments of the population, he tore asunder that unity with his partisan posturing. Divisions that should have been laid to rest in Israel's quest for peace were reinforced.

"It was the best of times." Benjamin Netanyahu, Foreign Minister Ariel Sharon and Trade Minister Natan Sharansky flew to the Wye River Plantation to eventually conclude a further agreement with the Palestinian Authority (see *Introduction*, page 19, footnote 1). It was clear that Netanyahu's government would have to rely on the opposition to secure the votes necessary for approval of the agreement. The opposition had already announced that, despite its desire

---

1. A set of agreements signed by the Palestinian Liberation Organization (PLO) and Israel on September 13, 1993, that set the stage for Israeli-Palestinian negotiations through mutual recognition.

to topple the Netanyahu government, it would support the agreement and postpone any no-confidence vote until after its implementation. Once again, it looked as if a potentially explosive and divisive decision would be moderated by a rare show of unity.

"It was the worst of times." As Netanyahu and his entourage landed at Israel's airport, news reports already indicated that those who signed the agreement had grave reservations. Before leaving the airport's arrival hall, Netanyahu launched into a scathing attack on the opposition, essentially blaming it for forcing him to agree to something that was clearly (to his mind) not in Israel's self-interest. Sharon placed conditions on the agreement which were not included in any of the negotiations, and Sharansky actually voted against it. The opposition voted with the government, but a few weeks later did its utmost to bring it down.

This "see-saw" approach to diplomacy is not only confined to the right wing of the Israeli political spectrum. It typifies the behavior of much of the political echelon in the country. Just as one feels that Israel is on the brink of compromise among the disparate factions within the country, someone sees fit to guarantee that dichotomies will rule the day. When a person's thought processes work against him or herself, then it is clear that the results can be unhealthy. This is different from running in two directions. Walking down two paths is something that falls within the field of normal contradictory behavior. There may even be a Machiavellian touch at work, in that it only seems that one is plotting different schemes, but in fact, all is well planned out in order to achieve the eventual goal at hand. But when one undoes that which he or she has already determined, then there is something clinically wrong in his behavior.

Personalities play a vital role in determining policies and relationships.[1] When one's personality harms relationships, thus impairing those policies, then the good of the country often becomes sacrificed for an individual's ego. This is true for any leader of any country. It is most dramatically expressed in countries where dictators, civilian and military, rule. Any country that has one-

---

1. In Israel's case, many of its leaders have loomed large as personalities in the international arena. Prime Ministers Golda Meir, Shimon Peres and Yitzhak Rabin enjoyed especially close personal relationships with its chief ally, the US government and its presidents, which clearly played a positive role in America's support for Israel. Prime Ministers Yitzhak Shamir and Benjamin Netanyahu had an adversarial relationship with the US and its presidents, which diminished support for Israel and damaged its image.

party rule, or is governed by a theocracy or a monarchy, serves as a further example of an ego dominated system of politics. There are few limits placed on leaders of these types of states.

While democracies are often led by people who may indeed be infused with a more than healthy share of ego, there are limits built into the democratic system that guarantee reasonable behavior, to be reflected in reasonable policies. Not always — as America proved in its errant war in Vietnam or as France proved in its adventurous war in Algeria. But time and civilian and political protest eventually directed the leaders of these respective countries to correct their ways.

This general rule applies to Israel as well. Israel is a vibrant democracy, which in many areas dwarfs the great democratic institutions of much of the western world; particularly given the constant threat under which it lives. Israel is diverse, giving expression to almost all political views, sometimes including the most contradictory of ideologies that bed down together under the same coalition.

Every Israeli government has striven to harmonize competing ideologies that dramatically infuse the body politic. There is a strong desire to establish stability in order to move forward on the peace front. On the surface this seems to be a healthy approach if one intends to reach a compromise among the dissenting elements within a society or, for that matter, within an individual who is driven to despair by a lack of psychological coordination.

As for Israel, the opposite seems to be the case. The fusion of the right and the left, of the religious and secular, only seems to exacerbate the dualities that exist within the Israeli character. This forces an Israeli government to march in place. Like the patient deep into therapy who refuses to follow one path, always clinging to his contradictory tendencies which drove him to seek help in the first place, Israel at times remains mired in its inner conflicts. Compatibility is the cure-all for a healthy constitution. When Israel strives for such compatibility, then it is able to move off of square one.

Indeed, such an approach has proven successful. Menachem Begin was able to conclude a peace agreement with Egypt by seeking the help of those in the political opposition dedicated to the same goal. Israel was able to pursue its policy of accommodation with the Palestinians by creating a government of like-minded ideologues. As narrow as the late Yitzhak Rabin's coalition government was, it was able to sign the Oslo Accords precisely because it saw that the best way to achieve some semblance of consistent behavior was by being single-minded. Harmony bred the Jordanian-Israel peace agreement and, it is hoped, will spur on further peace agreements.

Despite these far-reaching successes, unfortunately this rule of basic unity does not always pertain to the Israeli system of government. A coalition of differing personalities makes up the governments, splitting each down the middle. An imbalance pertains, and often, outlandish behavior takes place. It is the same imbalance that takes place in the human body when a person is taking two drugs, one canceling out the other, causing side effects that are anything but healthy. It takes much experimentation to find the correct chemicals to stabilize the unbalanced personality. In the end, it is either one drug, or a combination of compatible drugs, which leads one to the point where he or she can move on with his or her life.

When Israel has within its coalition an ultra-Orthodox rabbi and a secularist from a socialist kibbutz, then it is quite clear there will be a "drug imbalance." Each one wants to be the dominant factor in determining the direction of the government and so feels free to address all issues on the political agenda. Whether the issue at hand falls under his or her expertise or not is irrelevant. Each feels that only he or she possesses a "miracle drug." Therefore the ultra-Orthodox deputy-housing minister — who refuses to become a full minister because he and his party do not recognize the state as sovereign above God — will pontificate about matters of security. The ultra-Orthodox health minister will declare that the Russian minister of the interior represents a constituency of "non-Jewish whores and thugs."

While other democracies hold heated debates in their houses of parliament or congress, rarely does one minister comment about the affairs of another ministry. If he or she were to do so, the chances of being dismissed would be great in order to guarantee continued harmony, even if the harmony is at times tense.

What strikes one as unique to Israeli politics is that Israelis support this system of government. The two major political parties have lost numerical strength over the last few elections and the more sectored parties have grown considerably in numbers, strengthening their will to be part of the government, no matter who sits in the coalition with them. One is reminded of Tom Paxton's sarcastic song, made famous by folk singer Pete Seeger: "What did you learn in school today, dear little boy of mine? I learned our government must be strong. It's always right and never wrong. Our leaders are the finest men and we elect them again and again. That's what I learned in school today, that's what I learned in school."

The Culture of Language

I hold you Yitzhak, you Raful and you Motti[1] responsible. One of my daughter's teachers called her a "liar." The teacher must have heard how our political leaders speak. How else can I explain it?

My daughter misplaced an assignment, handing it in a day late. Upon telling the teacher what happened, the teacher replied: "Liar." Now of course, every father will defend his child, but my daughter is not a liar. If you don't believe me, ask her mother!

When my daughter and I complained about the incident to the school's principal, he refocused the issue in the most creative manner. He asked my daughter: "Do you really think your teacher genuinely believes that you are a liar?" When my daughter said that she felt humiliated and that she was owed an apology, the principal merely shrugged his shoulders and sighed: "Golda[2] never apologized for our failures in the Yom Kippur War." Returning home from that school meeting, I noticed a car, which did not stop for a pedestrian waiting patiently to cross the street at a clearly marked crosswalk. As the car passed, the seemingly mild-mannered individual hollered: "Maniac."

While Israelis do not swear very much, curse words not being indigenous to the Hebrew language, they have elevated to an art form other insults, like "greaser," "imbecile," "scuzball," and "idiot" — all words in the employ of elected officials as they refer to each other in political debate from the Knesset rostrum. Indeed,

---

1. Yitzhak refers to former prime minister Yitzhak Shamir; Raful refers to Raphael Eitan who has served as a minister in several governments and who was an army chief of staff; Motti refers to the late Mordecai Gur who served as a minister in several governments and was also an army chief of staff.
2. A reference to Golda Meir, the prime minister at the time of the Yom Kippur War, when Israel was caught off guard by an attack by the Syrians and the Egyptians.

Israeli politicians can be absolutely inventive in their use of the "holy tongue." They have an uncanny capability to use vulgar interpretations of the Hebrew language. Sometimes their verbal perorations make soccer locker room banter sound bland!

Routinely Israelis are known for interrupting each other, never letting the next person finish a sentence. News interviewers are only prepared to pursue their own agenda, never letting the politician they are interviewing answer questions, let alone state an opinion. The newscaster's desire to create sensational scoops dominates discussions. Israel once had a TV program that was supposed to foster understanding between those who held different opinions on a particular topic. The name of the program: "Confrontation!"

How did all this happen? Can the Jewish people, who have produced some of the finest literature throughout history, who have sustained an ancient language, thought by many to be holy, conjure up such uplifting expressions as "grasshoppers" (Yitzhak Shamir's reference to Palestinians), "cockroaches in a bottle" (Raphael Eitan's description of Arabs) and "whore" (Mordecai Gur's nomenclature for a female deputy-speaker of the Knesset)? Such exalted manifestations of speech flow ever so freely from our elected officials. Did these titular leaders have in mind Ahad Ha'am's[1] statement "the loftier the thought, the finer the language" when they uttered these remarkable phrases? One cannot help but feel that American jazz musician Mose Allison must have had Israel's political leaders in mind when he wrote for his friend: "Your mind is on vacation, but your mouth is working overtime!"

One must remember that words **can** kill. In extreme cases if one chants long enough and loud enough, "death to the Arabs," eventually an Arab will be killed. If one describes Arabs as "cockroaches in a bottle," then Arabs will be treated as such and Israelis will become immune to the dehumanization of a people resulting from such name-calling. If Yitzhak Rabin was continually labeled a "traitor," then the only act that can deal with a traitor is to eliminate him.

If one calls a student a "liar," particularly if the student is not lying, is not a liar by nature, then the clear indication is that one does not value the human

---

1. Pen name, meaning "one of the people," of Asher Ginsburg, a great Zionist thinker, writer and essayist who lived from 1856-1927.

worth of another individual. To paraphrase the saying: "Sticks and stones may break my bones, but names can demoralize and destroy me."

Where have you gone Eliezer (Ben Yehuda)?[1] Show how the Hebrew language is supposed to be used. Talk to Yossi and Ghandi[2] and tell them that they cannot refer to each other from the Knesset floor or in the Knesset cafeteria as "scorpion-face" and "ass-face," as was the case in one of their scintillating exchanges. Tell them that the manner in which they express themselves sets the tone for the way teachers speak to their students.

If Israelis cannot talk to each other with respect, then they will not treat each other with respect. Who should understand this better than the Jewish people who have suffered so long and so frequently from the most venomous types of verbal assaults? How does one explain such contradictory behavior, given the Jewish past that witnessed such vitriolic attacks upon the Jewish people? Israelis have to fine-tune the elements of democratic discourse and develop a culture of language that allows for dissent without creating bitterness. Chaim Nachman Bialik[3] expressed it best: "Language is the key to a nation."

"Baseless Hatred" (Sinat Chinam) — The Deri Case Part I

The verdict against Arye Deri[4] released a flood of reactions throughout the country. Reading the indictment sheet against Arye Deri and the later verdict, one got the impression that Deri had been pulling the wool over everyone's eyes from the time he entered the political arena. After years of investigation, the charges against him were devastating.

As a Reform rabbi, I admit that there is no love lost between Deri and myself. And here I must confess to a nasty, yet all too human emotion. I was pleased that he got "what was coming to

---

1. Hebrew lexicographer (1858-1922) considered the father of modern Hebrew.
2. Yossi refers to Yossi Sarid, a minister in several Israeli governments; Ghandi is the nickname of Rehavam Ze'evi who has served in the Knesset.
3. Outstanding Hebrew writer (1873-1934) considered the leading poet of the modern Hebrew renaissance and of the Jewish national movement.
4. A rabbi, a former minister in a number of Israeli governments and former leader of Shas, the Sephardic Orthodox religious party. He was tried and convicted of crimes such as fraud and theft. A controversial figure on the Israeli political scene, he found himself at the center of many of the major political controversies and scandals that rocked the country in the 1990s.

him." Like so many others in the country, I was delighted in the fall of one of the Orthodox establishment's leaders. Indeed, it is very human to try to build oneself up on the back of another person's shortcomings — even better on the heels of someone's criminal acts. But I would be foolish to believe that my stock as a Reform rabbi will rise because of Deri's woes.

Yet I am not the only one who gloated and is still gloating. It seems that the entire Israeli WASP community (White Ashkenazi *Sabra*[1] with "Pull") danced with joy when the word "guilty" was pronounced in court. Those of us who support religious pluralism felt we were finally getting even, because it was Deri and his Shas partners who sent our then liberal leader, Shulamit Aloni,[2] into the political wilderness. We are now particularly smug about Deri's ongoing miseries.

Shas leaders have hinted that the constant harassment of its ministers smacks of racial prejudice. They claim that an Ashkenazi establishment is out to get the Sephardi community. Liberals, who defend the rights of Palestinians, Israeli Arabs, gays and lesbians, as well as non-Orthodox religious Jews, scoff at such an idea.

The reality is that Deri's conviction by an Israeli court, a court system that is known for its integrity and objectivity, was free of any racial prejudice. In the past, Ashkenazi minister of housing, Avraham Ofer, committed suicide because of a police investigation into his alleged wrong doings. Yitzhak Rabin suffered because of his wife's illegal bank account in the United States when he served as Israel's ambassador to America. And Simcha Dinitz, the former chairman of the Jewish Agency/World Zionist Organization, considered "Mr. Ashkenazi," was driven from public life for a minor indiscretion for which he was later exonerated. In the pursuit of justice, the police and the judicial system have always risen above partisan and ethnic considerations.

But Shas' claim of racial prejudice is not without foundation. If prejudice has not appeared in the judicial arm of the government, it can appear in the political arena. Political revenge can become tinged with racial overtones. They are expressed in subtle ways. Worse, they touch not only upon stored-up prejudices against Sephardim, but also against Orthodox Jews. As aforementioned,

---

1. A native-born Israeli.
2. The leader and founder of the left wing Meretz party. By threatening to leave Yitzhak Rabin's coalition, Shas forced Shulamit Aloni to resign her post as education minister because of its opposition to her alleged anti-clerical ways.

because of Deri's difficulties, non-Orthodox religious Jews boast a certain amount of religious self-righteousness. They are joined by secularists who portray Orthodoxy as so parochial that the criminal acts for which Deri was convicted are to be expected. The implication is that "Black Hat Judaism"[1] breeds criminality.

The truth is that racial fuel has been added to this prejudicial fire. Exaggerated racial cartoons, mocking former Sephardic Chief Rabbi, Ovadia Yosef, the spiritual leader of Shas, appeared in a number of leading newspapers. In the privacy of one's living room, one hears expressions of an "I told you so attitude" in reference to "Moroccan Jews in Hassidic[2] drag." There are further racial slurs alleging that what Deri did is a result of a political culture endemic to "that community." The Deri affair has tended to condemn an entire ethnic group for the acts of one person.

Deri's actions reflect what he alone did — not what Orthodoxy is all about nor what Sephardic Jews are all about. For certain, his actions should have no basis for putting a positive label on secularists, non-Orthodox religious Jews or Ashkenazic Jews. Indeed, this would be reverse prejudice.

The behavior of any publicly elected figure, whether he is religious or secular, Sephardi or Ashkenazi, reflects upon the entire electorate, as do racial innuendoes by any segment of the citizenry. In the Deri affair, emotional expressions of anger, disappointment, shame and sadness are all legitimate. Emotional expressions that smack of racial prejudice are simply unacceptable.

"Baseless Hatred" (Sinat Chinam) — The Deri Case Part II

There is a reverse side to the Deri case, showing that prejudice can go both ways. Since the main thesis of this book is to demonstrate the split nature of Israeli society, the reaction of the Shas community to the guilty verdict serves this supposition quite well. It is the Sephardi racial response to an Ashkenazi one.

---

1. A reference to the dress of many ultra-Orthodox Jews, particularly members of Shas who wear black hats or black kippot (skull caps or yamulkes).
2. A reference to an ultra-Orthodox religious movement whose roots are Ashkenazic.

For me, the reaction of Arye Deri, Ovadia Yosef and all his followers within and without Shas, to the guilty verdict, taught me, an Ashkenazic liberal, something unique, contrary to my very human instinct. Those surrounding Deri declared that if Deri were found guilty, then all Shas members, all Moroccans, all Orthodox Jews and all Sephardim were guilty as well. By their syllogistic reasoning, they too were crooks, and the indictment of Deri was an indictment of an entire race of people, based on an unrestrained hatred of Deri and his cohorts. And who am I to disavow the plea of Shas leaders to hold every Sephardi Jew to blame for their political leader's dirty deeds? That would be "politically incorrect." And so I have been forced to be part of those "hate-mongers."

But in the name of fair play, I wish to prove that my hatred is spread equally, without the slightest hint of preferential treatment. I have to be consistent and apply the logic laid down by Shas whereby a guilty verdict against a leader of a particular party is a statement of guilt against all those who identified at any time with that leader. I will not give into double standards. And so I now hate Ashkenazim, not only because Deri told me to, but because Ya'acov Levenson, the Ashkenazi chairman of one of Israel's largest banks, Bank HaPoalim, was accused of criminal acts and Asher Yadlin, another Ashkenazi leader of the central kibbutz movement, was found guilty of fraud. Therefore, I truly detest Ashkenazim. Since both Levenson and Yadlin came from the socialist world of the kibbutz, I hate both socialists and kibbutzniks.

As for Orthodox Ashkenazim, I have absolutely no use for them. Baruch Goldstein has seen to that (see *Chapter 1*, page 40, footnote 1). Throw in Moshe Levinger[1] and the Jewish Underground, and you have further proof of why I should hate them all. I have no idea where to place Yigal Amir.[2] Oh, he studied at Bar Ilan University. I hate every student there.

And God knows how I hate all Palestinians, particularly Moslem ones — to say nothing about Israeli Arabs, Bedouins and Druse. But most of all I hate Russian Jews. Just one look at Avigdor Lieberman[3] or Gregory Lerner[4] makes me want to throw out of my house all those Russian Jews I adopted and supported. I feel like such a fool. How could I have had any one of them for a Sabbath meal? Bringing such hateful people into my home, what must I have been thinking?

---

1. A leader of the Jewish settlement movement in the West Bank who lives in Kiryat Arba, outside of Hebron. Known for his fiery rhetoric, he was found guilty of shooting and killing a young Palestinian boy.
2. A religious Jew enrolled as a law student in Bar Ilan University, who was convicted of the murder of Yitzhak Rabin.
3. A political strongman, who headed Prime Minister Netanyahu's office. Suspected of crimes, he was driven from his position. He was later elected to the Knesset as the head of a Russian party: "Israel is our Home."
4. The alleged head of a Russian Jewish "mafia" ring in Israel. Convicted of various crimes.

By the way, as a former United States citizen, I hate all Americans — Richard Nixon's crimes and Bill Clinton's infidelities providing sufficient reason to warrant my contempt. After all, more than any of Israel's leaders, these two men, presidents of the United States of America, truly represent all Americans.

It is amazing how someone can start out with a seemingly perfectly logical formula and misapply it so that it becomes a ridiculous piece of mischievous nonsense. Things equal to the same thing are not necessarily equal to each other. Though Deri, Yadlin, Levenson, Goldstein and Nixon are (or were) all members of the human race, they are not interchangeable; nor are they surrogate exemplars of the communities from which they hail. To accept such comparative drivel in order to make some lame social comment about universal guilt, but not individual responsibility, ultimately, through reverse prejudice, introduces wholesale discrimination.

It would seem that one side balances out the other with its equal doses of prejudice. In reality, what happens is that an emotional virus of racial discrimination festers, infecting the entire body. Prejudice alters sane thinking and can play itself out in unpredictable ways. For certain, bigotry of any kind does not reside in a healthy individual. When it spills over, it can only split a society in two.

Left versus Right

A draft press release was sent to human rights groups: "Israel and Palestinian human rights groups call for the Israel Defense Forces (IDF) to release the names and cause of death of unidentified Lebanese corpses buried in northern Israel."

The proposal was signed by an impressive group of human rights organizations: The Mandela Institute for Political Prisoners, Women's Organization for Political Prisoners, The Palestine Human Rights Information Center, The Public Committee Against Torture, Israeli and Palestinian Physicians for Human Rights, Hotline for the Defense of the Individual, B'Tzelem (Israel's Human Rights Monitoring Center).

There was good reason to sign the press release. It appears that approximately 150 Lebanese civilians are allegedly missing and presumed buried in unmarked graves near the B'not Ya'acov bridge in northern Israel. The signatories to the petition are demanding that the IDF "publicize the names, dates and cause of death of the unidentified Lebanese corpses... and calls on the IDF to notify the families of the deceased and return the bodies for proper burial." This is indeed a noble mission that should be embraced by all human rights groups.

However, matters relating to Lebanon do not exist in a vacuum. The cover letter is indicative: "... because we are concerned about the human rights of all in this area, we are demanding that information **about every victim of the Lebanese conflict be released.**" Where is the balance here? What about the Israeli missing who were **victims of the Lebanese conflict**? Why are the above-mentioned human rights groups reticent about including even a "throw-away" reference to the Israeli MIAs (missing in action)? When has the Public Committee Against Torture ever raised the issue of Zachary Baumel, Tzvi Feldman and Yehuda Katz, missing in action in Lebanon since June 12, 1982?

The petition begs to include these Israeli MIAs when it quotes relevant sections from the Hague Convention and the Third and Fourth Geneva Conventions on matters of human rights. Just as there are provisions in these Conventions that speak of proper burials and notification to families of deaths, so too are there parallel provisions for prisoners of war and/or missing in action. The inclusion of the Israeli missing in action does not weaken the demand for information about the Lebanese missing. Quite the opposite. It lends legitimacy, offering a credible and practical element to the plea. It lends balance.

But this one-dimensional approach to matters of human rights seems to be endemic to Israeli human rights groups. The same organizations rightfully oppose administrative detention, police brutality, religious abuses, etc., but only as they relate to the Palestinian population. It is true that abuses heaped upon the Palestinians far outweigh those experienced by Israelis. Also the Palestinians do not have the same avenues for protest and protection that Israelis enjoy. But this should in no way obviate the need to hold fast to the public defense of all who suffer from human rights abuses.

Kach, the extreme right wing movement founded by the late Rabbi Meir

Kahane, which was outlawed from running for the Knesset because of its "racist" ideological platform, truly was a hate-filled organization. Its very existence should have offended all. On several occasions, its members had been placed under administrative detention. Those on the left who oppose the use of administrative detention against Palestinians should also rigorously oppose administrative detention for Kach members. After all, if someone is suspected of a crime, whoever that person is and whatever ideological view he represents, he should be charged accordingly. This is a basic human right. The immediate round-up of right wing "hotheads" who praised the assassination of Yitzhak Rabin and were placed under administrative detention posed and still poses a real danger to a free society. It is during times of national emergencies that democratic rights become most vulnerable to abuse.

No one is asking Israeli human rights groups to dedicate an equal amount of time to protest offenses committed against Israelis. After all, Israelis are protected by government agencies, whereas Palestinians need the protection of private organizations. However, one should expect a verbal nod to the equal application of human rights concerns for all individuals, regardless of their political affiliation.

The area near the prime minister's residence in Jerusalem is often the scene of mass protests, from both the left and the right. In one of many such demonstrations by the right, the accusation of police brutality was made, although for the most part the Israeli police have displayed restraint in breaking up demonstrations. At this particular demonstration, some of the protesters exceeded the bounds of lawful behavior. The police, many mounted on horseback, waded into the crowd to disperse the people. Unfortunately, there were cases of excessive force used to contain the crowds.

Not a word of protest was raised by "leftist" who are active in human rights organizations and peace groups. The reason that these organizations and groups did not raise their voices in protest was that they did not (and still do not) understand the difference between "left" and "liberal." An individual with leftist leanings is concerned exclusively with the political correctness of his or her "cause" or "movement." A liberal is concerned with justice for all. For a leftist, it matters little if someone with competing ideological views is abused. In fact, in some quarters, there is almost a smug satisfaction that "these people" are getting a taste of their own medicine. But a group's political or ideological bent does not deprive the individual of his civil liberties.

Rabbis for Human Rights (RHR)[1] petitioned Israel's Supreme Court to block the construction of a housing and shopping development over a Moslem cemetery. This came on the heels of a protest over the building of a highway near the northern city of Haifa that would cut through another Moslem cemetery where Izzadin Kassam was buried, the founder of the military wing of the terrorist organization Hamas. Joining that protest too, RHR argued that Kassam's identity was irrelevant. What was relevant was the need to respect the dignity and sanctity of the cemetery.

Parallel to this petition to the High Court of Justice were ultra-Orthodox protests against the desecration of Jewish graves to allow for "technological advancement." In the eyes of these ultra-Orthodox Jews, the building of hotels, highways and bridges at ancient Jewish gravesites was a sign of blatant disrespect for the Jewish past.

The deep and abiding liberal concern for the dignity of Moslem gravesites was (and is) not translated to an equal concern for Jewish gravesites. Those on the left should not always see Orthodox protectiveness of Jewish tradition as a single-minded attempt to impose its religious will on an unsuspecting citizenry.

On many issues, the "unholy" alliance of politics and religion in Israel does lead to a cynical exploitation of the Israeli coalition system of government in order to bring the secular community to heel before the dictates of a religious minority. But it would be wrong to assume that such shenanigans pertain to Orthodoxy's concern for Jewish burial sites, or that they have any bearing on the merits of Orthodox insistence on showing respect for the Jewish past. The desecration of Jewish graves should be no less upsetting than the desecration of Moslem or Christian graves.

Sometimes one reacts to the form of protest rather than to the content of it.

---

1. A professional religious human rights organization in Israel composed of 100 rabbis from all streams in Judaism. RHR was established in December, 1988, to raise a moral voice in the name of the Jewish tradition against the violation of human rights.

This is only natural. But liberal thinking individuals usually pride themselves on distinguishing between the two. It is intolerable for many sectors in the ultra-Orthodox community to put out "archeological hit-lists." Its need to spill garbage bins on main thoroughfares, to hurl rocks at workers at building sites and to attack policemen who are protecting archeological digs are not acceptable forms of protest. This manner of protest most definitely gets in the way of the message that the ultra-Orthodox are trying to put across. The ultra-Orthodox community could better serve not only its cause, but also the cause of Jewish tradition if it brought its concerns to the public in a more creditable fashion. They should use the power of persuasion. Most Israelis, because of their rich history, have a basic respect for tradition. They realize that archeological research is necessary to uncover the past. They also recognize that this process must be carried out with the utmost of respect and dignity.

The debate over the excavations must take place within the confines of a mutual sensitivity for scientific progress and traditional concerns. Neither the ultra-Orthodox world nor the leftist secular world understands this. One would expect liberals to take the initiative; not just to enter into a dialogue with the Orthodox community, but also to show that respect for tradition is not contradictory to a liberal world view.

The most liberal (not leftist) of legal organizations in the United States, the American Civil Liberties Union (coincidentally staffed by many Jews and African-Americans) has defended the civil rights of such distasteful organizations as the American Nazi Party and the Ku Klux Klan. It does so because it knows that if any group is denied its civil rights, all groups can be subject to similar deprivation.

When excessive force is employed against Palestinians, Israeli leftists go "off the wall." By the same token, they cry "holy murder" when the police use tear gas to disperse Peace Now demonstrators. They assume that the "forces of evil" are arrayed against the "forces of good." Police brutality is ideologically blind. It must be protested no matter who is facing the billy-club. One's political persuasion must have no bearing on the purity of civil liberties.

It matters little that those on the right might never raise their voices against actions that would deny the full rights of those on the left. A genuine liberal acts according to absolute standards of behavior, not relative ones.

As a person who counts himself among the human rights activists for liberal causes, I want to reject the claim of our detractors who chide us for not according equal time to other people's human rights. I often ask myself, why can they not compliment us for the good deeds we do without pointing a finger at us for not working in other areas? At the same time, I must acknowledge that there is some justice to their argument. They may not see that they fall victim to the same inconsistency for which they fault us. Nevertheless, I would ask my human rights colleagues to be a bit less parochial and more inclusive. We should defend the rights of all to speak out for their views and to activate their right to protest, and to sign a petition not only on behalf of missing Lebanese civilians, but also on behalf of Israeli MIAs.

Those on the political left should go beyond their narrow reach. To qualify as good liberals they should defend the rights of those with a different political outlook, provided that that outlook is not predicated on seditious or violent acts. They should also enter into a dialogue. Gush Emunim's (see *Chapter 1, page 27*) passion for its views is justifiably equal to the passion of those in Peace Now. It is not enough to talk to Palestinians, one must speak with one's fellow Jews.

Israel's left, like Israel's right, has become too predictable. One can almost always expect a knee-jerk reaction whereby everything is categorized as those who are "for peace" (Peace Now, et. al.) or those who are "against peace" (Gush Emunim, et. al.). Applying such monolithic categories is dishonest.

Civil rights belong to everyone. Those who purport to speak in the name of human decency should be the first to recognize this. Unfortunately, this lesson is often lost on Israel's peace and human rights groups. It is time for those on the left to raise the liberal banner and to start worrying about all those whose civil rights are violated, and not just those who reflect their own ideological world-view.

Political and Religious Divorce

Israel is defined as a Jewish state. Israel's Declaration of Independence states twice that the "Jewish state" **is** Israel. First, it postulates that the "Jewish state" is synonymous with Israel and second, it defines the nature of this sovereign and democratic state. For Israelis, what constitutes the nature of that Jewish state is critical for its own self-definition and identity.

The challenge Israel faces is that the Orthodox community, as represented through its Orthodox political parties, has claimed the word "Jewish" for itself. They would have one believe that the sole essence of being Jewish and "living Jewish" is expressed through a religious (Orthodox) life-style. However, Jewish life manifests itself in many ways. There is a wider definition of Judaism that embraces concepts of land, state, people, culture, language and ethnicity, as well as religion.

Yet it is Orthodox Jews in the country who demonstrate on a daily basis a commitment to a Jewish life that can be measured — at least in the ritual realm. Their dress, their observances and their almost singular approach to social and political issues stand in sharp contrast to those of other Israelis. Expressions of ethical behavior, whose roots can readily be found in the history and literature of the Jewish people, are not always perceived as Jewish responses to events of the day, but as humanistic ones. One can argue quite convincingly that Judaism has always been pluralistic, and therefore has naturally produced a multi-faceted society. But when there is a plethora of views floating around, it is difficult to build a unity of purpose. Those holding varying approaches to Jewish life enhance the democratic nature of Israeli society, but they cannot compete with the single-mindedness of a religious movement in achieving specific goals that are a reflection of their world-view.

The percentage of Israelis who vote in Knesset elections is very high, usually hovering around the 75% mark. The percentage of ultra-Orthodox Jews who vote averages in the 90% range. Therefore, their political strength often outstrips their numerical representation within the general population. Since no political party in Israel has ever won a clear majority, coalition governments are built with the Orthodox parties, particularly the ultra-Orthodox parties, who are then able to wield tremendous power.

When a party has such a definitive ideological outlook, and is aware that a coalition is dependent on its support to stay in power, it flexes its muscles in order to gain as much as possible from the government to satisfy its constituents' needs. This is understandable. However, when that party goes beyond its voters' needs and tries to thrust upon a resistant citizenry its values and/or religious beliefs, then there is an abuse of democratic principles. Such is the case with the ultra-Orthodox parties, which have been part of many different Israeli government coalitions. In local politics, oftentimes the situation is far more extreme. For example, in Jerusalem the majority of the city is secular, yet the voting patterns are such that half of the city council is comprised of ultra-Orthodox members.

Recognizing the importance of maintaining the Jewish character of the state, most Israelis are opposed to a separation between "religion and state." They see religion as one of the expressions of the Jewish past and future, alongside the other Jewish personality traits aforementioned, of land, state, people, culture, language and ethnicity; and most importantly of Jewish values based on a prophetic vision of equality and social justice. However, given the power of the ultra-Orthodox parties, with their almost "missionary" agenda to turn Israel into a state ruled by Jewish law, which holds the government hostage in order to extract political favors, many Israelis do want a separation between "religion and politics."

Many Israelis see this separation as essential in one crucial area — the role that the ultra-Orthodox should play in the army. While one can argue that matters of religious belief and moral consciousness rise above national loyalty, all citizens in the country must share an equal burden in defending it. Approximately 30,000 ultra-Orthodox Jews do not serve in the Israeli army, for a myriad of reasons, the most prominent one being the Divine need to serve the country by studying in *Yeshivot*.[1] There are also many Orthodox women who do not serve in the army because it is felt in some Orthodox circles that it is not "fitting" for a woman to fill a "man's" role. Yet here, at least in the modern Orthodox world, many women perform acts of "national service." They work in various civilian fields that serve the state, such as teaching in disadvantaged schools, working on kibbutz, assisting in hospitals.

While the country has tried to address this issue through various governmental and parliamentary committees, virtually all recommendations made have yet to satisfy the vast majority of Israelis who do serve in the army, risking their lives to defend all citizens, secular and ultra-Orthodox alike. There

---

1. Institutions for Jewish learning. Oftentimes refers to a rabbinical seminary, modeled after the academies of Jewish learning in ancient Palestine and Babylonia.

is little question that one segment of the population cannot continue to be the sole bearer of responsibility for the country's physical survival. At some point in time, there will be a greater resentment and hostility than is currently the case. Ultra-Orthodox Jews cannot continue to benefit from someone else shouldering the burden for their continued safety. This is further exacerbated by the right-wing leanings of many ultra-Orthodox Jews. They seem ready to defend their political views to the last drop of someone else's blood. Religion in Israel can no longer dictate one's political obligation either to defend or not to defend the state.

The challenge Israel faces is from the ultra-Orthodox (and "moderate" Orthodox) religious parties whose understanding of Judaism is such that they believe it is their "Divine right" to make exaggerated claims which they hold to be good for the entire country. In order to achieve their goals they are even willing to put on hold one of the most sacred of religious quests, the quest for peace. As a result, "Divinity" has been reduced to a few sad anthropomorphic characteristics, which include such anti-religious personality traits as selfishness and intolerance. The opposite should be the case. Divinity cries out for a religious response to current issues that relies on persuasion, not coercion, compromise, not ultimatum.

The unholy alliance of politics and religion in Israel is just that — unholy. Politics is the art of compromise. Religion in Israel, as expressed through the ultra-Orthodox community, stands in contradistinction to this. Israel's multi-party electoral system requires respect for the pluralistic character of coalition building. Pluralism, however, is an anathema to every ultra-Orthodox party in Israel. It is an anathema not only because the ultra-Orthodox wish to retain control over matters of religious adjudication, but also because ultra-Orthodoxy, as interpreted by the religious parties, has produced a fundamentalist approach to religious beliefs that runs head on into the principles of parliamentary democracy. Those on the religious right who frequently argue that Judaism and democracy cannot abide each other are strengthened when they bring the government to a crisis. (For a small country, Israel has an extraordinary number of political parties. There are anywhere from five to seven different political entities that form any given coalition. As a result, almost any decision that comes before the government can create a crisis.)

Orthodoxy is based on Divine revelation. By definition, Divine revelation requires absolute adherence to God's commandments. No compromise is tolerated. Interpretation of Divine laws is permitted, but the parameters for maneuverability are extremely limited. Israel's Orthodox parties too often hold uncompromising positions in one area or another. All base their stances on a Divine dictate. Their actions are understandable as their religious beliefs determine their behavior; and religious belief is legitimate, particularly since such uncompromising faith in Divine revelation has served as a mainstay of Jewish survival.

However, what is no longer legitimate is the mixing of "milk and meat."[1] Politics and religion must be divorced from each other. Their marriage has tarnished both of them. At a time when confidence in Israel's political system is so crucial because of the ongoing peace negotiations with Israel's neighbors and the Palestinians, coalition crises, brought about by the Orthodox parties (and other small parties), create a disgruntled citizenry that is unable to trust its government. Trust is essential for compromise.

The continued coupling of religion and politics makes for schizophrenic decision making. This was given expression by Israel's past president, Ezer Weizman, when he said: "I would be willing to wear a 'shtreimel'[2] if it meant achieving peace."

What type of peace was he talking about? A peace that would include selling the soul of the Jewish state? Peace cannot come at the expense of freedom. Such division between these two lofty concepts reinforces internal contradictions that are already part of Israel's political system of government.

The pluralistic nature of Israeli society must be preserved. But pluralism cannot be maintained when one segment of the population rejects the very notion of pluralism because of an unbending theological view of the world. Such is the case with the ultra-Orthodox parties in Israel. If secular-led governments have to sacrifice too much of their political agenda to accommodate the ultra-Orthodox parties (like "being willing to wear a 'shtreimel' if it means achieving peace"), then they should display true pluralism by inviting the Arab parties to join them, something that has yet to occur in Israel. The advantage of such a

---

1. One of the elements of Jewish dietary laws (*kashrut*) is not eating milk and meat at the same meal.
2. A large fur hat worn by ultra-Orthodox Jews on the Sabbath and other religious holidays.

move would be three-fold: 1) a display of democratic rule at its best, 2) perhaps an end to exploitative horse-trading, as "Divine" demands would no longer be a part of the political constellation, and 3) a separation of religion and state. (Although even here, one should not be naive, as sectoral demands would also be made.)

Divorce may require alimony. But paying alimony is far superior to maintaining a marriage that is continually in crisis. It is psychologically unhealthy, even damaging, for the couple and for their children to have two contradictory forces dwelling in the same home. It creates a dysfunctional family. Politics and religion in Israel must go their separate ways.

Leadership and Accountability

Unable to quench his thirst for the beautiful Batsheva, King David sends her husband Uriah to his "forced suicide" by placing him in the front line of battle where he was certain to be killed. When Nathan, the court prophet, hears of this murderous act, he recounts for David that instructive parable where a rich man raids a poor man's flock in order to offer up a sheep to a passing stranger. Upon seeing David taking unprecedented umbrage at such a deed, saying the man should be put to death, Nathan turns to David with the famous words: "Thou art the man" (*II Samuel*, 12:7). Realizing the significance of the parable, David shrouds himself in sackcloth and ashes, entering a thirty-day mourning period for his evil act. Instead of passing the buck, or killing the messenger, he accepts his guilt.

The measure of true leadership should be judged by the degree of responsibility that a leader takes upon him or herself for his or her actions. Too often, responsibility and accountability are not part of the Israeli lexicon. Admissions of wrong-doing rarely penetrate Israel's political echelon. Israel's leaders simply ignore the Nathans of contemporary society. Israel's electoral process reinforces its peculiar system of government, allowing for its politicians to avoid any and all liability for their actions. (With the exception of the direct vote for the office of prime minister, one votes for a party, not an individual.)

Immediate electoral reform is needed so that Israel will not be condemned to continual unaccountable leadership.

If one takes the American model of leadership, with all its considerable flaws, there is a standard of accountability imposed upon its leaders. John Kennedy shouldered the blame for the "Bay of Pigs" fiasco.[1] Jimmy Carter, assuming full responsibility for the failed liberation attempt of US hostages in Iran, brought on his own presidential defeat. Lyndon Johnson retired in disgrace because of the Vietnam quagmire. Richard Nixon was forced from office over the "Watergate" affair. And Bill Clinton was impeached, although not convicted, for his wayward and dishonest behavior in his tryst with Monica Lewinky. Yet these events almost pale in comparison to some of the scandals that should have rocked Israel's political infrastructure.

After Aharon Abuhatzeira was convicted of embezzlement, he continued to sit in the Knesset. Yair Levy, convicted of financial irregularities, refused to vacate his Knesset seat. Tzachi Hanegbi,[2] former minister of justice, clung to his cabinet seat despite an investigation into his activities while he was the minister of justice. Former prime minister Benjamin Netanyahu appointed someone who was under police investigation to be his minister of finance. Only through the intervention of the courts were any of these leaders stripped of their duties. Despite a police investigation, Ezer Weizman clung to his Presidency until the attorney-general's report severely criticized his behavior. None took the initiative on his own. Shimon Peres, who led his party to one defeat after another, only stepped aside as the head of the Labor party when defeated by the late Yitzhak Rabin. And Arye Deri only gave up the leadership of Shas due to political realities and judicial procedures, not because of political responsibility.

More troubling is the way Israel's leaders flaunt their disrespect for national commissions of inquiry. Despite the Arganat Commission's findings on the Yom Kippur War "mechdal" (blunder/failure), the late Moshe Dayan, remained in government, defying the public outcry against his botched role as defense minister at the time. The Kahan Commission, investigating the Lebanon War, cited Ariel Sharon and Yitzhak Shamir as misleading the public during the war.

---

1. An attempt was made by the Kennedy administration to use Cuban exiles to return to Cuba in a covert operation to overthrow Fidel Castro's rule. The plot was foiled during the action.
2. Aharon Abuhatzeira was the leader of the now defunct Tami part, Yair Levy was from Shas and Tzachi HaNegbi from the Likud.

The Commission raked the then chief of staff, Raphael Eitan, over the coals. None of these men drew the honorable conclusion — to step down from public office. Army officers implicated in training accidents or misconduct are often given promotions. Again, it is the court that nevertheless stymies their career advancements.

In America in the early 1960s, not a week went by that I was not arrested for participating in some sort of protest rally. Whenever I went to join a demonstration against some government policy, I assumed that I might spend a night or two in jail. Not once did any of my comrades-in-arms claim that either the state or federal government was violating the principles of democracy by prosecuting those of us involved in disruptive acts of civil disobedience. Even at the height of the civil rights protests in the South, with all the rancid prejudice and violent confrontations that threatened civil rights workers, the legal right of the judicial system to arrest and prosecute us was not questioned. Even though we were protesting laws that we claimed were undemocratic and unconstitutional, we welcomed the mass arrests.

Contrary to this understanding of protest, those in Israel who commit an illegal act do not expect to, or feel they should, face the consequences of their actions. This is not just the case for those who lie down before bulldozers ordered to tear down a Palestinian home or dismantle a Jewish settlement, but is especially true for Israel's political leaders. Shamir, Sharon and Eitan are all very prominent figures to be reckoned with on the public scene. And so, like their elected officials, most Israelis do not like having to take responsibility for their actions.

The right to protest is an absolute democratic principle. This same right extended to those in *Yesh Gvul*[1] who refuse to serve in Lebanon or the territories must be accorded to those who refuse to dismantle Jewish settlements. It matters little if their motivation is based on matters of moral conscience or religious belief. As stated earlier, both must take precedence over national loyalties.

The problem arises when one believes that a democratically elected

---

1. A protest group within the army who, for reasons of conscience, refused to serve in Lebanon.

government has no right to respond. It is not too difficult to imagine what would happen in any major city in the world if, during rush hour, at different points on major roads leading into the city, burning tires halted all traffic. Protesters would be arrested. During the Vietnam War, those who refused to serve in the military were either arrested or fled the country.

Such a policy has not been applied in Israel. Only a handful of Yesh Gvul members served time in military prison. Most were either shifted to other units or released. When right wing protesters block major thoroughfares, holding the country hostage to their demonstrative whims, only a scarce few get hustled into paddy wagons. There are never the mass arrests that defined the American protest movements of the 1960s, which ultimately, and most importantly, affected policy.

Rabbis who clearly make inflammatory statements are never held accountable, nor are settlers chastised for their provocative behavior toward the Palestinian population. Moshe Levinger's four-month sentence for shooting to death an Arab boy in Hebron sent a clear message: "Do as you please, and expect to get away with it!" If one believes strongly in a particular cause, one should be prepared to go to jail for it. If enough people are willing to crowd the jails, eventually things will change. That is precisely what happened in the 1960s in the US regarding the civil rights and the anti-war movements.

In Israel, the arrest of protesters is expected neither by those who protest nor by those against whom the protest is directed. This is also the case with non-political protests, such as Israeli workers demonstrating illegally against the closing of a factory, or farmers spilling their produce on highways to protest a lack of government support, or students staging a sit-in in the middle of a city to bring to the public's attention the high cost of tuition. The expectation that Israel's government will do nothing to counter acts of civil disobedience, and the almost "Divine" understanding that it should do nothing, is unhealthy for the workings of democracy. It is the tension which exists between citizens and their elected government that strengthens democracy. And that tension is expressed through legitimate protest and an equally legitimate government response. The danger lies in the overreaction on the part of the authorities. Israel's police have not been above police brutality. Meting out harsh punishment on the spot is certainly unacceptable. But controlled arrests are possible.

In the US, as civil rights workers and Vietnam War protesters, we were often victims of police brutality. Many times we were arrested because of overzealous police action rather than because of any particular state law regarding public demonstrations. Also excessive police action was accompanied by violent reactions from other members of society who disagreed with our political positions. The hope, mostly in vain, was that the authorities would deal with these people. To the contrary, in too many instances the authorities instigated the violence. And while frequently having to attack the authorities on all levels, nevertheless we understood that the very act of civil disobedience would most likely result in arrest. We knew we were not above the law. If any of us did not understand this, then those on the other side of the picket line made sure we did. We knew that we had to take full responsibility for our actions.

Of all Israel's political leaders, Israel's late prime minister Menachem Begin stands out as a welcome exception to the rule where few if any elected officials assume responsibility for their actions. Begin had the decency to accept responsibility for the failures that occurred during the Lebanon War. A silent vigil was held outside Begin's prime ministerial home, where the number of deaths in the Lebanon War were recorded daily. Before entering his house at the end of the day, Begin always paused to pay homage to those who had fallen. Does anyone doubt that one of the reasons for his resignation was that he felt accountable for the Lebanese misadventure?

The unwillingness on the part of almost all Israeli leaders to assume any culpability for their actions raises two major problems: 1) by failing to admit mistakes, Israel is certain to repeat them, and 2) by refusing to be held accountable, the country is deprived of the moral leadership needed to instill confidence among the public. Until there is a change in Israel's electoral system, Israelis must rely upon the moral integrity of their leaders to demonstrate a commitment to the principle of responsible and accountable leadership. Understanding the implications of one's actions and contending with the consequences is a healthy sign of maturity and stability.

"Happy is the generation whose prince offers sacrifice for his faults"

(*Babylonian Talmud, Hodayot* 10b). During King David's time, the system of government also did not allow for direct representation on the part of the people, yet David possessed the basic decency and honesty to own up to his faults. Three thousand years later, does Israel deserve anything less?

For the Sake of Unity

Haim Yavin, Israel's premier newscaster, appeared on a special news broadcast. "A terrorist bomb has just gone off in the Ramat Eshkol suburb of Jerusalem, killing at least three people," he announced. After these brief, chilling words, came the additive: "This is yet another tragedy that has become routine — one that we have become used to."

It is a tragedy, but surely it is not routine, nor can anyone be expected to get used to such tragedies. How does one get used to murder? The only thing that becomes routine are the reactions that follow — not the reactions of the families and friends of the victims — but of the politicians and the arm-chair critics.

After the tragic bombing in Oklahoma City, Israel's prime minister at the time, Yitzhak Rabin, remarked that "we Israelis could learn a lesson from our American friends by reacting to terrorist atrocities with dignified unity." Of course, he left out the crass commercial abuse of the tragedy, whereby within hours of the bombing "I survived Oklahoma" T-shirts were being hocked. One must be grateful that this sort of warped capitalistic exploitation would never be tolerated in Israel.

But the political exploitation that follows every terrorist bombing in Israel must be considered intolerable. At the precise moment when fellow citizens are in a state of mourning, Israelis must not be pushing their own ideological agenda. No electoral calculations should be made. After the incident reported by Haim Yavin, Israel's then police minister, Moshe Shahal, drove to the site of the bombing. A crowd stormed the car, forcing him to leave the scene. Jerusalem's mayor, Ehud Olmert, pleaded for calm by stressing "that politics should not be a part of our immediate consideration," even as he immediately added the political caveat that the peace process should be stopped.

Anything short of peace will lead Israel back to the days of the Intifada. This time, an armed one. Achieving peace without the necessary security guarantees will unleash more terror. Sadly, peace will not prevent suicide bombers from carrying out their contemptible missions. In fact, no one, be it a newscaster, the police chief or the prime minister, should tell any Israeli that he or she must get used to a "routine" of suicide bombers. Division is what will hurt in the fight against terror. Terror does not distinguish between politics of the right or of the left. Islamic religious fanatics consider every Jew, no matter what his or her beliefs, as their legitimate target.

When terror strikes there must be a moratorium on all political posturing. Judaism has clear guidelines for moments of grief. In Judaism there is the tradition of the *"shiva,"* the seven-day mourning period. At such a time people visit the mourning house, offering solace and expressing unity.

Even when in mourning, Israelis are still very much afraid, because there is no routine response to death, especially death through terror. Should political bickering take place on the fresh graves of those who were killed in terror attacks, sadness and fear only increases. During such emotionally charged moments, when anger enters the Israeli psyche, partisan political exhortations only exacerbate internal divisions among the citizens. In some cases these exhortations can feed the anger to such an extent that it spills over into counter-violence and internal violence. There is only one thing that would give Israel's enemies the same satisfaction as their killing of Jews, and that is Jews killing one another. The pictures of Moslem extremists dancing for joy in Beirut and in Gaza City when Yitzhak Rabin was killed was not just because the leader of the Jewish state was gunned down, but because he was shot by another Jew. Terrorists try to destroy Israel from without, but are deeply gratified when their evil acts of collective murder sow destruction from within.

One cannot give in to this tendency, and start to spread the blame around for the actions of a suicide bomber. If the fragile commonality that exists among Jews in Israel becomes unraveled, they will never be able to combat not just terrorist atrocities, but acts of aggression like another Persian Gulf War.

There need to be frequent and demonstrative shows of unity. There must be a torch light march where all express solidarity with the victims of the horrible scourge of terrorist killings. A unified mission of Jews from all over the world, of every political and religious stripe, must join Israelis physically. The leaders of all political parties must issue a call to their professional colleagues and their public supporters to curtail all emotionally loaded rhetoric. All political leaders, inside and outside the government, should jointly call an emergency meeting where together they plan a bipartisan response to terrorism, not just in the practical sphere, but also on an emotional and psychological plane. Israel's prime minister, the president, the head of the opposition and the chief rabbis must address the nation. Even though Ehud Barak and Benjamin Netanyahu battled each other for the office of Prime Minister, their political differences should not have gotten in the way of their personal and shared memories. Barak was Netanyahu's commander in an elite army unit. In addition, it was Ehud Barak who delivered the eulogy at the funeral of Netanyahu's older brother, Jonathan, the commander and hero of the Entebbe rescue operation (see *Chapter 1*, page 39, footnote 1). Israelis are linked emotionally together in so many similar experiences. It is this commonality that should be tapped, for it is the basis for a deep and abiding unity.

If there is no sympathetic and unified leadership core to look to for strength and comfort during painful times, then Israelis will continue to feel betrayed, and ultimately orphaned. They will feel that not only can no one deal with security issues that abound in the country, but also that no one can deal with the emotional stress and tension that rips at the very core of their being.

"As the angel of death is licensed to destroy, he does not trouble to distinguish between righteous and wicked" (*Babylonian Talmud, Baba Kama* 60a). It is safe to say that the angel of death also does not distinguish between competing political ideologies. Those killed in terrorist bombings represent all sectors of Israeli society. After all, death is the great equalizer. The victims of any terrorist act find their way to death not because they differed politically or religiously or ethnically. They died because of a unity. They were all Jews living in a Jewish state.

For one moment, at the scene of the tragic bus bombing in that Jerusalem suburb, an almost surreal picture of unity flashed across television screens in every Israeli's livingroom. Ultra-Orthodox Jews of the *Chevra Kadisha*[1] were working side by side with secular Jews from *Magen David Adom*,[2] their political

---

1. Jewish Burial Society.
2. The Israeli version of the Red Cross. It means the "Red Jewish Star."

views and emotions cast aside. This image should serve as a paradigm for Israel's general behavior, not only in times of tragedy, but also in times of joy. It is not enough to display unity in death. One must display it in life.

Tragedies often draw people together. Sadly, the Jewish people have had more than their share of tragedy, as has the modern state of Israel in the short fifty years since its establishment. People are able to psychologically overcome loss when they receive support, when a familial and communal unity envelops them. It is the healthiest way for them to carry on with their lives. "Behold how good and pleasant it is for brethren to dwell together (*Psalms* 113:1).

CHAPTER 4

THE HOLOCAUST

Faded and Distorted Memories

In honor of the fiftieth anniversary of the State of Israel, a trivial pursuits game was produced: *Those were the Years*. There were six categories: Places and Sites, Heroism, Leaders of the Nation, Together in Pride (1948-1972), Together in Hope (1973-1998), From the Holocaust to Rebirth. What is most interesting about this game, which obviously was designed for fun, is that the majority of questions deal with tragedies.

Under the category "Together in Hope" (1973-1998), almost all the questions contradict the notion of hope. On each trivia card there are six questions. Here are the questions and answers on one of the cards:

> **Question**: "Who is Nachshon Waxman?"
> **Answer**: "A soldier who was kidnapped by terrorists and killed."
> **Q**: "What happened to soldiers Avi Sasportis and Ilan Sa'adon?"
> **A**: "Both were kidnapped by Hamas and killed."
> **Q**: "What attack happened on the Shore Road?"
> **A**: "Terrorists commandeered a public bus, directing it toward Tel Aviv. In the attempt by the army to free the hostages, 35 people were killed."
> **Q**: "Under what circumstances were soldiers Rachamim Alsheich and Yosef Fink kidnapped and what was their fate?"
> **A**: "They were kidnapped by Hizboullah (a fundamentalist Islamic group) in Lebanon and killed. Their bodies were eventually returned to Israel."
> **Q**: "What war began on Saturday evening, after the Sabbath?"
> **A**: "The Lebanon War."

Q: "Under what circumstances was reserve officer Uzi Yairi
killed?"

A: "In a confrontation with terrorists at the Savoy Hotel in Tel
Aviv."

In the category, "Together in Pride" (1948-1972), almost all the questions on
every card relate to Israel's wars. This is a classic example of a double message.
With all these tragedies, it is a tribute to the Israeli that he can still cling to some
flicker of hope. This is where the dichotomy of the Israeli personality works to
his advantage. It is either a sign of an "irrational genius" or a "warped
mentality" to term hopeful the kidnapping murders of Waxman, Sasportis,
Sa'adon, Alsheich and Fink.

If the categories of "Together in Pride" and "Together in Hope" can only
recount depressing events in the life of an Israeli, one can just imagine what
events are presented under the category "From the Holocaust to Rebirth." Yet
here it stands to reason (and rationality) that the saddest of questions are asked.
There can be no divided interpretation of the horrible events that gripped the
Jewish people from 1933, when Hitler assumed the position of chancellor of
Germany, until 1945 when World War II ended. The methodical slaughter of six
million Jews must be seen as the single most tragic event not only of the last
century, but of all human history. The genocidal murder of the Jews was
irrelevant to the war effort. It stood on its own. It must never be watered down,
given over to different understandings, doubted as an historical fact, distorted
by modern day anti-Semites, diminished by comparison to other events,
universalized beyond recognition and most importantly, because of the passage
of time, slowly erased from our consciousness, ultimately becoming a faded
memory.

Historians are always engaged in interpreting and reinterpreting the past. They
do so sometimes on the basis of newly found documentary evidence, sometimes
by reconsidering known data from a different political outlook, or sometimes
by taking into account a different time-span or even employing new

methodologies. With time, every historical subject has undergone some sort of revision as each new generation rewrites the historical past in light of its own perspectives and values.

As for World War II, one would assume that the universal revulsion against the Third Reich and the brutal massacre of the Jewish people would not create a hospitable climate for revisionism. Yet revisionist attempts manage to raise their ugly voice. The first and still primarily only major revisionist work on WWII by a supposedly "reputable historian" is A.J.P Taylor's book, *The Origin of the Second World War* (1961). Taylor argued that Hitler had not planned a general war, and that the conflict, far from being premeditated, was "an error, the result of diplomatic blunders of both sides to the conflict." Historians everywhere attacked Taylor's book and its thesis, but it nevertheless soon became the banner under which a swarm of Nazi apologists, cranks and anti-Semites rallied.

There is not a widespread conspiracy to deny the Holocaust. Yet attempts to alter the facts of the Holocaust appear, some with remarkable force. In the same year that Taylor's book was published, a revisionist work cropped up in Germany, written by an American, David L. Hoggan. The book had originated as a Harvard doctoral dissertation completed in 1948, but it was revised and "Nazified" in the ensuing years. Unable to find an American or bonafide German publisher, Hoggan gave his manuscript to a Nazi publisher. As any revisionist writer of the Holocaust must do in order to put forth the outlandish thesis that Jews were not sent to concentration camps and gassed there, Hoggan tampered with facts, distorting and willfully misreading those that did not fit his theories and prejudices.

Neither Taylor nor Hoggan is a match for some of the anonymous Internet writers who have denied the Holocaust. The Internet is full of web sites that distort the facts of the Holocaust. On one Internet site, only recently defunct, a "numbers theory," almost identical to that of Hoggan's, was presented: labeled "arithomania." Somehow it was calculated that precisely 4,416,108 of the six million Jews "said to have been killed" were actually still alive, and that the remaining were probably still in hiding so that they would not be charged with war crimes! Another Internet site claimed that the figure of six million was a total falsehood. It would have one believe that the chief blame for the misrepresentation of the facts rests with what Hoggan referred to as: "Those whom we call swindlers of the crematoria, Israeli politicians who derive millions of German marks from non-existent, mythical and imaginary cadavers, whose numbers have been reckoned in an unusually dishonest and creative manner."

Most recently, British historian, David Irving, not only denied the basic facts of the Holocaust, but also employed the worst kind of racism, by suggesting that the Jews should ask themselves why it is that they have been so hated. What is it in their national character that causes them to be persecuted? The clear implication of his remarks is that the Jews are responsible for whatever has befallen them. They are to blame for anti-Semitism. Irving lost his libel suit against American historian, Deborah Lipstadt, who, in her book, *Denying the Holocaust: The Growing Assault on Truth and Memory,* accused Irving of distorting facts to fit his anti-Semitic biases.

Does any of this matter? Would any sensible and decent person be taken in by the absurd malicious lie that Hitler's Germany never really murdered six million Jews? Who would believe such a monstrous falsehood that there were no gas chambers at Auschwitz? Yet as time passes, and the "survivor generation" dies, such lies may very well gain credibility. Attempts at rewriting the Holocaust may take on a renewed force. The further one gets from the Holocaust, the more clouded one's memory becomes. As a new generation of young people is schooled on the technological excitement of sitting at a computer, where one can instantaneously move from subject matter to subject matter with a flick of a switch (a mouse), the more tedious task of reading about historical events like the Holocaust or viewing video recordings of survivors' testimonies becomes less compelling. Even if the testimony were transferred to the Internet, with the passing of the survivor generation, it would not be "interactive" enough to satisfy the attention span of a generation that has been raised on "sound-bites" and twenty second commercial spots. Today, seeing is believing.

Lucy Dawidowitz, the late Holocaust historian, recalled one day that she received a phone call from a young man affiliated with Larry King's national talk-radio program. She was asked if she would be prepared to debate Robert Faurisson, a well-known anti-Semite who denies that Jews were killed in the Holocaust. Dawidowitz replied that Faurison should not be provided a platform for his virulent anti-Semitism, and therefore she would not debate him. The young man, puzzled, approached Dawidowitz again: "What is the matter with discussing 'controversial' matters on the radio?" To which Dawidowitz asked the young man: "Do you think the murder of European Jews is merely a 'controversial' matter? Had it not been established as an historical fact?" This twenty-first century young man answered: "I don't really know for sure. I am only twenty-two years old."

Sadly, this response may be coming more natural. Had that same young man visited the Auschwitz museum in Poland, the site of the Nazi's largest death camp, he would have read in the official guidebook: "Auschwitz symbolizes German terror and human suffering, but primarily Polish and Russian suffering." Not a word about Jews who were the overwhelming number of victims gassed to death at the camp. Indeed, Auschwitz is the symbol of Jewish suffering. Had he seen one of the most popular documentary films on the Holocaust, "Night and Fog," he would have been soothed by a film that gives no hint that Jews were killed in the death camps. Had he asked a random selection of 130 non-Jewish high school students in Cincinnati, Ohio, about the Holocaust, he would have been shocked that all but three students failed to mention that Jews were singled out for death; and that half of the students surveyed did not believe it when it was pointed out to them. Finally, had he accompanied the former US president, Ronald Reagan, to the Bitberg cemetery in Germany on his presidential visit there during his term of office, he would, in the words of Elie Wiesel,[1] have been "dumfounded by a political extravaganza that did not include one word relating to the fact that Jews were murdered by SS men buried in that same graveyard."

While one may be upset with Holocaust denial theories, they are less troubling than are the above-mentioned lapses in memory. Yet far more problematic is the perversion of the Holocaust to such an extent that it is turned against the Jews. During the days of the Intifada, the Israelis became the new Nazis, and the Palestinians the new Jews. This sort of transference is nothing less than abhorrent.

But such transference receives "respectable" cover through a more subtle, but equally distorted, interpretation of the Holocaust — and that is the

---

1. A Holocaust survivor, he authored numerous books about his experience, the most famous book being *Night*. A Nobel laureate, he has been called the "moral conscience of the Holocaust."

universalization of the tragedy. In the late 1960s in America, during the height of the Vietnam War, a number of plays appeared on Broadway by such notable playwrights as Arthur Miller (*After the Wall, Incident at Vichy*), Peter Weiss (*The Investigation*) and Robert Shaw (*The Man in the Glass Booth*). In each play, the writer used the Holocaust to illustrate mankind's inhumanity to man. During the 1960s, the Holocaust became equal to the napalming of the Vietnamese countryside, persecution against African-Americans, Communist baiting and the suppression of Arabs by Israelis. Years after Shaw's play was produced, he wrote: "I see Auschwitz as a universal instrument that could have been used by anyone. For that matter, the Jews could have been on the side of the Nazis... For example, in South Vietnam, a Nazi-style genocide took place. In its support for US policy in Southeast Asia, Israel displayed fascist tendencies."

With the passing of time, this attitude may surface more and more. The reelection of Kurt Waldheim as the president of Austria after his Nazi past was revealed, the rise of fascists in Switzerland, despite that country's admission of hoarding Jewish money during the Holocaust, and the meteoric rise of Austria's Joerg Haider are sad examples of how deeply rooted anti-Semitism still is in many parts of the world. Such attitudes still abound despite the recent production of popular and highly acclaimed Holocaust films, such as *Schindler's List* and *Life is Beautiful*.

The implications of all this should be clear, particularly for Israelis. But they are not. Often two opposing reactions are heard in the Jewish state. For some, the implications of the Holocaust prompt them to guarantee that Israel does nothing to indicate that they have adopted, even in the slightest way, the actions of those who haunt their worst nightmares.

Yet there are those whose experiences are so vivid and horrible that their memories dictate their attitudes. It is impossible to judge them. Their fear of another Holocaust in the Middle East, committed by Arabs against Jews, is born out of real experiences. Donning gas masks and sitting in a sealed room during the Persian Gulf War became a renewed trauma for many Holocaust survivors living in Israel. When the late prime minister, Menachem Begin, became angered at the world's response to the massacre of unarmed Palestinians by a Christian militia in the Sabra and Shatilla refugee camps in Beirut at the end of the Lebanon War, it had to be understood in the context of his Holocaust experience. He lost virtually his entire family. What was the world's response to the massacre? Because the refugee camp was under Israeli control, the Israelis were blamed. The coverage in the international media could lead the reader to conclude that Israelis had pulled the trigger that killed those Palestinians. Admittedly, Israel did shoulder much of the blame for what happened. But the visceral attacks on Israel prompted Begin to remark bitterly: "*Goyim* kill Goyim,[1] (Non-Jews kill Non-Jews) and the world blames the Jews!" (This was not the only time that Begin referred to the Holocaust to explain or justify Israeli behavior in the eyes of the world.)

Yet Begin's remarks, a reflection of a "Never Again" attitude on the part of many Israelis, was countered by a mass demonstration against Israel's complicit role in the Christian killing of those Palestinians. 400,000 Israelis crowded Tel Aviv's city square to protest what happened, to show the world that any comparison between Israelis and Nazis was blasphemous.

Rarely in history has a single event elicited such diverse public attitudes as has the wanton slaughter of six million Jews. With such a large population of Holocaust survivors living in Israel, the responses to anything relating to that dark time affects the entire country. The murder of the six million cannot be wholly accounted for either in terms of passion or of madness, or of overwhelming and irresistible social forces. The best one can do is to remember it, never letting it fade from one's consciousness. It is an obligation one has to the survivor generation which will soon no longer be among us to recount that horrible time.

The capacity to assume the burden of memory is not always practical. Sometimes remembering arouses guilt, brings on nightmares and induces depression. While the moral function of remembering cuts across the different worlds of art, knowledge, reason and history, it must always be compatible with basic truths. Whatever lessons an Israeli chooses to extract from the Holocaust, as contradictory as they might be, this basic memory must remain. The Holocaust has caused a great deal of psychological trauma for Israelis (and for all Jews). One need not add to it by judging another person harshly because his or her feelings conflict with one's own regarding that unspeakable horror.

---

1. A Jewish expression from the Hebrew and Yiddish language which is derogatorily used to describe non-Jews.

The world owes the Jews, and they owe themselves, the memory that the slaughter of six million of them is objectively the supreme tragic fact of modern times. This must be the prime remembrance of that dark period in history. Anything less will create a distorted memory.

Freedom of or from (Racial) Expression

If one has a choice between the protection of certain freedoms — of speech and of the press — and the protection against racial slander, and in the case of Jews, against anti-Semitic attacks, which one would a person choose? In a post-Holocaust era, there should be neither debate nor confusion about the answer to such a question. Jews are particularly sensitive to any private or public word or act that has the slightest hint of anti-Semitism. It makes good syllogistic sense that Jews should be quick to condemn bigoted remarks aimed at others because of their race or religious affiliation.

The collective experience of the Jews and the wealth of their value-oriented literature point to a people who have always waved the prophetic banner of social justice and equality. The short lists of quotes from the Jewish tradition include these two well-known phrases: "Love your neighbor as yourself" (*Leviticus* 19:18) and "What is hateful to you, do not do unto others" (*Babylonian Talmud, Shabbat* 31a). Experience and literature have fashioned Jewish responses to discrimination and prejudice. Over the last two centuries, Jews far outstripped their numerical presence when it came to joining in the universal struggle to protect the human rights of all peoples. In pre- and post-revolutionary Russia, many Jews were leaders in bringing into being and trying to maintain Communism, a system of government that was ideally based on principles of equality. It is most ironic that the Soviet Union, particularly in the person of Josef Stalin, waged an anti-Semitic campaign, which rivaled that of the Czarist eras. In America in the Sixties, a disproportionate number of Jews participated in the battle to secure full civil and human rights for African-Americans.

Not to defend the rights of all would run contrary to the heritage of the Jew as a freedom fighter. But a phobic duality sometimes strikes Jews, particularly those who live in Israel, and they fail to defend the rights of others, thereby forsaking their historical obligation to do so. A paradox arises where the victim of the racial slur fails to protest a racial innuendo hurled against someone else. Is this considered normative behavior? Should such "normative" behavior be acceptable in a Jewish state? Israeli Jews seem less aware of such a double standard than are Diaspora Jews. As a result, the dangers inherent in such contradictory behavior are far greater to Israeli society because Jews form a majority in the country. Israel could see its prejudices being used against a minority.

Despite David Frischman's[1] statement that "of all evils of our generation, I do not know one that obstructs justice or the moral development of mankind more than the Press," Israel's media is remarkably free and open. But it often works against its own self-interests. When it comes to matters of bigotry, there can be no discordance. Yet oftentimes, Israelis become confused. They understand one thing and do just the opposite. For a Jew, the protection against racial slander must overwhelm the protection of free speech and a free press. One can gauge public sentiments by what is written in the papers. When an Israeli newspaper editorializes against discrimination against Bedouins, and then prints an employment advertisement that stipulates "For Jews Only," then the symptoms of a split personality come to the fore.

(Joerg Haider, whose extreme right-wing Austrian Freedom Party is part of the ruling coalition of Austria, has taken a stand on foreign workers that borders on clear racism. While Israel has rightfully condemned Haider's cooption into the Austrian government, a little soul searching on its part might be in order. Israeli writer on the Holocaust and well known journalist, Tom Segev, referring to Rehavam Ze'evi, a former career army officer and a former minister in the Israeli government of past prime minister Yitzhak Shamir, who calls for the "transfer" of Arabs, wrote in the *International Herald Tribune* (February 4, 2000):

---

1. A well-known Hebrew writer (1859-1922), he edited various Hebrew periodicals and wrote a wide variety of works, including short stories, essays, poems and literary criticisms. This quote is from a letter in his diaries.

"Mr. Ze'evi represents a form of racism that's become a legitimate part of Israeli democracy. We have a long history behind us of systematic violation of the rights of Palestinians and others, so who are we to lecture the world about proper democracy and human rights?")

United States university campuses are often the battleground for ideological confrontations. At major state educational institutions such as the University of Michigan, the University of Wisconsin, Indiana University and Boston University, where there are large Arab student populations, anti-Semitic organizations place advertisements in school newspapers, sometimes denying the Holocaust and sometimes just promoting their anti-Semitic drivel. Most universities accept these advertisements despite intense lobbying against such action by local and national Jewish organizations.

The arguments for allowing these hate messages and blatant lies to find their way into papers are based on the sacred tenets of "freedom of press" and "freedom of speech." Furthermore, a paper can always distance itself from such advertisements by simply stating that it is not responsible for their content.

Yet such an approach is disingenuous at best when dealing with such an emotional subject as anti-Semitism. After all, if "truth in advertising" has any meaning, it needs to be scrupulously applied to such a sensitive matter as racism. A paper should also have the "freedom" to reject an advertisement with overt racial overtones. Not to reject the hate that appears in such advertisements could readily imply support for the view propagated. When appearing in a university paper, despite disclaimers, any advertisement might very well be seen as a reflection of that institution's policy. Any news story, editorial opinion, letter or advertisement promulgating a blatantly distorted view of a particular event or giving publicity to an unmitigated lie should be rejected by any reputable newspaper.

No doubt the owners and editors of any of Israel's papers would agree with this analysis. Indeed, on a number of occasions the Israeli press has raised objections to American campuses supplying a public forum for the likes of Louis Farrakhan[1] and his anti-Semitic cohorts.

---

1. One of the leaders of the Black Muslim Nation in the United States. He has often used anti-Semitic language.

Yet despite this, every so often, an Israeli may read in the newspaper some of the most vituperative advertisements imaginable: "Jewish Labor Only" or "A Declaration on Homosexual Abominations and Lesbianism." The content of these announcements is so extreme as to incite hatred toward non-Jews (Arabs), gays and lesbians — all three being lumped together as one. This lends itself to an orgy of bigotry that can become dangerously institutionalized. There must be moral limits to what is acceptable in a paid advertisement. The above displays a brutal insensitivity. They not only insult a specific population, but also impugn the architects of the advertisements.

When such notices appear in a "Jewish paper," they expose Judaism to accusations of exclusiveness and intolerance. Since Judaism is seen as the religious expression of the Jewish state, one could readily draw the conclusion that Israel is also exclusive and intolerant. This is most certainly the case in the aforementioned advertisements. How would a Jew feel if the *New York Times* carried an ad for social workers that called for "Christians Only" or worse yet, "Jews Need Not Apply?" The dominant view in a democratic society is that the inclusion of any and all advertisements is the highest expression of tolerance and liberalism. But often, the very opposite can be the case. Exaggerated respect for freedom of speech and press ultimately limits the freedom of an institution or a paper to say "no" to hate-filled propaganda and so preserve its right to be viewed as open and tolerant. It can also impinge upon and injure the respect and dignity of a particular minority — a respect that is an essential building block of democracy. Jews must guard themselves from going down that "slippery slope" where their country's media, in the name of "freedom of expression," fall prey to racial propaganda.

When one's respect for liberalism is curtailed by racism, then one becomes party to the clear misuse of democracy's benefits. It is in this area that one witnesses the abuse of democratic freedoms. The Jew, who now possesses the power of statehood, must never unleash any expression that harbors racial epithets because "Baseless hatred is as evil as three sins — idolatry, incest and bloodshed" (*Babylonian Talmud, Yoma* 9b). There can be no equivocation here. Racism has led to the slaughter of far too many Jews.

Hyperbole, Misuse and Abuse

What do Ehud Barak and Yasir Arafat have in common? What do Shimon Peres and Neville Chamberlain have in common? What do Yossi Sarid and Benedict Arnold have in common? Absolutely nothing. But given the road signs, placards and rhetoric that have come out of Israel as it pursues peace, it would seem that there is no distinction between the historical enemies of the Jewish people and Israel's leaders. Such confusion reminds one of the warning that the prophet Elijah gave to the Israelites when they were fighting among themselves causing further divisions within the people: "How long will you limp along on two opinions" (*I Kings* 18:21)?

During Yitzhak Rabin's tenure in office as prime minister, one was confronted with that despicable poster of him dressed up in a SS uniform. On the Jerusalem-Tel Aviv highway, a massive sign loomed high with the year "1939" written on it, a reference to the "year of appeasement" conducted by the British in their negotiations with Hitler. On Israel radio, one heard government ministers in support of returning either the West Bank to the Palestinians or the Golan Heights to the Syrians being called traitors.

There are two major difficulties with this comparative political posturing. It breeds hatred for fellow Jews and reduces the Jewish historical memory to cheap relativism. It is unacceptable to tap the most painful emotional experience of the Jewish people in order to make a political point.

One need not list the contributions of Yitzhak Rabin, Ehud Barak and Shimon Peres to the Jewish people to recognize that likening them to Yasir Arafat or Neville Chamberlain is nothing less than contemptible. To imply that Israel has returned to "1939" is to say that Israel's government plans to carry out a "Final Solution" for the Jewish people, that the Labor party is ushering in another World War, and that Israel is asking for other countries to invade it.

One is reminded of Menachem Begin's comparison of Syria's killing of Christians in Lebanon to the slaughter of the Jews by the Nazis. This sort of relativization takes away from the uniqueness of the Holocaust vis-a-vis the Jews. But one might forgive Begin this lapse, for he was attempting to whip up support for his planned attack against Syrian missile sites. What better way to gain support than by painting one's enemy in the darkest images possible? But to do the same to Barak, Rabin, Peres, et. al.? This is mean-spirited cynicism.

A number of years ago, the PLO almost scored an incredible public relations coup. To highlight the plight of Palestinian refugees, it planned to send a boat with "homeless" and "stateless" Palestinians aboard from Cyprus to Haifa. The boat was to be named the "Exodus II." The hope was that Israel would send its navy to block the ship from entering Israel's territorial waters and dispatch it back to its port of embarkation. The symbolism of such an event is almost too much to bear, and the reality too distorted to tolerate.

The Palestinians have often tried to portray Israel as a descendant of Nazi Germany and themselves as the Jews of Europe. This is the height of intellectual dishonesty and emotional offensiveness. How then could Israelis dare to do the same thing among themselves? But that is precisely what the opponents of the peace process are doing. Rabin was the "great appeaser," by inference ushering in another Holocaust; Peres is an "agent" of the Palestinian Authority and Ehud Barak a willing *Kapo*.[1] One could just imagine how a Jew would react if someone in the Christian community spoke in such terms. That Jew would immediately characterize the person as an anti-Semite. One should remember how enraged Jews were when President George Bush compared Saddam Hussein's invasion of Kuwait to Hitler's invasion of Poland.

These sorts of unconscionable counter-political attacks should be stopped immediately. Restraint is required. As emotional as is the debate as to what Israel should give up to secure peace with its Arab neighbors, this controversy must not breed exaggerated historical and personal comparisons. Indeed, if expressions of racism are outlawed in Israel (as is the use of the term Nazi to describe someone), then the deplorable appellations that have been attached to Barak, Peres and Rabin should be legally addressed. Such hyperbole lends itself to a distorted picture of reality.

---

1. A Jewish appointee, usually in the concentration camps, forced by the Nazis to carry out the ugliest of acts. Oftentimes he was considered to be a "traitor" by the Jews over whom he had been placed. Yet not to do the Nazi bidding would have meant certain death.

As a child of the Sixties in the United States, to justify my activism in every social and political cause imaginable, I would always apply the universal Jewish message of social justice, not only theologically, but also historically. Like others of my generation, I took the most tragic event in Jewish history, the Holocaust, and universalized it beyond recognition. As a "white" in America, I was as guilty as the Nazis in my perceived persecution of African-Americans. I remember participating in the moratorium against the war in Vietnam in Washington DC in 1969, "levitating" the Pentagon and stuffing flowers into the barrels of the rifles of National Guardsmen, all the while chanting Nazi insults at them with a vitriolic force. As I look back on that phase of my life, I am amazed that I behaved like those playwrights Miller, Shaw and Weiss who I now realize were abusive in their glib universalizing of the Holocaust.

From the founding of the United States until the enactment of the Civil Rights Bills of 1964 and 1965, African-Americans were lynched with impunity in many Southern states. This fact rarely made news. The political powers-that-be were infrequently moved to action or protest. It was not until two "white" Jewish boys from the North, Andrew Goodman and Michael Schwerner, were kidnapped and killed that the general populace became aroused. That an African-American, James Chaney, was also murdered received significantly less press than did the death of his white co-workers.

Israeli army officer Gamliel Peretz, an Orthodox Jew, was dismissed from his duties because of his outlandish comparison between Reform and Conservative Judaism and the Holocaust. Unknowingly, he made his comment in a lecture to a group of female soldiers that included two girls from these two religious movements. Yet such an abuse of the Holocaust was understandable because he was merely parroting that which Israel's chief rabbi, Bakshi-Doron, had said earlier. Dancing abusively on the graves of those who died in the Holocaust, Bakshi-Doron said: "Reform Jews are creating a Holocaust greater than that of Hitler." Peretz just refined these ludicrous comments by arbitrarily claiming that Reform and Conservative Jews have caused eight million Jews to assimilate, therefore causing a greater Holocaust than the Nazis. Saying that Reform or Conservative Jews have created a Holocaust greater than that of Hitler dwarfs any embarrassment that liberals around the world may feel for misusing the Holocaust. There is no universalizing the Holocaust by Bakshi-Doron. He knows exactly what he is doing. He has learned the lessons of the Holocaust well, and in so doing, unwittingly reveals a type of anti-Semitism.

So the dismissal of Peretz from the army was swift and just. Fortunately, there was no collision between the forces of those who claim that Peretz's world-view is legitimate and those who hold that, legitimate or not, it must not be expressed in a public forum. Israelis were of one mind that this type of outburst is intolerable. But Peretz's comments, backed as they were by Bakshi-Doron's remarks, set the stage for uninvited parallels. Too many in the world stood silent during World War II. Bakshi-Doron enjoys a silent complicity, as none of his Orthodox colleagues protested his words.

But there is a flip side to this whole sorry event that harkens back to the murders of Goodman, Schwerner and Chaney. Inciteful statements made by some army officers against the Ethiopian community rarely result in the same sort of disciplinary action that was enacted against Peretz. The two "white Ashkenazi" girls knew how to activate their political connections and get immediate results. But some poor Ethiopian immigrant, who is barely aware of his or her rights, continues to suffer declarative statements as derogatory as those suffered by the two girls. Only when the "white" and "privileged" class in Israel is no longer singled out for preferential treatment will equality reign in the country. This applies not only to how Jews relate to each other, but also to the relationship between Jews and non-Jews.

Israelis witness countless demolitions of Palestinian homes by the Israeli army, based on the technicality that the house was built or a room added illegally. The order to destroy the house is carried out with efficiency, with little concern about what happens to the family. A very different standard applies to a house built illegally by a Jew.

There are approximately forty-two illegal settlements in the West Bank. The government decided to dismantle only between ten and twelve. Note the terminology. One **demolishes** an illegal Arab home, but **dismantles** an illegal Jewish settlement. The word demolish indicates violence, the word dismantle implies compromise and delicacy. This plays itself out in the field. Almost all demolitions of Arab houses are accompanied by the firing of rubber bullets or tear gas, with Palestinians usually counting their wounded. For example, in dismantling the settlement of Maon, one noticed that negotiations preceded any army activity. Despite the violent opposition of some of the protesters, they were treated with kid gloves. Not one volley of ammunition was fired.

Prejudice and discrimination cannot become the public policy of a state, which in many respects was born out of the ashes of Holocaust. It is legitimate, even necessary, for Jews in Israel to apply the lessons of the Holocaust to their own reality. In many ways, Israeli Jews are the ones who have the greatest right to do so. If the Holocaust has taught anything, it is that class or racial distinctions are dangerous. **This is the only fair comparison that must be allowed.** Less than that would be a perversion. When applied to Israeli society, the question must be asked if Israelis measure up favorably to one of the most significant lessons of the Holocaust — to be rid of all persecution and discrimination?

To be certain that this is the case, Jews in Israel must be singularly unified in their understanding of the Holocaust. Jews in Israel cannot prevent others from causing the depreciation of the Holocaust by misusing it for their own political agenda. However, they can honor those who died in the Holocaust by so discrediting those Jews who would make facile use of the tragedy that they will no longer make odious comparisons between other Jews and Nazis.

If any event could have produced a paranoid personality, none could have done better than the Holocaust. But so many Jews who survived the Holocaust managed to rebuild their lives because of a basic resiliency that Jews have acquired during centuries of persecution. Sanity emerged out of a world that went insane. Together Jews emerged with a psychological stability that overcame the alienation, which is an almost natural outgrowth of such a terrible nightmare. The key word is **together**.

When a siren sounds throughout the country on Holocaust Memorial Day, all Jews in Israel stand still for a moment of silence and, as one, pay tribute to those who died. For the entire day, as a collective entity and on the deepest level, Jews in Israel commemorate the tragedy of the Holocaust. There is no divergence of opinions. The great divide between right and left, religious and secular, Ashkenazi and Sephardi, veteran and immigrant evaporates. The legacy of the Holocaust must not be discordance, but harmony, not division, but unity.

CHAPTER 5

RELIGION IN ISRAEL

Orthodoxy: The Only Game in Town

Contrary to popular belief, Orthodox Judaism in Israel is not monolithic. Within the Orthodox community, there are wide varieties of expression. Only a surface understanding of Orthodoxy would make one think that Orthodox Jews are less prone to divisiveness than other sectors of Israel's population. While their world-view is such that both religiously and politically one can well predict what their stance will be on any given issue, one should not draw the conclusion that they are blissfully unified. Like other segments in Israeli society, they suffer from paradoxical behaviors. **However, this chapter will primarily discuss the role of ultra-Orthodoxy in Israeli life, for ultra-Orthodoxy is a brand of Judaism that is growing in adherents and increasing in influence. Modern Orthodoxy, which for the most part is religiously moderate (though not necessarily politically so), is *not* the subject of this chapter.**

In general, Orthodox Jews seem not to be as conflicted as their secular counterparts because they believe in a God who set down the "Divine law" at one revelatory moment in time (at Mount Sinai). For Orthodox Jews, this law is seen as immutable, despite historical evidence of changes that have taken place in the understanding and interpretation of Judaism since the Written and Oral law (Torah and Talmud) were handed down to Moses at Mount Sinai. With God on their side, it would seem that Orthodox Jews have a clearer picture of what they should say and how they should act than do many in the non-religious world.

Yet despite their notion that they are divinely commanded to behave in certain ways, contradictions abound. These contradictions are exacerbated by a dual chief rabbinate, one Sephardi and one Ashkenazi, which represent a different cultural, historical and ethnic background. Their behavior often seems to be in conflict with the spirit of Judaism. It is here that Orthodoxy seems to swim upstream and downstream at the same time. Some Orthodox Jews, often taking the lead from their titular spiritual guardians, say and do things that leave the average individual dumbstruck, muttering out loud to himself: "This person can't be a religious Jew!"

The late Rabbi Hugo Gryn of London used to tell a story about a keynote speech he had given at an international conference in Japan. Just before he was to address the gathering, he was informed that a translator would be appointed. Gryn assumed that after every few sentences his words would be translated. However, he was told that he should speak in intervals of ten minutes, and after each ten-minute portion of his speech the translator would render into Japanese what he had said. Though surprised, Gryn thought the interpreter was probably blessed with a photographic memory.

So Gryn began his speech, being careful to stop after exactly ten minutes. The translator got up, spoke a few words and then sat down again. People in the audience nodded in agreement. A bit baffled by the brevity of the synopsis, Gryn continued for another ten minutes; and once again the man uttered a few words and sat down. Knowing smiles appeared on the faces of those in the audience. After another ten minutes, came another thirty-second translation. Completely bewildered, Gryn approached the podium for the last time and ended his speech in a climactic ten-minute flourish. The translator looked out at the crowd, spoke five words and sat down. There was a thunderous applause.

At the reception, people came over to Rabbi Gryn to congratulate him on a brilliant talk. After a while, his curiosity level at a peak, he turned to his Japanese host and asked him how it was possible that he could speak for ten minutes and the interpreter for less than thirty-seconds. Gryn acknowledged that Japanese was an economical language, but he was still stunned, curious to know how the translator managed to capture his speech, particularly the end of it with only five words.

After some hesitation, Gryn's Japanese host revealed the secret. The first time the translator got up to speak he said: "Our speaker has not said anything new." The second time he said: "He still has not said anything new." The third time he remarked: "I do not think he will say anything new." And the last time he reported: "I was right. He didn't!"

In *Chapter 3*, the matter of religion and state was discussed. The focus was not to necessarily break new ground, but rather to sharpen the conflicts that exist between "the politics of religion" and "the religion of politics." In contrast, as stated earlier, this chapter will refer to the religious behavior of ultra-Orthodox Jews, not regarding their political or institutional effect on Israel, but rather their societal influence on the state. The novelty in this approach is that it is intended to address ultra-Orthodoxy, the almost "official" religious expression in Israel and most certainly the most influential, in ways it is rarely portrayed: as a self-possessed ecstatic movement that distorts normative Judaism rather than represents it. What is new is that Israel is contending with a theological phenomenon that has produced an over-confident and self-indulgent ultra-Orthodox community, which is trying to return the country to a time of religious medievalism.

Israel's ultra-Orthodox community is the only Jewish sector in the country that is growing numerically. Ultra-Orthodox Jews take quite literally the first Divine commandment that appears in the Bible: "Be fruitful and multiply" (*Genesis* 1:22). Since the rest of the Jewish population in Israel is, for the most part, "fruitless and subtracting," it is no surprise that in Jerusalem, for example, fifty-five percent of all entering first-graders come from ultra-Orthodox families. There is a sad sociological downside to this reality. Large families cause overcrowded housing and neighborhoods. In addition, many of the adult males study full-time in Yeshivot (receiving limited government subsidies to support them) and their wives stay at home to tend their families. The poverty level among this sector is quite high. In recent reports on poverty in Israel, B'nei B'rak, an almost exclusively ultra-Orthodox town, and Jerusalem, with its large ultra-Orthodox population, were ranked among the places in the country with the greatest number of people living below the poverty belt.

Because they live in a relatively isolated community, not wanting to come into contact with the "corrupt" secular world, a general lack of sophistication makes ultra-Orthodox Jews vulnerable to all sorts of "spiritual" pronouncements by their religious leaders. These pronouncements are publicly addressed not only to the ultra-Orthodox community but also to the general populace. When a bus load of school children is hit by a train, killing a number of the passengers, one hears the most revered rabbis claim that the real cause of the accident is not careless driving, but that the family of each child who was killed did not have a "kosher" *mezzuza*[1] on its door! To the outsider, this does not sound like the enlightened statement of a religious leader, but more like the ranting of an evangelical impostor.

At times, Judaism as expressed by some of the most prominent rabbis in the ultra-Orthodox world does not seem like Judaism at all. It seems like a tribal cult that is stuck in a medieval time warp. From the most extreme examples of exorcising *dybbuks*,[2] fashioning *golems*,[3] declaring a mezzuza as having supernatural powers (to prevent traffic accidents), to the troubling examples of relegating women to a secondary status or claiming a particular tract of land "holy," for many Jews in Israel, Orthodoxy seems foreign to any sane understanding of Judaism.

Most Jews in Israel understand that this expression of Judaism is not normative. But the rise of these "ecstatic" phenomena is at times shocking. Even more surprising is the manner in which they creep into the secular world, and especially into the political world, as even "socialist" politicos try to curry favor with an Orthodox constituency by trying out the latest model of religious absurdity. From its earliest stages, Judaism has always seen itself (and is portrayed as such) as a religion that found a healthy balance between spiritual excitement and rational consideration. Jews created for the world the notion of monotheism, which was an essentially reasoned response to paganism and dualism. It would seem then that the current brand of Judaism expressed in Israel by many of its ultra-Orthodox proponents suffers from a form of "psychic" imbalance.

---

1. Small parchment on which are written the first two paragraphs of the *Shema*, the single statement of the Oneness of God (*Deuteronomy* 6:4), which is rolled into a case and affixed to every doorpost in a Jewish home (*Deuteronomy* 6:9).
2. A popular legend (and belief) that the soul of a disembodied sinner, which finds no peace after death, enters the body of a living person. The concept evolved in mystical circles in the 17th century, and "appropriate exorcism" was practiced by "wonder-workers."
3. The legend of a creature, usually in human shape, magically formed, especially through the use of the Divine name. The concept was developed in the 12th century. Legends that such creatures had been created spread in the 15th century and the best known story was associated with Rabbi Yehuda Loew of Prague.

Look Forward to Yesterday

Concerned by the political and diplomatic leaks emanating from his office, former Prime Minister Benjamin Netanyahu was encouraged to have the mezzuza to his office checked. It was postulated that such leaks could only come about due to an unkosher mezzuza. (Perhaps someone put a "bug" in the mezzuza.) Dutifully, Mr. Netanyahu sent off the mezzuza to some rabbinic authority to be checked. No sooner did the news of the prime minister's worry about the status of the mezzuza hit the press, then out trotted his press secretary to deny such an act.

While this was going on, a petition to the High Court of Justice was taking place. The claim was that Mr. Netanyahu had wasted state money on a $500 bottle of wine when he was on an official visit to the United States. There is no kosher bottle of wine anywhere in the world that costs $500, so the claim that he spent that much money could not possibly be true, especially considering his concern about the purity of the mezzuza that adorned the office of the Prime Minister of the Jewish state. Unless the bottle of wine was not... Perish the thought!

Why perish the thought of Mr. Netanyahu ordering a bottle of unkosher wine? Because like all of Israel's prime ministers, he stands prayerfully at the Western Wall on the 17th of *Tammuz*.[1] The only problem with his and other prime ministers' presence at the Wall is that their sudden religious awakening on such a fast day is usually preceded by a breakfast of juice and yogurt!

In Mr. Netanyahu's case, his religious posturing was more hypocritical than that of Israel's other prime ministers. One is reminded of this "devout" man whispering into the ear of the revered religious leader, Rabbi Yitzhak Kaddouri, that "the left is not Jewish," all the while violating the commandment that forbids rumor-mongering.

Everyone knows that this is just a religious game, a controlled, yet false, attempt at piety. If the Torah forbids adultery, then Benjamin Netanyahu, a confessed adulterer, cannot be "good for the Jews" — the campaign slogan promulgated by the ultra-Orthodox community in urging its constituency to

---

1. Fast day marking the breaching of the walls of Jerusalem in the year 70 CE. The date begins the traditional three weeks of mourning, to the 9th of *Av* when the Holy Temple was destroyed by the Romans.

vote for him. This should neatly fall into the category of a split personality. It is a perfect example of "saying is not believing." The Torah says one thing, but those who hold the Torah to be absolutely true and immutable, not subject to changing sociological realities, act differently and support a man who openly violated no less than one of the Ten Commandments: "Thou shalt not commit adultery" (*Exodus* 20:14).

But there is a way out of this contradiction. Maybe Mr. Netanyahu's capricious ways were a result of a blemished mezzuza. What is a $500 bottle of unkosher wine compared to adultery? Nothing Mr. Netanyahu did wrong was his fault, or for that matter nothing any political leader does is wrong. If school children killed in a bus accident or in a bus bombing outside another school cannot be explained away rationally, blame it on the mezzuza! This is reminiscent of the song "Gee, Officer Krupke" from the Broadway show *West Side Story*, where sociology excuses all manner of aberrant behavior. The system is to blame, not the individual.

> Gee, Officer Krupke,
> We're very upset.
> We never had the love
> That every child otta' get.
> We ain't no delinquents,
> We're misunderstood.
> Deep down inside us
> We are good!

Mr. Netanyahu's and other political leaders' pseudo-religious piety receives encouragement from the general Orthodox community, and sometimes from the general community. One witnesses secular Knesset and prime ministerial candidates kissing the rings and beards of rabbis and viewing with bemusement "hoaxed" exorcisms of a dybbuk from a woman in Dimona. Non-believing politicians invoke God's name in every speech ("with the help of God"), and socialist kibbutzniks row out into the middle of the Sea of Galilee with some *"Kabbalists"*[1] to

---

1. Kabbalah is the overall designation for Jewish mysticism. Kabbalists looked at Divinity as a pure, infinite, spiritual light, whose emanations account for all creation. They also held that man's soul was formed in the "upper spheres" and that the goal of the soul is to come closer to the Divine source. Today, Kabbalists attribute to themselves supernatural powers to cure seemingly unexplainable human behavior.

pray for rain. It would be one thing if fringes in the ultra-Orthodox community supported such fanciful religious eclecticism, but its support finds its way into the mainstream. Judaism, is turned into voodoo and its ultra-Orthodox rabbinic interlocutors into magicians, reminiscent of those who served in Pharaoh's court.

Jewish national identity, forged in the experience of Egyptian slavery, was supposed to produce a "holy nation," not a nation of magicians. Jews in Israel are being treated to a brand of Judaism that is being exploited by rabbinic ghosts and goblins.

The "God Squad" — Part I

the internet

With Orthodoxy being the "only game in town," one must watch out for its long arm. The ultra-Orthodox reach is incredible. They have become a moral "God Squad!" Their concerns for the sexual mores of the Jewish people know no boundaries. They are willing to do virtually anything to "save the Jewish people."

There it was in big bold type, strung across a major thoroughfare: **"BEWARE!"** Beware of what? "Our girls are wearing translucent stockings!" Help! Everyone knows that translucent stockings drive ultra-Orthodox men wild. Quick, before their sexual fantasies are aroused beyond control, get them to a cold *Mikvah*.[1]

What is going on here? Is this too fanciful to be believable? Not really. A supermarket, located in a primarily, but not totally, ultra-Orthodox neighborhood, does not want to admit women shoppers who have exposed elbows. Now, any fool knows that a bony and craggy elbow is the most enticing part of a female's body, sending lascivious chills up a *haredi*[2] male's spine. What to do? Issue those women full-length robes to cover themselves up so as to

---

1. A ritual bath for purification used by men and women (separately).
2. Literally meaning "fearful," as in fearing God. It is a designation of an ultra-Orthodox Jew.

prevent these haredi men from going directly to the produce section to fondle grapefruits and bananas.

The concern of the ultra-Orthodox community to limit any behavior that might hint of sexual arousal is so great that it has begun to widen its scope of activity to include the high-tech world of a computer society. Somehow, ultra-Orthodox Jews are aware that pornography is available via the Internet. While ultra-Orthodox Jews live successfully without television and cinema that often offer up a fare of sexual entertainment, they also wish to avoid the sexual attraction that Netscape, Yahoo and Alta Vista can offer.

Indeed in computer literacy, unlike in some other parts of their lives, ultra-Orthodox Jews are well into the 21st century. And so one would think that they would be undaunted by the opening of a Cafe Internet in Israel. Cafe Internet is that chain of cafes set up around the world to offer the possibility for young people traveling to be in touch via e-mail with their family and friends. It also helps them to find out what is going on in the world, which they cannot glean from foreign-language newspapers.

Contrary to common sense — in that Orthodox kids also travel substantially — the elders of the ultra-Orthodox community are unhappy with the opening of a Cafe Internet in Israel, especially in Jerusalem. They would prefer that the future really be the past when it comes to Cafe Internets (not only). Why? Because they fear that their young yeshiva guys, foreign and local, will begin to frequent Cafe Internet in order to plug into the web-sites of "Porn Incorporated" or "Sex City, USA" or who knows what other types of "Sex. Com."

The ultra-Orthodox community is so disturbed by the Internet's seductive capabilities that almost the entire ultra-Orthodox Council of Torah Sages signed a binding rabbinic opinion, which sounds a "serious warning against the terrible dangers within computers, compact disc players and the Internet" (Ha'aretz, January 6, 2000). The ruling presents a long list of tough restrictions on computer usage and imposes a strict ban on hooking up to the Internet, which is said to constitute a terrible threat to the Jewish people. Israel's ultra-Orthodox religious parties have weighed in with their own invective against the Internet world. *Degel HaTorah*[1] has claimed that the "Internet is the world's leading cause

---

1. An ultra-Orthodox political party.

of temptation. It incites and encourages sin and abomination of the worst kind. Internet users expose themselves to the morbidity of a corrupt culture." Some ultra-Orthodox groups have claimed that the Internet is a "deadly poison" and "burns the soul" (*Jerusalem Report*, February 17, 2000).

Since Cafe Internet in Israel, like others around the globe, tries to create a relaxed atmosphere by serving light refreshments and providing some sort of entertainment, it is dependent on the state's good graces to receive an operating license. And since Cafe Internet in Israel is interested in attracting as many young people as possible, it naturally wants its premises to be kosher. Here is where the "God Squad" enters. Israel's Cafe Internet can only open its doors if it lets haredi whiz kids scramble all the pornography in its computer programs. If a block is not put on the computers, then Cafe Internet can forget about getting a kashrut certificate. It is interesting to note that if there were no computers on the premises, then the haredi world would probably leave Cafe Internet alone, as it has done with so many restaurants that are, for example, unkosher. (Just let McDonald's set up an Internet station in the corner of one of its franchises, and one can bet that the haredim will see to it that its operating license is revoked, not because of the lack of kashrut, but because of an absence of moral righteousness.)

Pornography is disgusting. That it fouls one's visual airwaves and dirties one's computer screen offends one's basic sensibilities. So what is the problem? Not just this, but rather blackmail, and verbal and sometimes physical abuse. Too many ultra-Orthodox Jews are trying to increase their hegemony over the moral behavior of Israeli society, democratic freedoms be damned. Censorship in one area leads to censorship in others. If the social and technological advances of tomorrow are offensive to the ultra-Orthodox world of today, then it will do everything in its power, which is considerable, to turn the clock back to yesterday. (Ironically, the rabbinic ruling against the use of the Internet was posted on the Net!)

It is one thing to erase the computer program at Cafe Internet. It is something else to eradicate the basic elements of democracy. Perhaps it might be helpful to call up the ultra-Orthodox community on one's computer. One would then have the option of deleting it or even trashing it. Better yet one should probably just send it to the recycle bin in the hope of restoring it when it finally understands what it means to live in an open and pluralistic society. If not, then all manner of aberrant behavior will continue to take place. For as things stand at present, virtually anything in Israel that displeases the ultra-Orthodox community is not suffered in silence, particularly if it considers the offense to have negative moral overtones.

The "God Squad" — Part II

women: separate and unequal

I took my ten-year old daughter to the Burger King at the Jerusalem Mall and ordered a "kid's meal." While my daughter is not particularly wild about hamburgers, she knows that with the "kid's meal" she will get a surprise. Before giving us the surprise, the girl behind the counter asked me if I was ordering for a boy or for a girl. I asked coyly: "What does it matter?" Stunned, she began to stutter. Was the choice between a G.I. Joe and a Barbie, between a blue toy and a pink one?

I told her that I believed in an egalitarian approach to life, and resented the suggestion that my child would choose a particular toy based on her gender. I asked the cashier to show me the choices without indicating which was for boys and which was for girls. I then asked my daughter to choose the one she preferred. I personally could not tell the difference, and, apparently, neither could my daughter, because she picked the "wrong" toy. She picked the one that Burger King, in its infinite "politically incorrect" wisdom, had designated for the male of the species.

This would almost be a humorous anecdote if it were not for the sad fact that children in Israel are trained at a very early age to countenance stereotypes. In fact, if someone accuses Israelis of not being "PC," they think that they are being told that they do not own a personal computer. Israeli kids confront this sociological reality virtually everywhere in their adult world. In too many government institutions, women are almost invisible. The Knesset looks like the locker room of a national soccer team. The number of women cabinet ministers barely satisfies tokenism.

The male domination of Israeli society, accompanied by its "macho" image, stems from a number of reasons. But there is one clear area where it is most dramatic, and that is in the ultra-Orthodox community. With the continued rise of ultra-Orthodoxy, a *"mechitza"*[1] ideology has strengthened its impact on the secular world. Non-Orthodox women have to submit themselves to halachic rulings in the area of *aguna*,[2] *chalitza*[3] and purity inspection before marriage. Not only does a woman have to use the mikvah before marriage, but, former chief rabbi, Ovadia Yosef, in a further plunge into superstitious religious experimentation, claimed that any married woman who does not immerse herself in the mikvah with regularity will give birth to "whores and criminals." And yet another occurrence has reinforced the inferior status of women in Israeli society — a relatively new law that would outlaw virtually all abortions. With such a demeaning attitude toward women spilling over from the ultra-Orthodox world into the secular world, it is little wonder that women are treated as unequal. The religious powers-that-be must feel that the secondary role women play is so ingrained that they can get away with further institutionalizing it. Women simply are forced in the religious world to literally take a back seat to men.[4]

So here comes the "God Squad" once again, this time lurking behind trees to watch women who work at the Ministry of Education, located next to an ultra-Orthodox area, to make certain that they are not wearing sleeveless blouses, sometimes physically attacking them to make their point. Some stand outside that supermarket, accosting women who they deem are dressed immodestly.

> **Man #1** (ultra-Orthodox): "Hi. What are you doing?"
> **Man #2** (ultra-Orthodox): "I am out for a walk with my wife."
> **Man #1**: "Oh. Where is she?"
> **Man #2**: "Half-a-block behind me!"

1. A divider set up in Orthodox synagogues that separates men from women. It was established so that a man could pray with necessary fervor, and not be subject to distractions by women who do not share equally in the worship requirements, and who may cause a man to conjure up impure thoughts.
2. A woman who is not allowed to remarry though her husband has abandoned her, or because he is believed to have died, but there is no certifiable proof.
3. Ceremony performed when a man refuses to marry his brother's childless widow. Prior to this ceremony the widow is not allowed to remarry. At the ceremony she takes off her brother-in-law's shoe, spits in his face and makes this declaration: "So shall be done to the man who will not build his brother's house" (*Deuteronomy* 25:9).
4. The ultra-Orthodox *Agudat Yisrael* party proposed a Knesset law that a woman wearing a prayer shawl and *yarmulke* (skullcap) be sentenced to seven years in prison (equal to the sentence for rape). The law passed a first reading.

The above conversation is not fanciful when one considers Ovadia Yosef's likening "the walking of a man between two women to walking between two donkeys!" In its behavior, the haredi world — and here I am inclusive because not one haredi leader has condemned some of the outrageous attacks by some haredi men on secular women, making them complicit supporters — is contributing to an atmosphere that sees women beaten down in Israeli society. Apart from a general contribution to a belittling attitude toward women, haredi behavior points to another reality.

One need not be an expert in psychology to understand what is going on. For fear of the sexual wiles of the modern day Eve, women are forced to sit behind a "mechitzah" during prayer, are invited to dance through the sanitized holding of a handkerchief and "to walk humbly with your God" (*Micah* 6:8), but humiliatingly behind one's husband. It is the beguiling ways of a woman that must be tamed so that men do not give into their sexual urges. Such an attitude lends credibility to the view that no woman is ever raped. A woman who exposes her wrists or ankles may be raped because of her alluring style of dress. She is to blame. Since man cannot control his inner sexual drive, a woman must be caged. This stands in contradiction to the ultra-Orthodox view that women hold a special place in Jewish life. What could be more "schizophrenic" than to place a woman on a pedestal at the same time one suggests that walking side-by-side with her could somehow be physically inappropriate.

One might be sympathetic if the haredi community opposed the exploitation of women's bodies, for example, in advertising. Merchandising women to sell Amstel Beer, Levi jeans, and yogurt is truly objectionable. But when a haredi hooligan burns down a bus stop that has a poster of a woman in a revealing outfit, he does so not because he feels that this is a vile abuse of a woman's body, but rather because it is an offense to his sensibilities. (Such crass merchandising of a female's body is far more offensive to women then to haredi men, yet one does not see women taking the law into their own hands whereby the most active feminists would hurl a crow-bar through the glass enclosed advertisement.)

A woman wearing a short-sleeve blouse and skirt on a hot summer Tel Aviv day does not suggest ill behavior or moral turpitude on her part. But an ultra-Orthodox man who understands this to be so is suspect of ill, perhaps even clinically sick behavior; and most certainly of moral turpitude and criminal activity, given the resultant assault on women. Ultra-Orthodoxy's attitude toward women, no matter how cloaked it is under the catch-all rubric of "religious freedom," hurtles one back to a darker time in human history. It clearly has a negative impact on Israeli society.

I know that what follows will be interpreted as a psychological rationalization in order to cope with the fact that I live among five women (my wife and four daughters). For certain, as the only male in a sea of females, I confess to having been sensitized to all the issues relating to the opposite sex. Therefore, I am greatly troubled by the secondary status that women are accorded in traditional Judaism.

A sixteen-year old girl leads services at a Reform synagogue in Jerusalem. In a secular society that sees the Orthodox world as too extreme for its taste, Reform (and Conservative) synagogues fill a critical spiritual need. What is unique about Reform houses of worship is that a woman can stand in front of a congregation and lead it through prayers. She is an equal partner in helping to create the religious atmosphere that enables Jews to reach God. This is the Reform Movement's greatest contribution to the Jewish world.

In referring to the Jewish world and not specifically to the religious Jewish world, one should understand that it is a Divine imperative to institute egalitarianism for one and all. The consequence of such a theological world-view will produce improved relationships between men and women, and thus a better society.

Many liberals see pluralism as the crowning achievement of a democratic society. But pluralism as a concept must be second to equality. Pluralism connotes tolerance, which by definition is a grudging, almost negative term. Religious freedom, which is another code phrase for liberals, is no more helpful in setting the parameters of a truly democratic society. For under its banner, every manner of behavior would have to be justified, including discrimination against women.

Over the centuries, male rabbis, schooled in the sociological realities of their time, interpreted Halacha in a way that served their male egos. Orthodoxy's understanding of the Jewish tradition regarding women is based on this acquired sociological development, not a Divine decree. At Creation, man and woman are created equally: "...in the image of God... male and female did He create them" (*Genesis* 1:27, see *Introduction*, page 14). They totally disregard the Divine thrust toward equality of the sexes that was clearly present at Creation. Equality is a God-given right. Therefore, to indulge in a theme of pluralism, which would grant one the right to fully accept women or to fully reject them is to reduce the glorious creation of the universe and the Divine spark in each individual to a political parlor game.

An observant Jew would agree that fulfilling Divine commandments is the highest goal that any Jew can achieve. Yet women are forbidden to perform many ritual commandments, particularly those that relate to matters of worship. And then, there is the small matter of the blessing that an Orthodox male says every morning: "Blessed are You (God) for not making me a woman" (*Morning Prayer Book*, preliminary blessings). Imagine a Protestant Evangelical starting out a morning worship with the words: "Thank you God for not making me an African-American, a Jew, a Sufi or a Buddhist!"

By claiming that observing all the commandments is the highest religious goal attainable, preventing a woman from partaking in this quest is to confine her a priori to an inferior status. The argument is that the woman is given different (sacred) tasks within the family structure that are considered to be life-shaping. Yet these male defined roles for women are not as religiously significant as the higher Divine world of "Mr. Macho Man." The fulfillment of many Divine commandments excludes half the population of the Jewish people.

Is one to believe that women are incapable of achieving full sanctity? Is a woman really incompetent to lead a religious service or to chant from the Torah? Worse, there are psychological mind-control games that men who opt for this sort of religious outlook maintain over women. A woman who wants to recite the mourning prayer for her dead father is prevented from doing so because there is not that ten-man quorum (minyan), and she could not be counted as the tenth person. What power these Orthodox men wield, dictating when a woman can mourn, when she can cry.

What are Orthodox men afraid of that they would perpetuate a religious system, which renders women as inadequate? The tragedy is that these women are held hostage in the most meaningful aspect of one's life — the accessibility to the Creator through a communal act of worship that includes, for example, reading directly from the Torah, the written word of God. Would a man really claim that a woman does not possess an equal spiritual feeling to lead a community in prayer as does he?

A man's insecurity is being played out at the expense of a woman's integrity. If a woman is humiliated in one area of life, she will be abused in others. When such an absence of parity between the sexes is institutionally sanctioned, it is an easy jump to perpetrate discriminatory measures against others. Perhaps the most painful example of this type of prejudice is demonstrated in the Orthodox relationship to the Ethiopian Jewish community. Despite the political, historical, social, cultural and physical discrimination that Ethiopian Jews withstood in order to hold on to their Judaism, upon their arrival in Israel it was determined by the Orthodox Rabbinate that they would have to undergo conversion because they had not had access to Rabbinic Judaism. They were not "real" Jews. Their religious leaders were not recognized as legitimate because of this lapse in their religious development.

Assenting to the demand, thirteen Ethiopian religious leaders enrolled in the Meir Yeshiva in Jerusalem, underwent ritual immersion, steeped themselves in Halacha and eventually received rabbinic ordination. These "black" Jews satisfied the same requirements as did their "white" Ashkenazi colleagues. Yet no rabbinic council has accepted their authority. Why? Their ordination certificate determines that they can only serve the Ethiopian community, whereas the non-Ethiopian graduates can serve all segments of the Jewish community.

Such prejudice can readily spread further. Orthodox members of the Knesset have called for a bill to be passed that would exclude democratically elected Israeli-Arab Knesset members from voting on any issue of "Jewish significance." (This could mean not only matters of who gets a certificate of kashrut, but also whether Israel should return land for peace.) Every male, who relegates a woman to a secondary status in any area of life's interactions can become a complicit supporter of the above kinds of discrimination.

The Kabbala expounds the theory that before releasing a soul for life on earth, God splits it in two; and when these two parts find one another in life, their encounter is true love, and their union fulfills the biblical saying: "And they shall be as one flesh" (*Genesis* 2:24). That unity — **two divinely inspired and equal halves, making up one whole** — dates to the beginning of time. Any religious movement that refuses to embrace this expression of the Divine removes itself from the protective cover of religious freedom, pluralism, and most important, equality.

Just as the political party of the late Rabbi Meir Kahana[1] was outlawed because of its racist ideological platform, so should any Orthodox political party be declared outside the sphere of influence if it has a discriminatory doctrine against women. The wealth of the Jewish tradition must not be used to the detriment of Israeli society.

"If you miss me at the back of the bus, you won't find me nowhere. Come on over to the front of the bus, I'll be sittin' right there" (1950s American civil rights song).

The late entertainer, Sammy Davis Jr., who was black and Jewish, told the story that in the late Fifties he once got on a bus in the heart of the Delta Basin in Mississippi. The bus driver took one look at him and said: "Get to the back of the bus." Davis protested: "But I am Jewish." The bus driver responded: "Then get off!"

The ultra-Orthodox community's desire to run separate-seating buses for men and women through ultra-Orthodox neighborhoods jolts the memories of those immigrants from the United States who participated in the bus boycotts in the deep South in order to end separate seating for African-Americans and whites on public transportation. This is yet another example of "looking forward to yesterday." How does one integrate Jewish law into a democratic state? What should be the balance?

Interns for Peace (IFP), a program that encourages cooperation between the

---

1. The leader of the extreme right-wing Kach party in Israel, Kahana, an Orthodox rabbi, who immigrated to Israel from America, spewed out racist hatred for Arabs. He was assassinated during a visit to the United States on November 6, 1990.

Jewish and Arab sectors in Israel, matches schools from both communities. A number of years ago, IFP had to forego these meetings if they included the religious school system. Apparently there is an obscure halachic ruling determining that no mixed social gatherings can take place between Jews and non-Jews lest one drinks from the same glass of wine, thus causing unwarranted fraternization.

Much of Jewish Law is a Diaspora creation (not the *Mishna*[1]). Despite the Divine decree that requires strict adherence to both the Oral and Written Law, the sociological realities of living as a minority determined the need for certain laws to be instituted in order to protect the integrity of the Jewish people against the intrusion of foreign beliefs. This made perfect sense as Jews could readily be overwhelmed by a majority society that was not Jewish. It is difficult to hold to one's sense of identity when one is a minority. The dizzying rise of assimilation and mixed marriage that plagues the American Jewish reality is ample evidence for the need to enforce rules of Jewish tradition to maintain one's Jewishness.

Yet once the Jewish people secured their own independent sovereign state where they form the majority, the application of these laws to today's realities leaves a prejudicial taste in one's mouth. Imagine the outcry should the United States Congress pass a law that would forbid socializing between Jews and Christians because of the latter's fear that such social integration might lead to the dissolution of Christian integrity. Imagine if the state of Texas, which is dominated by Southern Baptists, established separate seating on buses for Baptists and Jews, whereby Jews were forced to sit at the back of the bus.

Once laws that fit another era become universally applied to a new age, the result can hurt the workings of democracy. One must single out those halachic rulings, without threatening the theological force behind them, that, when transferred to Israel, may cause harm to another individual or group, thereby violating perhaps progressive halachic dictates.

Historical symbols play an important role in the life of a people. While mixed seating on buses that traverse religious neighborhoods offends ultra-

---

1. Codification of Jewish law compiled by Judah HaNasi around 200 CE. It contains the basis for Oral Law. The Mishnah is divided into six parts (orders), each one being sub-divided into tractates, and each tractate further subdivided into sections, which in turn contain paragraphs; also called Mishnayot.

Orthodox sensibilities, it is also clear that such separation creates an image of discrimination in the eyes of the general public. But image and reality touch each other when there is no such thing as the "purity" of bus lines. No single bus line begins and ends in an Ultra-Orthodox area. This reality will force non-religious women to sit in the back of the bus, setting off a whole range of black images.

There are certain red lines that cannot be crossed. There is already sufficient public religious coercion in Israel. Further coercion, which goes beyond the realm of religious consideration, and which touches upon the social fabric of society, must be prevented. No matter what the sensibilities of the religious community in Israel might be, the enforcement of separate seating on buses violates the very democratic **and** Jewish character of the country.

Having four daughters, I was naturally intrigued by the 1995 remake of the film of Louisa May Alcott's novel, *Little Women*, about the trials and tribulations of four sisters. The surprising element of this latest re-issue was its feminist thrust. Despite the March family's commitment to a revolutionary life style, neither the novel nor the original movie catered to female independence. Yet in this remake, Marmi preaches pure feminism to her children. She makes it clear in one of her many wise "woman-to-woman" talks with her daughters, that despite their obvious intelligence, ingenuity and forbearance, the March girls would be prevented from achieving certain advancements in life because of their gender.

Therein lies the obvious eternal truth in Marmi's sad wisdom — women are essentially oppressed. And most men, wittingly and unwittingly, maintain this contemptible reality. In Israel, ultra-Orthodoxy, run by and for males, has created a system of belief that runs contrary to the expressions of equality that are the very essence of Judaism. If such a belief structure is not a manifestation of schizophrenic tendencies, it most certainly is an expression of a double standard.

The "God Squad" — Part III

burn, baby, burn

They are burning down the bank. Now one might ask, what could possibly motivate someone to set a bank on fire? Loss of money in a savings scheme, the fall of bank shares, high interest rates? Any one of these reasons could push a "psycho" button in an individual, causing him to torch a bank. But to burn a bank for religious reasons? It does not make sense. But then again, there is a lot in the ultra-Orthodox world that can confuse one. What can be the halachic reasoning that gives one the religious go-ahead to physically destroy something or harm someone?

A haredi group called *"Keshet,"* a formal "God Squad," tried to burn down Bank Leumi in an ultra-Orthodox neighborhood because the bank had ties with an Africa-Israel holding company. The latter was allegedly involved with contractors building a mall near some sacred Jewish grave sites. Apparently, this supplies sufficient motivation — and a justified reason — to burn the bank to the ground.

Now comes the halachic question: What is the traditional Jewish text that gives the okay for such action? Perhaps the ultra-Orthodox world is more assimilated than one thinks. Maybe religious syncretism plays a pivotal role in the haredi community. The Keshet hooligans must have learned well from those who torched the homes of African-Americans in Alabama.

A non-kosher Chinese restaurant that bordered an ultra-Orthodox neighborhood was burned to the ground. After numerous threats by some ultra-Orthodox students at a nearby yeshiva to set the restaurant ablaze, one evening the place went up in flames. Can anyone quote me the Jewish chapter and verse indicating that to burn down this Chinese restaurant was a religiously pious act? Indeed, in the area of kashrut, Orthodoxy in Israel, not just ultra-Orthodoxy, demonstrates new heights of contradictory behavior.

What is the legal responsum that warrants some haredi group to pour kerosene all over an apartment of two Christian women who are suspected of being missionaries, and then set a match to the place? Which tractate in the Mishnah allows these bullies to beat up a former ultra-Orthodox Jew, still living in a haredi neighborhood, because they objected to the "sinner" watching television on the Sabbath in the confines of a private apartment? Where in the Jewish tradition is one permitted to take the law into one's own hands by violent means?

Public burnings reached a new hight when a kindergarten of the Reform Movement was torched and when a Conservative synagogue witnessed firebombs destroying part of its sanctuary and a number of its sacred texts. "If there is one vice that a Jewsih state might be thought to be free of, it would be anti-Semitic violence. There is no other name for the burning of Congregation Ya'ar Ramot, a Conservative synagogue in Jerusalem's Ramot neighborhood... This was not just the burning of a 'building', as Ashkenazi Chief Meir Lau curiously called it... Lau, while strongly condemning violence in any form, was careful not to call Ya'ar Ramot a synagogue, but a 'building specified for prayer of a stream.' This type of refusal to recognize other legitimate streams of Judaism creates an atmosphere that may have led to the attack" (*Jerusalem Post*, June 27, 2000).

One has to search far and wide to find consistent halachic dispensation for such actions. One has to opt for a minority view to reveal that one commandment in the Bible, or a law in the Mishnah, or its elaboration in the *Gemara*,[1] or a quote from later traditional Jewish sources would allow for the continuous abuse of a halachic system that, for many religious and non-religious Jews, reflects the richness and beauty of the Jewish tradition. It is clear that ultra-Orthodoxy is working at cross-purposes. If, according to the tradition, there is a continual struggle between the *"Yeitzar HaTov"* and the *"Yeitzar HaRa"* (good and evil inclinations), then it seems that within the ultra-Orthodox world evil is winning the day. The balance that is suppose to exist in the ultra-Orthodox Jewish world between the letter and the spirit of the law has ceased to be a guiding force.

When such an imbalance spills over into the political realm, the chances of extremist behavior increase. The fusion of nationalism and religion is a powder keg waiting to explode. In the name of Jewish religious chauvinism, a Jewish underground, made up of extremist Orthodox Jews, is formed and carries out

---

1. Comment on and discussion surrounding the Mishnah. The Mishnah and the Gemara constitute the *Talmud*.

deadly acts of violence against Arabs. Orthodox Baruch Goldstein enters an Arab mosque and guns down 29 Moslem worshippers, and Yigal Amir, receiving instructions from some of his Orthodox rabbinic luminaries, assassinates the late Prime Minister Yitzhak Rabin. One wonders what awaits future Israeli prime ministers should they also opt to trade a "piece of land" for a "land of peace." Such an imbalance tips the scale from sanity to lunacy.

The "God Squad" — Part IV

you are what you eat

There was Moses sitting at the top of Mount Sinai, copying down God's commandments. As one can learn from the biblical narrative, Moses often challenges God, entering into a spirited dialogue with the Almighty.

> **God**: "Moses, thou shalt not boil thy kid in its mother's milk."
> **Moses**: "Dost Thou mean that one must have separate dishes for milk and meat?"
> **God**: "Moses, just listen. Thou shall not boil thy kid in its mother's milk."
> **Moses**: "Dost Thou mean that one must wait several hours before eating meat after drinking a glass of milk?"
> **God**: "Moses, I told thee already. Thou shalt not boil thy kid in its mother's milk."
> **Moses**: "Dost Thou mean that one must never have a Big Mac with cheese in the holy city of Jerusalem?"
> **God**: "Okay. Do what you want!"

Something went awry these past few thousand years since God introduced this commandment. Of course, with the intervening years, there were attempts to fine tune God's intentions. Indeed, that simple singular sentence set in motion an entire set of laws regarding kashrut.

Big Macs have invaded "kosher-tight" Jerusalem. While other non-kosher restaurants operate in Jerusalem and its environs, it is difficult to imagine

McDonald's in the heart of Jerusalem, the spiritual center of the Jewish people. Not only does McDonald's represent "high *treif*" (unkosher) at its tantalizing best, it also symbolizes the ultimate American invasion of the Jewish land. So how was McDonald's allowed to open its door in "Orthodox" Jerusalem? How is it that the ultra-Orthodox parties that make up fifty percent of the municipality's coalition have barely uttered a word of protest against McDonald's incursion into sacred territory? Why have there been virtually no ultra-Orthodox demonstrations?

How do some places in Jerusalem, which have kashrut certificates, stay open on the Sabbath for business? Here the intention is not to mention movie theaters and discotheques, but rather cafes and bars where there is electric jazz, boogie, blues and acid rock, where tickets are sold at the door and hard cash is used to booze it up.

Anyone with even the most rudimentary understanding of Jewish law knows that someone's kashrut cannot be trusted if he or she does not observe the Sabbath. Yet many of these places maintain a certificate of kashrut. Perhaps when Moses failed to raise this scenario at Mount Sinai, it was eventually to be understood that such blatant violations of the spirit of kashrut would be tolerated.

Everyone loves Chinese food. The advantage of living in Israel is that there are numerous kosher Chinese restaurants. In most countries throughout the world, Chinese food is quite economical. It is inexpensive. In Israel, it is a rich person's fantasy. In addition, with all the Vietnamese and Thai cooks who do not have the slightest idea of the rules governing kashrut, it is impossible to believe that there are not kosher "mix-ups."

Israel's steak houses are very popular. There is not necessarily a direct halachic relationship between the ritual observance of kashrut and the spiritual purity that might stem from cleanliness. Yet, no less a halachic authority than Maimonides provides hygiene as one rationale for the dietary laws: "I maintain that the food forbidden by law is unwholesome" (*Guide to the Perplexed*, 3:48). However, at many of Israel's steak restaurants, any notion of "cleanliness being next to Godliness" (*Babylonian Talmud, Avodah Zarah* 20b) is cast aside, as the cooks, making good on the menu that offers the famous "Jerusalem mixed grill," drop their cigarette ashes into the food. But apparently according to Jewish law, such untidiness does not disqualify these restaurants from being considered kosher. Once a kosher certificate is issued, the restaurant is licensed, even if it could not pass the standards of the Health Ministry.

What do all the above-related places have in common: McDonald's, a kosher Friday evening entertainment spot, a kosher Chinese restaurant and a kosher steak house? With the exception of McDonald's, circumstances do not favor any of the above restaurants observing kosher purity. Indeed, how is a kashrut certificate issued to eateries that sport an electronic "at the hop" gig on the Sabbath? As for the exaggerated prices at kosher Chinese restaurants, one must assume that there is a very high salaried *mashgiach*[1] employed by the state to insure that the non-Jewish Oriental cooks are not "treifing" up their Jewish clientele. Regarding Jerusalem steak houses, it is impossible to figure out, given the filthy state of some of their kitchens, how they secure their certification of kashrut. As far as McDonald's is concerned, Jerusalem's mayor must have extraordinary skills in keeping his ultra-Orthodox municipal cohorts under wraps as streams of Jerusalemites order McDonald's cheeseburgers with a milk shake on the Sabbath!

All this means is that the norm of religious blackmail is alive and well. For the right price, one can be kosher. Inconsistencies abound, which is ironic because Orthodox Jews would hold that their entire halachic world-view is immutably consistent. This is the classic definition of a split personality. Yet there should be no illusions, leniency in one area of religious observance may not indicate tolerance in some other area, even if political or monetary favors are part of the deal. Righteous indignation among ultra-Orthodox Jews cannot always be assuaged, and so reactions by the haredi world too often reflect a violent response that is completely contrary to the spirit of Judaism. If a Conservative Synagogue was burned down, there should be no surprise to wake up one morning and see an ashen skeleton of the McDonald's arch.

---

1. An Orthodox man (often a rabbi who specializes in the dietary laws) authorized to supervise restaurants to guarantee that they enforce the regulations surrounding the laws of kashrut.

The "God Squad" — Part V

they shoot horses, don't they

It seems that anyone and anything that is not in absolute sync with the haredi community can be subject to physical attacks. Intoxicated with their electoral growth, ultra-Orthodox Jews are flexing their political muscle in order to put forth their religious/moral agenda. Because of their increased entrenchment in the workings of government, they feel confident that what they cannot achieve in the political arena, they are entitled to implement on the streets. Too many in the ultra-Orthodox community feel that it is their God-given (and politically empowered) right to put those they perceive as morally lame out of their misery. And so haredi vigilantes roam the back alleys of Israel's moral corruption, waiting to strike. They would probably call it "mercy attacks." Sadly, it is virtually impossible to find a time when the haredi community or its leadership has condemned any of these increasing violent acts.

Now, one might ask, is this any way for religiously upright Jewish boys to behave? Apparently so. If that Chinese restaurant really serves *"glatt* treif" (exceedingly unkosher food), why bother with legal niceties to get it to change its ways when one can torch the place? If suggestive advertisements at bus stops offend one's sensibilities, why employ judicial procedures to register a protest when, instead, one can take a sledgehammer and smash them to smithereens? If an archeologist is digging too close to a sacred grave, why wait for a Knesset law to set the parameters for archeological excavations when one can just slug the uppity son-of-a-bitch so that he or she can no longer lend validity to one's Jewish roots in the land? If one gets palpitations when a car accidentally drives near an Orthodox neighborhood on the Sabbath, why wait for the police to deal with the matter when a rock, hurled through the windshield of the car, can teach the wayward driver a lesson once and for all? Upset by an integrated minyan at the Wall? Why turn to the authorities to enforce the accepted etiquette at the Kotel when one can crack a chair over the head of a woman deep in prayer?

It is little wonder that such violence exists. On far too many occasions, ultra-Orthodox leaders — but also some in supposedly mainstream Orthodoxy — boldly declare their intention to not abide by Supreme Court rulings, thus attesting to what they consider a "higher" rule of law, the law of the Torah. Such a view is a direct call for incitement to violence. In recent years, there have been increased security measures taken to protect government ministers, Knesset members and judges. This increased security came about not only as a response to Arab terror, but also (possibly primarily) because of a concern for the actions of Jewish religious fanatics. As if it were not enough that Yitzhak Rabin was killed by another Jew who decreed that Rabin was acting against the Divine will of the Jewish people, now judges who carry out their judicial duties are intimated by threats.

It would seem that the haredi world is trying to turn Israel into a Jewish Iran. If the ultra-Orthodox community would adopt a "live and let-live" attitude, then most Israelis would be perfectly satisfied to let Orthodox Jews hermetically seal off their neighborhoods on the Sabbath. But that does not seem to be what the ultra-Orthodox Jewish world wants. It wants to take control of the everyday life of society: what one eats, how one dresses, how one practices his Judaism. If it takes physical violence to implement their grandiose scheme of installing a Torah-based society, then many in the haredi community have no compunctions about attacking one and all.

What is going on? Is there a higher law than the civil law that guides Israel? If there is, then it is one that finds a narrow interpretation of Jewish law. What has occurred in Israel is that ultra-Orthodoxy has adopted an eisegetical approach to Jewish life, whereby one forces the Jewish tradition to fit one's prejudices. Such a "one size fits all" approach does not create unity. However, it does and will continue to tear asunder any semblance of balance in Jewish life. In behaving in ways that clearly contradict the thrust of the Jewish tradition, ultra-Orthodoxy is also causing a real split within Israeli society.

Mutual Respect and Compromise: A Therapy for Repair

At an international religious peace conference, the leaders of the three monotheistic religions — Islam, Christianity and Judaism — met in an unprecedented attempt to solve the world's conflicts through compromise.

The first speaker was the titular head of the Moslem world. His words: "In order to guarantee peace, I hereby proclaim in the name of the nation of Islam, that Moslems will no longer look to Mohammed as the descendant of the Almighty. I have also instructed every preacher of our sacred faith to eradicate from the holy Koran all reference to violence and 'holy wars.'"

His remarks were met with thunderous applause. Not to be outdone, the Pope approached the rostrum: "In the name of the Holy See, the Catholic Church and the entire Christian world, for the sake of peace, let it hereby be known that Jesus Christ will no longer be considered the son of God. Proselytizing will be a thing of the past. All people shall be as one."

The conference hall erupted in cheers, shaking at the raw emotion generated by the Pope's incredible sacrifice of Christian religious doctrine to meet the demands of peace. Huddled in the corner were a number of haredi rabbis, chosen to represent the Jewish people. They were confident that their announcement would be so far-reaching that it would literally dwarf the religious compromises of these two courageous leaders.

The head of the Jewish delegation walked dramatically to the podium. "In deference to my co-religionists, I am about to announce to you that in the name of Judaism, the most ancient of our three religions, we, the Jewish people, are willing to make the ultimate sacrifice for peace, reflective of the magnitude of the sacrifices made by my clerical colleagues. For the sake of compromise, to advance the cause of peace, to bring harmony to this troubled world and to reconcile all conflicts that divide us, we, the guardians of our ancient Jewish faith, are willing to forego the recitation of the obligatory prayer for miracles in the blessing after the meals on the first night of Chanukah." (The rabbi was almost stoned to death by his own constituency for suggesting such an exaggerated compromise.)

In order to move toward healing, compromise is an absolute necessity. By definition, this means that Jewish life cannot be set into a particular time-frame. Judaism cannot become static. Judaism must and can speak of tolerance and respect. Even respect for haredim, provided they do not decorate the walls in their neighborhoods with graffiti that reads: "Zionism = Racism" or "According to the dictate of our holy Torah, serving in the Israeli army is a grave transgression, whereby one must be killed for such an act." Such blasphemy contradicts the Divine commandment: "You shall not hate your brother in your heart. Rather you shall reason with your kin so that you do not bring sin upon yourself. You must not seek vengeance, nor bear a grudge against your kin. You shall love your neighbor as yourself; I am the Lord" (*Leviticus* 19:17-18). These underlying moral truisms of Judaism are the ones that should serve the test of time. It is upon their foundation that compromise, tolerance and respect can rest.

Yet, with time, these heavenly directives have become perverted. Over the years, God's instructions got in the way of human beings' authority, particularly the authority of too many ultra-Orthodox rabbis, who have set themselves up as "pretenders to the Throne." A rabbi's power became more important than the Almighty's intentions, thereby denying equal access for all Jews to God. It is not a Catholic hierarchy de jure, but it is one de facto.

The first step that needs to be taken is the dismantling of the offices of the Chief Rabbinate, under whose authority rest all life cycle matters. "Womb to tomb" ceremonies are the sole domain of the Orthodox in Israel. For example, there are no halachic restrictions that would forbid a Reform or Conservative rabbi from performing a wedding. Preventing this from happening in Israel is a matter of political protection, not religious purity. According to Jewish law one does not need a rabbi at all to make a marriage Jewishly binding, but rather two kosher witnesses (who observe the Sabbath and adhere to the laws of kashrut).

I am an Israeli Reform rabbi. Because of this Orthodox monopoly, it is illegal for me to perform marriages. That which my profession entitles me to do in any other country in the world is denied to me in a Jewish state. How ironic that legitimacy and basic democratic rights are bestowed on me as a minority in a Christian world, but denied me in a self-contained Jewish world.

As aforementioned, I have four daughters. I performed the weddings of the two older ones. While opposing the draconian law that confines marriages to the officialdom of the Ministry of Religion and the Office of the Chief Rabbinate, I suggested to both girls that they register at the local Rabbinate, and seek an Orthodox rabbi who would perform the halachic elements in the ceremony, yet allow me to participate in the wedding in some meaningful way.

Both girls flatly rejected this suggestion. They refused to give in to the Orthodox stranglehold on religious matters in Israel. They also wanted their father, who for them is a rabbi in the full sense of the word, to be the singular religious figure to sanctify this extremely emotional and sacred moment in their lives. And so, in front of hundreds of guests, on two separate occasions, I performed the weddings.

When the ideals and standards of parents and children are in conflict, the marriage of a child is a departure and a separation. But when there is an identity of ideals, of basic commitments and Jewish values, then marriage does not separate parent and child, but leads them to greater closeness. Neither my children nor I would let the Orthodox establishment derail that overwhelming familial closeness that we all felt at the wedding of our daughters. Within the confines of this deeply religious ceremony, a dynamic present and an evolving future were linked together by a common, **but not static**, past.

The wedding ceremonies that I performed, and that other Reform and Conservative rabbis in Israel like me have performed, made relevant this sacred moment without, in any way, letting go of the traditional aspects of Judaism. Such an act was not only important to me as the father of the brides, but as a rabbi; it was crucial in guaranteeing that the progressive forces within Judaism will keep pace with the historical progression of our people. It is clear that most of my Orthodox colleagues in Israel have proven themselves incapable of doing this. Ultra-Orthodoxy in Israel is **married to the past**. My daughters who underwent a Reform wedding ceremony remained **engaged to the past**, but **married to the future**.

Perhaps the fault lies in the understanding of what constitutes a religious individual, or rather what criteria are used to define a religious leader. For some, a religious leader is one who adheres to the ritual aspects of the Jewish tradition, and for others, it is one who tends to the ethical teachings of the Jewish heritage. Too often Orthodoxy becomes bogged down in the minutiae of religious expression that it fails to see the forest through the trees.

An Orthodox guest ran frantically around in my house prior to the beginning of the Sabbath, to make certain all was prepared so that he would not do anything that would be considered in violation of the Sabbath laws. Concerned about not doing any work on the Sabbath, he unscrewed the light bulb in the refrigerator so that it would not go on when he opened it, and he prepared individual strips of toilet paper so as not tear anything. With his great concern for the details of the Sabbath, he was going to be late for the evening services. In the middle of his frenzy, I grabbed him and said: "You are so concerned about keeping the Sabbath, that you will have no time to enjoy it!"

While not denying the place of ritual in the life of a religious Jew, it should be noted that a completely literal interpretation of Jewish law can lead one to such a self-righteous and narrow view of the world, that virtually any manner of aberrant behavior can result.

No one would consider a halachically observant Tel Aviv rabbi convicted of sexually assaulting his women parishioners as a religious leader. On the other hand, the Reform rabbi who founded Interns for Peace is most certainly a religious person. But one need not choose extreme cases to put forth the argument of the need for balance and moderation. This can be found among the pantheon of religious leaders who have occupied the recent stage of Jewish history. Non-orthodox rabbis such as Leo Baeck, Mordecai Kaplan, Abraham Joshua Heschel and Stephen S. Wise fare quite well as religious leaders when matched against Orthodox rabbis like Avraham Yehuda Kook, Adin Steinsaltz and Yosef Soleveichik. To compare either grouping to the most extreme rabbis in different religious streams is unfair.

Unfortunately, ultra-Orthodoxy in Israel suffers from a psychological disruption. For example, according to Jewish law homosexuality is an abomination: "Do not lie with a male as one lies with a woman; it is an abomination" (*Leviticus* 18:22). Based on this, gays and lesbians are not regarded as worthy to carry out certain roles within the Jewish community. (This did not prevent some Orthodox rabbis from ruling that Dana International, the transsexual who represented Israel in the Eurovision song festival, could be counted in a minyan if there were only nine males.) One should ask how is it that Rabbi Moshe Levinger, who was convicted for shooting a Palestinian boy, Rabbi Dov Lior, who praises Baruch Goldstein, the murderer of twenty-nine Moslem worshippers, and that Tel Aviv rabbi, who abused his parishioners, are all permitted to fulfill roles of religious responsibility? Was not their behavior abominable? Can one imagine a declared homosexual being accepted as a *Shaliach Tzibur*,[1] a Torah reader or a *Shamash*?[2] Such selective interpretations of Jewish behavior set off a host of contradictions as one attempts to reach an understanding of Orthodoxy.

---

1. A male in Orthodoxy who leads the congregation in prayer.
2. The sexton of the synagogue whose learning is often extensive but not of the same caliber as the rabbi's, and who helps facilitate the everyday running of the synagogue.

There are many Jewish laws, whose universal import are morally so powerful, and whose ritual significance so meaningful, that they span generations. But what does one do with those laws, fashioned centuries ago and applied to today's reality, that perpetuate a situation where women are regarded as inferior, that cast Ethiopian Jews in the role of second-class citizens and that refer to those whose sexual preferences are not perceived as "normal" as abominations? It is here that the halachic world is less than honest. Their intrusions into the non-halachic world are dependent upon the legal force of a secular Jewish state as much as on Halacha itself. It is the Orthodox establishment's cynical manipulation of a secular political system that helps it to force some pretty distasteful Jewish laws down Israelis' throats against their will, therefore bending the lifestyles of all Israelis to fit its own.

Judaism is an extraordinary religion. There may be other religions that have persisted longer, but there is no other religion that has mastered the complex art of survival through every phase of western civilization, subsequent to its emergence at some unknown time in the ancient Near East. Jews succeeded in maintaining themselves as a people because of a commitment to a unity principle — historical monotheism. Exposed to radical shifts in history, Judaism demonstrated its powers to reshape itself without relinquishing its basic identity. Belief in the one God was continually redefined to cope with natural phenomena, scientific advancement and historical developments. Since Jewish awareness and experience constantly underwent change, concepts of God were widened so that God might remain adequate, and Judaism could become simultaneously involved with the past and creatively innovative. Under Orthodoxy, Judaism in Israel has surrendered its **traditional** paradigm of ideological growth and historical and sociological development for **tradition**.

The general community in Israel, eighty percent of which is not Orthodox, is in need of moral and spiritual guidance. Since most Israeli leaders do not provide the type of moral direction that is needed, one would hope that those entrusted with the "spiritual" welfare of the state could provide Israelis with some sort of moral compass. Unfortunately, ultra-Orthodoxy in Israel, the most vocal of religious expressions in the country, seems mired in halachic minutia. More problematic is that they seem only to be able to fashion ritual responses to the existential questions that Israelis face. They have created a "ritual reality."

Such an approach has offset the healthy balance that must be maintained between tradition and change. But such a sane balance can only endure when the Orthodox monopoly in Israel is broken. Its singular control, reinforced by the official combination of religion and politics, has emboldened Orthodoxy's "chutzpah" to legislate the moral will of all Israelis (thereby affecting non-Jewish Israelis as well). Ultra-Orthodoxy in Israel too often speaks with a "schizophrenic voice." It has produced a real paradox whereby a Jewish tradition that speaks of respect and decency finds its expression in intolerance and coercion. This must be altered immediately. Otherwise, not only will the psychological equilibrium of the Jewish people teeter, but also its physical well being will be scarred. **The balance of tradition and change is Judaism at its authentic best**. Their harmonious combination is the singular cure that will lead religion in Israel out of its disruptive and divisive state.

CHAPTER 6

ISRAEL AND DIASPORA JEWRY

Here, There and Everywhere

Israel and the Diaspora are intimately entwined. Yet over the years, the relationship between Israel and the Diaspora has dramatically changed. At the very beginning of Israel's establishment, the American Jewish community supported Israel virtually en masse, and blindly. Whether American Jews planned to move there or not was irrelevant. Israel was the fulfillment not only of the ancient longing to return to the Jewish people's ancestral homeland, but also of the desperate need to have a physical refuge for those Jews who survived the horrors of the Holocaust — as well as a place for all Jews who suffered persecution. In helping Israel, Jews around the world felt good about themselves.

Yet the heroic image of the Israeli as portrayed by Ari Ben Canaan of Leon Uris' *Exodus*, reinforced in the film version of the book by the ever handsome and dashing Paul Newman, has long since evaporated. In the 21st century, Israel is now exposed as a country, like others, whose flashes of brilliance and ingenuity are offset by its failings. Israel no longer automatically "turns on" American Jews. Many American Jews become disappointed when Israel does not live up to its mythic image of perfection. They expect Israelis to be "Jewish" as they understand "Jewish" in the American experience — an expression of religiosity. For these American Jews, a secular Israeli is an oxymoron. For an Israeli who speaks Hebrew, studies Jewish history, literature and Bible, fights in a Jewish army, secularism does not contradict one's Jewishness. One gets a sense that vicarious Judaism defines much of the American Jewish reality. What many American Jews do not do Jewishly for themselves, they expect others to do for them: rabbis, the synagogue and the religious school. Once Israel was part of that equation, but now most American Jews consider Israel no longer a necessity for fashioning their Jewish identity.

Of course, should one open a prayer book, one would think that Israel occupies a central theme within American Jewish life. In any given worship service, Israel "runs a close second to God" in the amount of space accorded to it in the prayer book. But as might befit the schizophrenic mind, believing and practicing what one preaches (or prays) need not necessarily go hand and hand. Because of the role that it plays in the prayer book, a general disinterest in Israel would indicate a disregard for one of the most important theological tenets of Judaism — the centrality of Israel for the Jewish people.

As much as American Jewry would like to walk its independent course, Israel still looms too large on the international screen, if not on the Jewish screen, to ignore. Barely a day goes by when Israel is not a news item in the American media. However, the average American Jewish reaction (or non-reaction) to Israel does not reflect the views of the American Jewish leadership. For these leaders, both professional and lay, Israel is a constant force in the shaping of Jewish identity. While some religious movements in the Diaspora relate to Israel only as it affects their own parochial concerns, for most American Jewish leaders, Israel is **a** central, if not **the** central force in impacting positively on the perpetuity of the Jewish people. And so, they turn to Israel to help them counteract what they perceive as a slow dissolution of the American Jewish community.

The concern for Jewish survival in the Diaspora weaves a myriad of contradictory notions. On the one hand, the American Jewish leadership readily admits that one of the surest ways to guarantee the survival of the Jewish community is to incorporate into one's life a trip to Israel. Yet on the other hand, the very fact that American Jews view an encounter with Israel as one of the best guarantors for Jewish survival points to a certain bankruptcy in Diaspora Jewish existence vis-a-vis its own ability to self-perpetuate. That being the case, why not just call for wholesale *aliya*?[1]

Jewish continuity and/or survival cannot be a selfish consideration. To access Israel only in American terms leaves out the possibility of drawing upon the fullness of the Jewish state as a tool to maintain one's sense of Jewish belonging — a belonging which necessarily serves as the mainstay of any Jewish

---

1. Literally, aliya means "ascent." It refers to immigration to Israel.

future. This leads to the question of definition as to what constitutes Jewish continuity and survival. If Israel, as an expression of Jewish self-sufficiency in its own right, is excluded from that definition, then one is left with a narrow understanding of Jewish life — one that sees Judaism as a religious expression only. If American Jews believe that they can speak about Jewish continuity or survival without the inclusion of land, people, state, culture, nation and language — characteristics that Israel represents — then they are out of sync with the reality of the collective Jewish experience.

Given the increased rate of assimilation and the steady rise in mixed marriages, as well as the desire to hold onto the children of these mixed marriages, it is understandable that faith would be the primary determining factor of one's Jewishness. But faith devoid of national commitment will eventually become so diluted that while a new Jewish reality will be created in the Diaspora, it will have virtually no link with any recognizable historical Jewish past.

The challenge here is that many of these genuinely well-intended American Jewish leaders want to dictate the nature of the relationship between Israel and the Diaspora. Consequently, the two worlds collide, causing a psychological breakdown. The intensity of each community's involvement with one another is such that it often takes on the dimension of a love-hate relationship. Each community claims it knows what is best for the other.

During the last year of the late President Richard Nixon's administration, a rabbi was asked to give the Sunday morning sermon at one of the ecumenical services held at the White House. When word got out that a rabbi was invited to preach before the President of the United States, the first phone call the rabbi received was from the late Yitzhak Rabin, then Israeli ambassador to the US. Rabin proceeded to dictate to the rabbi what he should or should not say. The rabbi's response was to politely hang up the phone. When the shoe is on the other foot, and American Jews criticize Israel, Israelis do not hang up politely. They slam down the phone.

At a *Tikkun Magazine*[1] conference in Jerusalem, its editor, Michael Lerner, an American Jew who lives in Oakland, California, called on Israelis to refuse to

---

1. An intellectual liberal Jewish periodical.

serve in the territories. In response to this clearly presumptuous and self-righteous statement, the Israeli press generally overreacted. Israelis took what was basically a "chutzpadik" comment and blew it into a general broadside against "Diaspora interference" in Israeli affairs — a broadside that defied all reasonableness. The view that a Jew has to live in Israel in order to offer opinions on Israel's behavior makes no Jewish sense.

Wittingly or unwittingly, what is done in Israel is done in the name of the Jewish people. The image of the Jewish people and the perception of Judaism are often determined by how Jews in Israel behave. That is the reason that Mr. Rabin felt free to impose his views upon that American rabbi. Israelis are forever telling Diaspora Jews how to educate their children, how to lobby for Israel, how much money to send to their state. Israelis even tell their Diaspora Jewish brothers and sisters who among them can be Jews![1]

American Jews respond by criticizing Israel for its lack of religious pluralism, for its chauvinistic tendencies, and its violations of the human rights of Palestinians and other minorities in Israel. Many American Jews have been at the forefront of the struggle to safeguard human rights. It is unreasonable for Israelis to expect American Jews to do their bidding in the halls of Congress when the former institute policies that are deemed an embarrassment to the American Jewish community. More so, it is not difficult to imagine Diaspora anti-Semitism raising its ugly head because the world perceives Israel, rightfully or wrongfully, as a country that routinely abuses human rights. It is painful for Israelis to be called on the moral carpet by Diaspora Jews.

It is here where Diaspora Jews must be honest in their criticism. They must always keep in mind the geographical locale from whence their criticisms come. American Jews must not confuse their existential relationship to Israel with the empirical reality of living there. American Jews must also be prepared for Israelis to point a finger back at them, criticizing their lack of Jewish education and their lack of Jewish commitment.

---

1. This is a reference to the halachic question: "Who is a Jew?" According to Jewish law, only the child of a mother born Jewish or halachically converted is considered a Jew. According to many American Jews, the Reform Movement in particular, a child's Jewishness can be determined by the father as well as by the mother. In addition, both the Reform and the Conservative Movements consider their conversions as binding, but these are rejected by the Orthodox establishment.

The bottom line is that many American Jews, for the most part, live a minimalist Jewish existence. They understand this, yet somehow try to devalue the Israeli experience to fit their own reality. With their eye to future generations of Jews, the American Jewish leadership concentrates on sending its youth to Israel. But rather than sending young people on long-term programs to Israel, they concentrate on lightning visits. Given the paucity of Jewish knowledge among most Diaspora Jews, they seem to be working at cross-purposes: wanting to put intellectual flesh on spiritually weakened Jewish bones, but not allowing the investment in time to realize this. Israelis tell American Jews to accept them as they are, Jews living in a self-contained Jewish state according to a Jewish calendar. American Jews tell Israelis to accept them as they are, a dispersed community, which essentially can afford a part-time Jewish life at best. The two do not go hand in hand. As such, a dysfunctional relationship develops. Like toddlers, both communities are engaged in "parallel play." They look beyond each other and not at each other. They talk about each other, not with each other.

Israel as the Jewish People's Birthright

A Jewish student at a university in Boston, Massachusetts, approached his Hillel[1] rabbi, confessing that he had sinned.

> **Student**: "Rabbi, I ate a pork sandwich on Yom Kippur."
> **Rabbi**: "What happened to you? Don't you know that it is forbidden to eat on Yom Kippur?"
> **Student**: "I know. It slipped my mind."
> **Rabbi**: "Don't you know that pork is not kosher?"
> **Student**: "I know."
> **Rabbi**: "Then why did you do it?"
> **Student**: "I forgot that I was Jewish!"

Terrified of the idea that American Jewish college students are forgetting that

---

1. The Jewish student activity center on many university and college campuses.

they are Jewish, Yossi Beilin[1] gave birth to an idea. Charles Bronfman and Michael Steinhart, two extremely wealthy Jewish philanthropists, adopted it. They determined that it is every Jewish child's "birthright" to come to Israel; thus the name of the project which has become the new "savior" of the North American Jewish community. The idea is to bring approximately 50,000 college-age students, primarily from North America, over the next several years, for a ten-day visit to Israel. These students are considered the future of the Jewish Diaspora, and their numbers are rapidly diminishing on the Jewish scene. The Birthright type of cure-all for this phenomenon is paradigmatic of the conflicting and contradictory approach of the American Jewish community to many of its social ills.

The headline of this dramatic effort is — it's free. That's right. Judaism is on sale. Israel is "on-the-house." There is one condition. The kid must never have been to Israel (on an organized educational program). For certain, the American Jewish leadership knows that if college students were charged for the trip, no one would come. In and of itself, this fact is a sad commentary on the state of affairs of the American Jewish community, particularly given its extreme wealth.

This is called outreach. If you are an unaffiliated Jew, never having been involved in Jewish life, you get rewarded. It is your "birthright" to come to your homeland. Those who support this idea would be well advised to read the biblical story of Jacob and Esau. Esau gave up his birthright to Jacob with barely a thought — for a bowl of lentil soup. He counted on his legacy serving him, having done nothing to merit what he was born into. But the mere acquisition of the birthright did not entitle Jacob to hold on to it. It was only after years of struggling, during which he served his uncle Laban as little more than a slave for twenty-one years, that he ultimately earned the name Israel, legitimately inheriting the birthright (see *Introduction*, page 17, footnote 1).

Nothing comes easy like water from a faucet. A person does not arrive at wisdom at short-range. One has to work hard to achieve anything, to earn something of worth. To crown someone with such a grand Jewish prize as a trip to Israel for doing virtually nothing is to tell that person that Judaism is cheap. This stands in sharp contrast to what Israel is all about — the living proof that

---

1. Current Israeli minister of justice, Yossi Beilin was one of the architects of the original Declaration of Principles drawn up by the Israel government and the Palestinian Liberation Organization.

throughout Jewish history Jews have sacrificed their lives to sustain themselves as a people. Herein lies the contradiction between what Israel can offer and what American Jews want of Israel.

Such a "quick-fix" is supposed to solve the issues of assimilation and mixed-marriage, save the Diaspora Jewish community and guarantee its perpetuity. This will be about as successful as the supplementary Jewish educational program in America where a Jewish child dedicates two to four hours a week to Hebrew, Jewish history, Bible, Holidays and life-cycle events. (This all takes place on an afternoon, after the kid has had a full day of public school.) Not only does a Jewish child cognitively learn virtually nothing, but also gets a clear psychological message: Jewish life sits on a shelf, dusted off for a few hours a week, then placed back on the shelf to gather more dust. A Jewish child is taught that a minimal investment is all that is needed to nurture Jewish life and foster Jewish commitment. This supplementary approach to Jewish education is the primary exposure to Jewish learning for the overwhelming majority of young American Jews.

In order to bypass cognition as a tool to strengthen Jewish identity, a flash trip to Israel is planned, predicated on the notion that these kids will be so emotionally impacted that the long-term results will be truly positive. But these youngsters lack any Jewish memory. There is no such thing as a United Jewish Appeal (UJA)[1] mission for the unaffiliated, whereby one can expect to smother college-age students in exaggerated emotionalism in order to simultaneously open Jewish tear-ducts and Jewish pocketbooks. In many ways, Israel is turned into a Jewish Disney World — instant entertainment that will provide momentary pleasure, and little lasting effect.

The idea to accord everyone the right to come to Israel is essentially a good one, even an admirable one. A short visit to Israel can be very powerful, even for the Jewishly uninitiated. Also the godfathers of Birthright are correct in their assertion that a short-term program for college-age students has a greater impact than one for high school-age students. No one should fault the American Jewish leadership for its noble attempts at securing a Jewish future through the use of Israel. Yet, how does one measure the success of such a grandiose venture

---

1. The main fundraising organ of the American Jewish community.

as Birthright? According to numbers? If so, then even its success will be failure. Approximately eight thousand students came on the program in its first year. Those who gave birth to the idea are claiming success beyond their wildest imagination. The numbers are dictating their euphoria.

They forget they were giving something away for free. If one really wants to measure the success of this "give-away" program, offer the same students a free trip to the Bahamas. The promoters of the program are boasting that for those 8,000 places there were 15,000 candidates. Considering that there are an estimated 400,000 college-age Jewish students in North America, and considering that over one million dollars was spent on marketing this free trip, one should be careful about braggadocian claims. (Out of 6,000 Jewish students at the University of Michigan, only 150 signed up for Birthright, despite an all-out effort at recruitment. The greatest challenge will be to find the 50,000 students that Birthright plans to bring to Israel every year.) But those free ten days give another message: "I've filled my life-time Jewish quota of involvement." Sure, kids might come to Israel for free. But when something is given away for free, syllogistically it means it is not worth anything!

And of course, when these "ten-day visits" do not make the slightest dent in the area which most threatens the perpetuation of the Diaspora Jewish community, mixed marriage and assimilation, the creators of Birthright will point the finger at Israel. They will claim that Israel let them down: as if the impoverishment of Jewish education and Jewish family life in the Diaspora, coupled with the sociological reality of being an insignificant minority in a sea of Christians, has little to do with the sorry state of Diaspora affairs. It is always easier to blame someone else for one's own shortcomings.

If one needs any proof of what effect a short-term Israel program has on North American Jewish youth, one only has to examine the statistics of sociologist Erik Cohen's study, commissioned by the Jewish Agency, of tens of thousands of summer participants in Israel programs over the last few years. While 80% or more of those who came to Israel responded positively to such questions as; "Did your Jewish identity increase?" "Do you feel more religious?" "Are you a Zionist?" the same number said that marrying a non-Jew who would not convert would suit them just fine!

Is Birthright's ten-day trip to Israel an act of desperation? Since the price tag of this idea is two hundred million dollars, one might draw the conclusion that the American Jewish community is indeed in dire straits. It is amazing how such an enormously wealthy Jewish community can be so Jewishly impoverished. Those philanthropists willing to donate such large sums of money to "save the Diaspora Jewish world" are truly dedicated and unselfish individuals. Their motivation is to be praised. But the question is not one of intent, rather one must ask, is this the best use of so much money to increase awareness of Jewish identity? Is it wise to spend such an amount of money on this project if one takes into account the genuine economic needs of so many areas of the world-wide Jewish community? Is it justified when ninety-nine percent of the students who come on such a trip can afford to pay their own way? Is it fair that certain Israeli institutions are being pressured to contribute toward this venture, thereby, for example, diverting money earmarked for Ethiopian immigrants? Many Israelis are incensed because a large portion of the matching funds is to come from their government — out of their taxes. And this comes at a time when millions of dollars are being cut from Israel's budget — cuts that affect the quality of education, social services and security concerns. It is difficult for an Israeli to justify bringing a kid from Beverly Hills to Israel for free when a child in one of Israel's development towns cannot afford to go on the school's class trip.

Then again, perhaps Israelis have no right to criticize these philanthropists as they do their own government's contribution to this effort, since one is talking about these men's private monies, and they are entitled to do what they want with their fortunes. Israelis should be grateful that they are pouring their considerable wealth into Jewish/Israeli causes. But criticism comes not only from Israeli quarters. Isi Leibler, the chairman of the World Jewish Congress wrote: "Birthright will not bear positive results beyond providing many young Jews with a publicly funded good time and, at best, a memory of a pleasant Israel encounter" (*Jerusalem Post*, January 14, 2000). However, what is surprising is that Birthright's co-sponsor, Michael Steinhart, asks: "Will it (the Israel experience) reach the majority of them (participants)? Probably not. Will it reach some of them and have an impact on their Jewishness? I think so" (*Washington Post*, January 17, 2000). Two hundred million dollars later, and only to "think so," strikes one as a pretty good bet that the whole project may be a massive waste of the Jewish people's money.

In principle, Israel should support the education of the American Jewish community — through educational emissaries, curriculum development and serious intensive long-term programs in Israel. Perhaps the better use of money would see the American Jewish community investing in itself. The two hundred million dollars could be used to subsidize children to go to Jewish Day Schools from the earliest ages. Since most non-Orthodox Day Schools only go to the eighth grade, an influx of money would enable Jewish Day School education to continue through the 12th grade, and thus influence the most formative years of a teenager's growth.

In Dallas, Texas, for example, many Jewish parents, dissatisfied with public school education, send their children, in the high school years, to private schools like: Hockaday, Greenhill, Saint Ursiline Academy, the Episcopal School of Dallas. The mere fact that a child attends one of these "prestigious" private institutions gives him a jump start into getting into a top university. Why should there not be elite private Jewish high schools?[1] The Dallas reality is true for many other US cities.

As part of the Jewish curriculum, long-term programs in Israel should be included and subsidized, whereby a Jewish child can experience the fullness of the Jewish calendar in a self-contained Jewish community. This will foster a knowledgeable and dedicated Jewish leadership for the Diaspora world, as well as seriously plant the notion of aliya. This is a far better way to develop a core group of committed Jews in the Diaspora whose ties with Israel would reflect a natural outgrowth of their learning experience.

But the argument holds that the masses of the unaffiliated need to be reached. While many of those who came on the first "Birthright" programs were marginal, they were not unaffiliated. By definition, it is virtually impossible to reach the unaffiliated. Numbers are indeed "sexy." Yet the survival of the Jewish people has never depended upon masses, but on an elite leadership. Returning to the Jewish biblical heritage, Esau represented the masses and Jacob, the elite. And it is Jacob (Israel), not Esau, to whom Jews refer for their ancestral legitimacy.

But one is led to believe that the two hundred million dollar investment will

---

1. Such a school is being established in North Carolina.

be well worthwhile if even a small percentage of the participants are Jewishly excited. When the Jewish Agency[1] was faulted for subsidizing the simulative "Exodus" journey[2] of North American Jewish teenagers (to the tune of $500,000), the professionals' response: "One person making aliya as a result will justify the expenditure." What nonsense! The same sort of Jewish minimalism that has devastated the Diaspora Jewish community should not be transferred to Israel and Israel programs. Life in Israel is just the opposite, and that is its attraction — a full-time Jewish life.

One wonders what happened to the educational advisors for these Jewish philanthropists. Are they so awed by Jewish wealth that they become sycophantic fodder for every idea that rich Jews put forth? What best can be done with the two hundred million dollars? At a Jewish Institute in Kiev, young Jewish students, who come to study for a year in order to serve small Jewish communities throughout the Ukraine, receive a subsidy of $100 a month. Should Birthright funds not be diverted to these committed Jews, who are also potential immigrants? Perhaps the money should be invested in immigrants and Israeli youth. There is little guess work here. Such an investment has yielded and will continue to yield positive results. Jewish philanthropists would be served well if they were advised to stop throwing money away on dead-end schemes that have a history of failure, and start investing in a population and a state that has a chance of succeeding.

As for follow-up, there should be no illusions. Those who come on Birthright type programs will not rush to join the organized American Jewish community. Upon graduating college, they are at an age when they find themselves in places and positions where they have little access to any Jewish framework — socially or religiously. The momentary excitement of their brief stay in Israel will probably turn them off even more than before to organized American Jewish life. After all, the sum total of these students' Jewish experience took place in Israel, and it is in the Israeli environment that they saw their Judaism expressed. Therefore, the only follow-up that might have any impact and chance of success is that which builds upon the Israel experience. Yet

1. The organization that receives Diaspora funding to carry out projects for the Jewish community worldwide.
2. This program is designed to simulate the period of illegal immigration during and immediately after World War II.

funding for a Birthright graduate to return to Israel for a longer, more intensive and meaningful encounter with Israel is not in the offing. Once again, American Jewry will opt for the path of least resistance: a ten-day shot of Jewish adrenaline in Israel and attendance at a lecture in America on Jewish wines!

On paper programs like Birthright look and sound great. The founders of Birthright view the American Jewish community as being on the brink of disintegration, and turn to Israel to bail them out. But they err in their dictation of the type of Israel program that should be instituted. One cannot provide a short-term solution for a long-term problem. A doctor does not prescribe an aspirin for a cancer patient. The scales are not even. And therein lies the ultimate manifestation of "schizophrenia" — trying to have it both ways. In order for American Jews to reclaim their Jewish self, they will have to follow the path of the Jewish tradition, which will require them, like Jacob, to earn their "birthright" through hard work, not by quick-fixes. One needs a long-term solution for a long-term problem.

CHAPTER 7

HOLIDAYS IN ISRAEL

An Annual Check-up

A teenage boy hurriedly ran into a pharmacy to use the public phone there. He promptly began to make his call. Since the young man spoke rather loudly, the druggist could not help but overhear the conversation:

> **Boy**: "Hello, is this 647-3583? It is? May I talk to the boss? Oh, you are the boss! Well, then you can tell me, do you need a good office helper? You have one? Well, wouldn't you like to make a change? You don't care to make a change? I see. That's alright, thank you."

The young man was about to walk out when the pharmacist stopped him:

> **Pharmacist**: "I apologize for eavesdropping. I am really sorry you did not get the job."
> **Boy**: "Thank you for your interest, but I have the job anyhow."
> **Pharmacist**: "What do you mean?"
> **Boy**: "That was my own boss I was talking to. I was only checking up on myself."

Every person wants to find out where he or she stands. Everyone needs a mental and moral check-up no less than a physical one. The Jewish High Holidays (Holy Days), *Rosh HaShana*[1] and *Yom Kippur*,[2] meet this need for a self-inventory. For those who attend religious services only once a year on these two Holidays, which occur virtually back-to-back, this would be called an annual check-up.

A great Italian actress, arranging a contract with her manager for

---

1. The beginning of the Jewish New Year, ushering in a ten day period of reflection and repentance, ending with Yom Kippur. Tradition holds that the world was created on Rosh Hashana.
2. The most solemn day in the Jewish calendar when a Jew recounts his past year, asking for forgiveness for sins committed against God and man. It is commemorated by a full day of fasting and intense prayer.

performances in the United States, insisted on the inclusion of the stipulation that every hotel room in which she stayed would be kept at exactly a temperature of 72° (Fahrenheit). This was in the days before air-conditioning and automatic thermostats. Realizing that this demand could not be met, the manager was in a real quandary as to what to do, until someone suggested that he extract the mercury from the thermometer and fill the tube with red ink up to the marker that read 72°. The actress was tremendously impressed by the comforts of American hotels, but did remark on one occasion how strange it was that 72° in Chicago seemed so much colder than 72° degrees in Miami!

At Rosh HaShana and Yom Kippur, one would expect an individual's official religious temperature to be set very high, but in fact, there is a wide devotional temperature range among individuals. Such is the case with the many Holidays that fill the Jewish calendar in Israel. Unlike in the Diaspora, where Jewish Holidays are celebrated at home and/or in the synagogue, in Israel, in addition to the home and synagogue, they are celebrated on a state-wide basis. Businesses and schools are closed, places of entertainment and restaurants do not operate and Israeli television and radio are inundated with Holiday programs. While this is a natural occurrence in the Jewish state, the seriousness of the Holidays seems to vary in "degrees" of importance based on events that took place over the years at Holiday time.

Yom Kippur will forever be linked in the Israeli psyche to the Yom Kippur War. Purim will be inexorably defined by Baruch Goldstein's slaughter of twenty-nine Moslem worshippers in the Cave of Machpela, the end of the Persian Gulf War and *Operation Shlomo*.[1] Rosh HaShana reminds one of *Sabra* and *Shatilla*.[2] *Shavuot*[3] returns one to the Lebanon War. *Sukkot*[4] conjures up the

---

1. Reference to the lightning operation that brought 14,000 Ethiopian Jews to Israel out of war-torn Addis Ababa on Purim, 1991.
2. On September 6, 1982, Lebanese Christian Phalangists entered the Palestinian refugee camps of Sabra and Shatilla in the outskirts of Beirut, and killed over 200 unarmed Palestinians. Israel was accused of turning its back while the massacre took place. The massacre prompted a state inquiry (Kahan Commission). As a result of the committee's findings, Defense Minister Ariel Sharon was forced to resign. The largest public protest demonstration in Israel, which was held in Tel Aviv's Municipal Square, was prompted by the massacre.
3. Feast of Weeks. Also one of the three pilgrimage Holidays. Shavuot falls exactly seven weeks after Passover, thus giving it its name, which means seven. It celebrates the receiving of the Torah and the giving of the first fruits.
4. Festival celebrating the completion of the fall harvest. Also known as the Feast of Tabernacles or Feast of Booths, the Holiday reminds Jews of their wandering through the desert. It is another of the three pilgrimage festivals.

image of Moslem worshippers being shot at the Temple Mount while a hail of stones filled the Western Wall Plaza.

While many Israeli Jews view themselves as secular, as they reflect upon these dramatic events, which are so identified with certain Holidays, their attachment to them varies greatly. While they may choose to distance themselves from celebrating the Holidays, they nevertheless are forced to confront them. And so their reactions to them run a myriad of emotional responses, from "hot to cold." Many Israeli Jews only acquire a surface knowledge of the Holidays. While many of the Festivals recount occurrences in ancient Jewish history, they also touch upon more recent events, and should say something about what takes place in Israeli society. It may be coincidental that over the last decade so many dramatic events have taken place on specific Holidays. But it is not coincidental that each Holiday carries with it a universal and timeless message. The overriding theme of each Holiday is one of tolerance and freedom, and as such, can readily help Israeli Jews relate to the events surrounding them.

It is rather surprising that many Israeli Jews have only a perfunctory understanding of Jewish Holidays, considering that the study of the Holidays is part of the general school curriculum and an integral part of the national landscape. But more troubling is that those who are elected to interpret the Holidays, those who sit on the thrones of rabbinic leadership, seem to view them in an extremely parochial and exclusive fashion.

And so, an "annual check-up" is needed. In one of his "Letters of Consolation," Maimonides wrote: "There are two kinds of Jews, those who hold on to their religion. grasping it firmly like a person will hold on to a rope to keep from drowning, and then, there are those Jews who cling to the Torah only with their fingers — not enough to be guided and helped by it, just barely enough to keep in touch with their faith."

Herein lies Israel's schizophrenic application of the Jewish Holidays. While Orthodox rabbis, who represent the state at all public Holiday events, be they religious or national, "hold on to their religion... firmly like a person will hold on to a rope to keep from drowning," they actually "cling to the Torah only with their fingers." Orthodoxy in Israel has presented Israeli Jews with "fingertip Judaism." The understanding of the Holidays is reduced to a recollection of past historical events with little relevance to present realities. They are forever contradicting themselves, steeped in all the minutiae of observance related to any given Holiday, but unable to make it applicable so that the moral message of each Holiday can serve as a guide for Israel's behavior.

In understanding the importance of the Jewish Holidays for Israeli society, an annual check-up would reveal that on the outside — and to the outside world — the celebration of Jewish Holidays in Israel looks good. The entire country comes to a halt on Yom Kippur. The approach of Passover engages every household in a spring-cleaning. Purim finds the streets crowded with school children dressed in Purim costumes. Israel Memorial Day for Fallen Soldiers witnesses everyone standing in silent reflection as a siren sounds throughout the nation. There is indeed something comforting, unifying and even exciting in communal celebration or commemoration of the Holidays. But one must ask oneself: Does Yom Kippur really usher in a personal soul-searching?[1] Does Passover yield a national soul-cleansing? What can Purim mean when, after Baruch Goldstein killed those twenty-nine Moslem worshipers on Purim, Knesset member Hanan Porat can parade the streets of Kiryat Arba, the neighborhood adjacent to where the massacre took place, smiling and refusing to let such an "incident" spoil his Holiday spirit?

While on the outside the Holidays look good, oftentimes on the inside there is festering illness. A narrow and chauvinistic presentation of the Jewish Holidays renders them unhealthy in spirit, if not in body. It is only their outer trappings that look good. Too often their inner workings have been stripped of their moral importance.

In 1977, when Sinai was still in Israel's hands, I was enrolled in an army artillery course at a make-shift base near Parker Junction, located not far from the Suez Canal. At night we were all required to take our turn at guard duty, each for a two-hour shift. When we finished our

---

1. In the book of *Isaiah*, the meaning of the Fast of Yom Kippur is spelled out in clear terms that go far beyond the mere ritual of refraining from eating. "Is this the fast I look for? A day of self-infliction? Bowing your head like a reed, and covering yourself with sackcloth and ashes? Is this what you call a fast, a day acceptable to the Lord? Is not this the fast I look for: To unlock the shackles of injustice, to undo the fetters of bondage, to let the oppressed go free, and to break every cruel chain? Is it not to share your bread with the hungry, and to bring the homeless poor into your house? When you see the naked, to clothe them, and never to hide yourself from your own kin? If you remove the chains of oppression, the menacing hand, the malicious word; if you make sacrifices for the hungry, and satisfy the needs of the afflicted; then shall your light shine in the darkness, and your night become bright as noon; the Lord will guide you always..." (58:5-7; 9-11).

duty, we were to wake up the next person. One soldier went to wake up someone who was to assume guard duty after him. Roused from a deep sleep, the soldier refused to get up. The other soldier woke the commander who in turn tried to shake the boy awake. At that point, the young soldier got up from his bed, took his rifle and threatened to shoot both of them if they did not leave him alone. The next morning, the soldier was dragged from his bed and rightfully placed under arrest.

While awaiting a military field trial, he was suddenly brought out to the center of the encampment. With the entire unit standing around, his head was shaved and he was ordered to stand at attention for hours in the hot sun. **It was Holocaust Memorial Day**. I could not help but remember that moving passage from Elie Wiesel's *Night*, about the young boy who was suspected of sabotage by a Nazi commandant. Shaven, he was led to the gallows to be hung in public, others being forced to watch.

Outside the Old City of Jerusalem, just west of the Jaffa Gate, developers are trying to get around the historical building preservation codes by buying up old buildings and gutting them, except for their facade. They then build high rises right behind the old buildings. In reference to Jewish Holidays in Israel, Israelis are becoming not just "fingertip Jews," but also "facade Jews." The universal historic grandeur of the Holidays has been knocked out. Nothing is left inside. Such aberrations that find a boy (Jewish or non-Jewish), no matter how heinous his crime, shaved as a form of public punishment and humiliation must never occur in a country whose people are truly sensitized to the horrors of the Holocaust. A different and more moral (and balanced) understanding of the Holidays must become part of Israel.

When the Festivals see a veneer Judaism conflicting with substantive Judaism, then a split interpretation of the Holidays prevails. Israel has to go from an understanding of Jewish Holidays that are morally pretended to ones that are ethically practiced. Israelis need to close the psychological gap between what the Holidays are and what they should be.

Rosh HaShana:
The Holiday of Sacrifice — Israelis Missing in Action

On Rosh HaShana, a Jew reads the Torah portion that recounts the birth of Abraham and Sarah's son, Isaac and his "sacrifice" by his father (*Genesis*, chapters 21-22). While the sacrifice was eventually averted, Abraham's willingness to slaughter his own son at God's behest serves as the definitive paradigmatic commitment of an individual to his absolute faith in the Almighty. Whether someone's theology abides such a view is almost irrelevant. To begin the Jewish New Year in such a dramatic fashion is almost too difficult to bear. There is nothing more painful than the loss of a child. When a parent dies, one loses the past. When a child dies, one loses the future.

Sacrificing one's child on the altar of war and violence is a sad part of the Middle East reality. Israelis are prepared to do this because they believe in the efficacy of individual and personal sacrifice as necessities for the survival of the Jewish people. In reference to Rosh HaShana, infrequently does one hear this theme resonate within Israeli society. Rosh HaShana either represents a day of prayer in the synagogue for religious Jews or a day at the beach for secular Jews. Rarely does either segment of the population draw any real applicable message from the Holiday.

It is incredibly easy to relate the message of this Holiday to the realities of everyday life in Israel. A visit to Israel's central military cemetery, Mount Herzl, reveals on the graves the ages of the soldiers buried there, the youngest being ten-years old. Rare is the family in Israel that has been spared the sacrifice of one of its young members to some hostile act prompted by war or terrorism. Therefore, there is no greater act of diplomatic wisdom and mercy that a political leader can display than to alleviate the emotional and psychological devastation of these families. The best way to prevent such pain and loss in the future is to hasten peace. Yet the esoteric enticements of peace leave the actual harmony among nations far off. One would think that those religious Jews who hold unique insights into this Holiday's meaning would stand at the forefront of the peace movement. After all, Abraham is also known as "the seeker of peace."

For a Jew, peace is the ultimate religious quest. To support this view, one can turn to the famous priestly benediction, also known as the "blessing of peace," which is part of the daily liturgy. "The Lord spoke to Moses: Speak to Aaron and his sons; thus shall you bless the people of Israel. Say to them: The Lord will bless you and keep you. The Lord will light up a Divine Face to shine upon you and be gracious to you. The Lord will bestow Heavenly Countenance on you and grant you peace" (*Numbers* 6:22-26). The three daily services reach a theological climax with a prayer for peace: "Blessed are You God who blesses the people Israel with peace" (*Daily Prayer book*). Finally, the sacred prayer for the dead, the *Kaddish*, the prayer that has been repeated by so many Israelis at the graves of their fathers, brothers and sons (and daughters), ends with a plea for peace: "May God Who makes peace in the heavens, make peace for us and all of Israel." Therefore, given the emphasis placed upon peace as a Holy aspiration and mandate, one would expect religious Jews to be "dovish" by nature. But the very opposite is the case. Most religious Jews in Israel have developed a real polarity between what Rosh HaShana and the general liturgy should teach and what they choose to learn.

While one could readily expand the theme of Rosh HaShana, for Israel it is the matter of "child sacrifice" which is most compelling. It is difficult to narrow this theme, but there is one area where it seems most pertinent — Israeli soldiers missing in action (MIA). Since June 12, 1982, a few days after the outbreak of the Lebanon War, three particular Israeli families have been living with the loss of their children. The Katz, Feldman and Baumel families have given their sons for what they perceived to be the greater good of the state of Israel, without knowing what has happened to these children they sacrificed. Their pain is inconsolable. So far, there has been no "happy ending" such as was the case with the biblical Isaac.

There is an additional missing soldier, Ron Arad, who fell into captivity in 1986. Two other missing soldiers, Yosef Fink and Rachamim Alsheich, whose bodies had been discovered, were returned for proper burial in Israel. The long held hope that both Fink and Alsheich were alive came to an abrupt end, but the pain of the unknown was resolved — an unknown that is perhaps more debilitating than the fact of their deaths. "To perish by the sword is worse than a natural death, to die of hunger worse still and captivity worst of all" (*Babylonian Talmud, Baba Batra* 8b). If captivity is "worst of all," then immediate attention must be focused on the MIAs. This must be one of Israel's highest priorities as it continues along its delicate path toward peace.

Why does not the Chief Rabbinate use Rosh Hashana to call upon Israelis and their government to act more steadfastly in the search for the missing soldiers? Why not hold a "Rosh HaShana rally" with the MIAs as the theme of the demonstration? Why not make the Holiday relevant?

Israel's religious (Orthodox) guardians seem to be stuck, seemingly incapable of relating the Jewish Holidays to the realities of modern day Israeli life. Like all people, Israelis are in desperate need of spiritual guidance. Since Rosh HaShana is the Holiday of renewal, leading to Yom Kippur, which is a day of personal reflection (as opposed to *Tisha B'Av*, which is a day of national reflection[1]), Israelis need to recreate a new approach to the Holidays. Rosh HaShana, the Holiday that begins the Jewish New Year must serve as both a spiritual and an educational guide to prompt social and political self-awareness. Indeed, all the Jewish Holidays have within them the potential for providing excellent psychological and medicinal care, and ultimately the possibility for the improvement of Israeli society.

Chanukah — The Maccabean Revolt

Virtually every Jew knows the story of the miracle of the cruse of oil burning for eight days. After the Maccabees prevailed against the Greco-Syrian pagans, they found in the Holy Temple only one undefiled flask of oil with the seal of the high priest. The vial contained just enough oil for only one day's lighting of the Temple's *Menorah*.[2] But miraculously, its oil lasted for eight days. The following year, the Maccabees designated these eight days for giving thanks and praise to God (*Babylonian Talmud, Shabbat* 21b).

The Chanukah lights have come to symbolize the Jewish belief in the gradual progress of spiritual enlightenment. Starting with one light the first evening and

---

1. The 9th day of the Hebrew month Av, the traditional day of the destruction of the First and Second Temples, commemorated by a national day of mourning and fasting.
2. Seven-branched candelabrum described in the Bible and used in Temple days. Today it is the official emblem of the State of Israel. Most synagogues utilize a Menorah as part of the decor in the sanctuary. The special Menorah used for Chanukah has eight candlesticks and a ninth for the *shammash* (server). To distinguish the two types, the latter is nowadys called a *Chanukiyah*.

increasing the number of lights by one each night, the Jewish people mark the slow but steady victory over the violent storms, which have raged against them throughout the centuries.

While Chanukah is considered a minor Holiday in the Jewish calendar, its significance has soared because of its historical relevance. (It has also gained major importance in the Diaspora in order to compete with the enticements of Christmas.) The lesson to be culled from the Hasmonean[1] revolt is that Jews must always strive to overcome any attempts to delegitimize Judaism. The Hellenism that the Maccabees fought against had a devastating effect upon the moral life of Judea.[2] All religious precepts were prohibited upon punishment by death. Copies of the Torah were destroyed, the Temple itself was converted to the worship of Zeus, harlots were brought within the sacred precincts and heathen altars set up in villages and towns. With such a list of outrageous violations against the precious ethical center of Judaism's faith-heritage, it is little wonder that the Maccabees went on a rampage to restore Judaism's dignity and integrity.

The Maccabees should serve as a shining example of a people dedicated to fighting the evils that threaten the very fabric of Jewish belief and practice. But just as Israelis see Chanukah as dedicated to warding off those enemies who would hasten to destroy them physically, so too must they dedicate themselves to thwarting the "enemies within" who would hasten to undermine their moral and spiritual essence. The tradition hints that the Temple and the Second Jewish Commonwealth were destroyed by "baseless hatred." It is here where the relevance of Chanukah is most significant. It is often difficult to recognize a moral and religious strength at the center of Jewish life in Israel. There seems to be a Hellenization of Israel's "Temple," the Divine acceptance of a false god — Nationalism. The fusion of extreme nationalism and Divine exclusivity provides a script for the perversion of the Jewish tradition. Worse, it presents a recipe for explosion. Israel is engaged in delicate negotiations with its neighbors that include the return of occupied lands. The combination of chauvinism and Divinity elevates land to such theological heights that anyone who would

---

1. Family name of the priestly family, popularly known as the Maccabees, who organized the revolts against the Syrian-Greeks, leading to the cleansing and rededication of the Temple.
2. Reference to the name used for the south-central region of ancient Palestine, in which are found the Judean Hills and the Judean Desert.

contradict the supposed "holiness" of physical claims to the entire land of Israel must be understandably subject to abuse at the least, annihilation at worst. After all, who would dare go against the Divine Will?

Herein lies the inherent contradiction in understanding the Holiday. The miracle of the Maccabean revolt is conveyed in the prophetic lesson recited on the Sabbath that falls during the eight days of Chanukah: "Not by might, not by power, but by my Spirit, says the Lord of Hosts" (*Zecharia* 4:6). While Israelis may understand Chanukah as the recounting of the courage of the Maccabees, which serves as a source of inspiration and strength for the Jewish people's longevity and persistence, they must be wary of turning a lofty spiritual and essentially allegorical account into a physical charge of total purification. Applied to today's realities, the combination of these two interpretations of the Holiday can produce dangerous psychotic episodes. How else can one explain Yitzhak Rabin being gunned down by the "hand of God" because he dared to entertain the possibility of returning the "land of God." And so with all the bravery that marks much of Chanukah, and which can lead to extreme applications of the Holiday, one should perhaps view the "Festival of Lights"[1] in a more balanced and sane manner.

The stage was set. Officials representing the Greek authorities arrived at Modi'in,[2] stood in the city square, and invited the local residents to join in the pagan sacrifice to the Greek gods. Mattathius, as the eldest and most respected among the local populace, was accorded the "right of first opportunity" to perform the sacrifice in order to serve as an example to the others. Mustering all his strength and courage, Mattathius refused to violate the "laws of our fathers." No sooner did his words echo throughout the village when a Jew from the crowd stepped forward, offering to carry out the sacrifice. Perceiving him as a "collaborator,"[3] Mattathius rushed forward and seized the man's sword, slaying

---

1. Another name for Chanukah.
2. Town in ancient Israel where Mattathius and his sons, the Hasmoneans, lived.
3. Today, the word "collaborator" refers to those Palestinians who, during the occupation of the territories by the Israelis and during the days of the Intifada, cooperated with the Israeli authorities against their own people.

him. Then, turning his anger upon the Greek representative, he killed him and smashed the pagan idols.

Fearing violent reprisals, Mattathius and family fled to the hills in order to carry out their struggle for national liberation that would see its realization in the purification of the Temple in Jerusalem. After his death, with the ascendancy of his son Judah to leadership, the Maccabees raced from victory to victory in their rush toward Jerusalem. It can be assumed that, along the way, anyone who was perceived as a "Jewish collaborator" fell prey to their mighty war machine.

When reminded of such acts in the Jewish past, Israelis tend to rationalize and justify them, even to the point of exonerating the most obvious errant behavior displayed by Jewish "heroes." One need not go very far to show where even in the Bible God condemns and admonishes those of His people who committed criminal acts. As noted earlier, no less a heroic figure than King David is punished, having to leave the building of the Temple in Jerusalem to his son, Solomon, because of his zealous pursuits of the Jebusites in his conquest of the city.

What should the legendary stories of Jewish heroes mean for the modern state of Israel? More importantly, what should they tell Israelis about what is happening today? As uncomfortable as it might be at times, Israelis must draw upon their Jewish past, as so often expressed in their Holidays, in order to gain insight into the Jewish future. At times throughout Jewish history, Jews have faltered, sometimes committing intolerable acts in the name of Jewish national interests. That still pertains, as warped understandings of national interests led to the killing of an Israeli prime minister. Yet despite these aberrations, one can still acknowledge the basic legitimacy of the Jews to exist as people in an independent and sovereign nation. Rightfully, Israelis should never permit the Jewish state to be condemned because of Mattathius' abuse of "Jewish collaborators" or because of King David's excesses. More so, the wayward behavior of great Jewish leaders should not diminish the significant role they played in shaping Jewish history.

It is vitally important to avoid simplistic readings of Jewish Holidays. It is irresponsible to justify one's ideological views based on a self-serving interpretation of Jewish texts. At the same time, however, often the basic plot-line of a story is so straightforward that it cries out for immediate (and universal) application to present day realities. That is the beauty of the Jewish Holidays. They have in them relevant lessons that span generations.

Even as Israelis justly ask the world not to judge them by the crimes of certain personalities in their past, or even in their present (Baruch Goldstein), so too must Israelis, for example, not judge the entire Palestinian people on the basis of the vicious acts of those who would kill "collaborators," or even the more bestial acts of Hamas fanatics. These killings are a tragic reality that reflect a sad phenomenon of virtually every rebellion that sees itself as a liberation movement.

It would be a sad commentary if the Palestinians took a chapter out of the story of the Maccabean revolt as a paradigmatic primer for gaining Jerusalem as the capital of the Palestinian Authority. A genuine reappraisal of the past regarding the manner in which the Maccabees retook Jerusalem lends historical legitimacy to Israel's forceful condemnation of and actions against the heinous acts of Hamas in its attempt to claim exclusivity over Jerusalem, Israel's eternal Jewish capital.

The first step on the road to sane behavior requires an honest examination of past behavior. Israelis need to look objectively at their own history as the best way to confront that which surrounds them. After all, the word Chanukah has within it the meaning "to educate." Israelis must reeducate themselves to comprehend the fullness of the Maccabean revolt — its heroic and aberrant elements. An open and critical examination of Israel's past will provide it with better insight into the Palestinian struggle for its own national identity. Objectivity, cool analysis and a somewhat detached view of the world break down stereotypical understandings of the world, eliminate one-sided and extreme actions and eventually lead to balanced and sane behaviors.

Who's Afraid of Christmas?

I bought my eight-year old daughter the video of Tchaikovsky's *The Nutcracker Suite Ballet.* I felt this would be both an educational and enjoyable way to spend an hour in front of the television set.

Unfortunately she watched the video with some of her friends — unsupervised. Having been born and raised in Israel, she and her friends did not understand the Christian religious significance of Christmas that is central to the *Nutcracker* story. They were thoroughly enchanted and entranced by the story. When her class was asked to decorate the foyer of their religious school with winter scenes, recalling the *Nutcracker* video, she and a few of her buddies drew Christmas trees, Santa Claus and reindeers. The teacher, not paying attention to what the kids drew, included these pictures as part of the hallway mural. Needless to say that I, Rabbi David Forman, was mortified when I saw my daughter's signed masterpiece in the school corridor.

I blame myself. I have never taken the time to explain to my children what the Christmas and New Year Christian Holiday season is all about. Since Israel provides for Jews such a welcome relief from the onslaught of Christmas and New Years that a Jew suffers in the Diaspora, I always preferred to lock myself up in ignorant bliss. The only point of reference my children had to Jesus Christ was when they heard their father yell his name when he stubbed his toe!

Living in a Jewish state, there is a tendency to become overly insular when it comes to understanding other religious expressions. By avoiding the issue of the Christian Holiday season, Israelis are doing a disservice. As Israelis move along toward their shaky path to peace, it would be in their own interest to try to understand their co-religionists, especially when dealing with the sensitive religious issue of Jerusalem. Also, with cable TV being a constant in most Israeli homes, it is no longer possible to cut oneself off from Christmas and New Years. Christmas movies such as *A Christmas Carol* and *A Wonderful Life* crowd Israel's television screens, and Bing Crosby's *White Christmas* and Nat King Cole's *The Christmas Song* fill the airwaves.

Those Israelis who live in Jerusalem have a rare opportunity to engage in serious interfaith exchanges. Jerusalem is the focal point of Christianity's earliest historical development. In the Old City's Holy Sepulchre Church, Jesus is allegedly buried. The Stations of the Cross are clearly marked on the Via Dolorosa. Hundreds of churches, monasteries and convents dot Jerusalem's landscape. While Jerusalem is free of Christmas trees and Christmas lights, it is not free of Christians. What is true of Jerusalem is also true of the Galilee where most of Christ's ministry took place. Bethlehem and Nazareth are also easily accessible to Israelis.

It would seem reasonable that the first line of information about Christianity should come out of the schools. And what is true regarding the acquisition of a basic knowledge about Christianity is applicable to learning about Islam. One should not fall back on the issue of separation of religion and state as an excuse not to address matters relating to other religions. After all, even in the most secular of Israeli public schools, the teaching and often celebrating of Jewish Holidays are an integral part of the educational system. Unlike other western countries, which value the separation between "church and state," Israel cannot avoid the integration of religion and state because of the intimate relationship that exists between religion and this country, in both a historical and a political context.

Given some of the built-in prejudices of the vast majority of Israel's ultra-Orthodox practitioners, there would be rigorous opposition to the slightest notion that Israeli Jewish school children become educated toward some understanding of Christianity. But burying one's head in the sand will no longer suffice. The world is getting smaller, and Israelis owe it to the next generation of Jews to be far more open than they are. Jews who maintain a majority in their own sovereign state should not be afraid to expose themselves and their children to learning about other religions and cultures. Israelis have rejected a Diaspora existence and so should feel fortified enough not to be threatened by concerns of assimilation or frightened that mixed marriages will invade their borders.

Christians know quite a bit about Jewish Holidays (Christian and Moslem Israeli Arab schoolchildren learn about Jewish national and religious Holidays), and so it would seem only reasonable that Christians, as well as Moslems, who are Israeli citizens, should receive a fair hearing among their fellow Israeli Jewish citizens. And here Israelis should not rely on their own resources to teach about the importance of the winter Holiday season to the Christian community. Israel is a veritable educational laboratory for interfaith understanding. Christian clergy should be invited to speak at pubic schools. Israeli school children should visit Christian Holy Sites (as well as Moslem ones). This should all be part of a school's curriculum, as should a perusal of the New Testament and the Koran. This should be done over the objection of the vast majority of the Orthodox community.

Once again, one sees ambiguities abound. The almost total exclusion of Christianity, and to a lesser extent, Islam, from the Israeli public mind clearly points to a real inconsistency. While the fear of excessive fraternization with non-Jews is a definitive consideration for the Orthodox community, it should not be the same for the rest of Israeli society. After all, fears of intermarriage in Israel should not be exaggerated. Jews form the vast majority of the country's population; and more so, Jewish culture is so embedded in Israeli society that it is difficult to imagine assimilation ever becoming the agenda item it has become in the Diaspora world. Israelis can rightfully feel secure in their Jewishness so as not to worry about being proselytized.

As a minority people who were continually cast in the part of being society's religious pariahs, they must not become guilty of similar prejudicial behavior. Such contradictory behavior creates a real imbalance, relegating the other to a secondary and often inferior role in society.

Keeping Purim in Perspective[1]

On Purim, 1994, Dr. Baruch Goldstein entered a mosque in Hebron and gunned down twenty-nine Moslem worshippers. He was killed by the frightened crowd of Arabs present in the mosque. A memorial grave site was established, only to be legally torn down by the Israeli authorities. But every year, mourners, who see in Goldstein's crime the Divine hand of God, seek to memorialize his name in various demonstrative ways. There is an attempt by a few within the Orthodox community to confer a quasi "sainthood" on Goldstein. Because the notion of attributing any sort of praise to a person who would commit such a repellent act is abhorrent, it would be instructive to understand Goldstein's actions in light of the Holiday during which they occurred. There is absolutely no way that one could use the story of Purim, or any interpretation of it, as justification for Goldstein's actions. What he did and what the story demands stand in direct conflict.

---

1. Partially excerpted from the author's book, *Israel on Broadway; America: Off-Broadway — Jews in the New Millennium*, pages 218-221, Gefen Publishing House, 1998.

There is a genuine difficulty with the story of Purim. While there is legitimacy in the satisfaction that Jews were saved from Haman's[1] wicked rule, the manner in which that satisfaction is expressed indicates true schizophrenic leanings. The celebrations on the Holiday manifest themselves in two simultaneous and yet contradictory behaviors — of exuberant joy and sinister hatred. The joy is born out of the ultimate defeat of the enemy of the Jewish people. But too easily that joy becomes an expression of a vengeance that is embarrassing at best, mean-spirited at worst. The idea that at Purim Jews rejoice with such fervor at the expense of someone else's misery may be natural enough, but it exposes a human frailty for which the Jews were dramatically chastised at the moment of the greatest single event in Jewish history — the exodus from Egypt. After a narrow escape from Egyptian bondage, the Israelites, once safely ensconced on the other side of the Red Sea, danced with joy as they watched their Egyptian enemies drown. A famous Talmudic comment points out that God was so upset with the Israelites' behavior that they were sternly admonished (see *Introduction*, page 16, footnote 2).

One of the signs of insecurity or indications of having an inferiority complex is the attempt to build oneself up on the back of someone else. Such an attitude ultimately fails to increase one's own self-worth, instead reinforcing delusions of self-improvement. Jews who have been so downtrodden over the centuries surely should recognize the inherent ill-will in such erratic forms of behavior.

No one is suggesting that the fun be taken out of Purim. It is exciting to see Israeli streets filled with children in Purim costumes. But one must wonder what message Israeli children absorb when they are encouraged to fly into fits of ecstasy at the public hangings of Haman and his family. Although the Jews are reminded to blot out the name of Amalek,[2] is this the manner in which to do it? How easy is it for Israelis to extrapolate an errant lesson for their Purim behavior and sound the trumpet of exhilaration at the death of any enemy of the

---

1. Vizier of the Persian emperor Ahasuerus. According to the *Book of Esther,* he planned to kill all the Jews in the Persian Empire, but his plan was foiled by Esther and her uncle Mordecai. Haman and his sons were hanged in punishment. The story is the basis of the festival of Purim. Haman became regarded as the arch-enemy of the Jewish people.
2. Leader of a nomadic people living in the Sinai Peninsula in early biblical times. When the children of Israel were crossing the wilderness, they were attacked by the Amalekites at Rephidim, but after a hard fought battle, the latter were driven back. The Amalekites, and their leader, Amalek, were regarded as an inveterate foe of the Jewish people who should be obliterated (*Exodus* 17:16, *Deuteronomy* 25:19).

Jewish people, be it the late Syrian president Haffez Assad or Palestinian Authority chairman Yasir Arafat, or a perceived enemy — Yitzhak Rabin? In a pre-Purim sermon, former Sephardi Chief Rabbi Ovadia Yosef used the Purim story to vent his anger toward an Israel Education Minister Yossi Sarid. Yosef proclaimed that even as one curses Haman, so should one curse Yossi Sarid; even as one is commanded to wipe out the remnant of Amalek, so should the same be done to Sarid. The next day, Yosef claimed that he did not mean for any physical harm to come to Sarid. This is "schizophrenia" at its best: call for Sarid to be hung like Haman, but don't cause him physical harm!

The relevance of Purim is most significant for Israelis. In 1991, when Purim began just as Israelis stepped out of their sealed rooms, it seemed to make good sense to rejoice in the defeat of a modern Haman, Iraq's Saddam Hussein. But today, as Israel attempts to negotiate peace agreements with men whom many consider to be Haman's reincarnation, like Yasir Arafat, the drunken happiness that Jews experience at the killing of Haman and his entourage seems terribly out of place. It contradicts the Jewish truism: "Who is a hero? He who turns his enemy into a friend" (*Avot d'Rabbi Natan* 23). The behavior on Purim contradicts the behavior at other historical events that also commemorate the victory of the weak over the strong. Remembering the defeat of the Greeks at Chanukah or the mortal blow encountered by the Egyptians at Passover is not accompanied by a parallel sense of excitement at their respective suffering. During the Passover *Seder*,[1] ten drops of wine are taken from the wine cup in order to express a sense of remorse that the ten plagues had to be inflicted upon the Egyptians in order to secure the Jewish people's ultimate freedom.[2]

It could very well be that one of the reasons that Jews are commanded to get so drunk on Purim that they cannot distinguish between Mordecai and Haman is because as sober individuals, they would be truly ashamed that they took such delight in capital punishment. Indeed the Talmud forewarns: "A drunkard praying is like an **idolater**" (*Babylonian Talmud, Brachot* 31b). How ironic.

---

1. Literal translation means "order." It is the ritual meal that begins the Passover Holiday and at which the *Haggada*, the book that recounts the story of the Exodus, is read.
2. The story of the ten plagues raises all sorts of contradictions. God sends the plagues upon Egypt to let the Israelites go, only to harden Pharaoh's heart each time. It would seem that God is working at cross-purposes.

According to the Jewish tradition: "Of any sin spoken of in the Torah, if a man is told to commit it, and does, he will not die; save **idolatry**, incest and bloodshed" (*Babylonian Talmud, Sanhedrin* 74a). In short, to get drunk, pray, and rejoice at the shedding of blood (even of one's enemy), is **idolatrous** and therefore worthy of death. So while in a drunken stupor, rejoicing at the death of one's enemy, one is really hastening one's own end.

Perhaps it is for the above reason that the name of God is excluded from the Purim story. Perhaps God felt uncomfortable with the brutal public hangings that took place. In fact, that the hangings took place in front of such an enthusiastic crowd in all likelihood forced God to withdraw Divine sanction for such a public act of revenge. God seemed not to want any part of such a cynical charade. God prefers Holidays where the positive is emphasized, not Holidays that are clouded with double messages and neurotic aberrations.

Passover — The Longest Liberation Movement

At Passover, Jews read the dramatic story of the Exodus from Egypt — the single most significant event in Jewish history. Out of that experience was forged Jewish national identity. It was against the background of the Jewish collective suffering as slaves in Egypt that the Jews were born as a people. The escape from Egypt was the authoritative rejection of the social model of power and its abuse, as symbolized by Pharaonic despotism. The maturation process that took place in the desert would eventually lead to the "promised land" and give birth to a nation. The story of the Exodus is essential for any understanding of the realities of modern day Israel.

At the time of the escape from Egypt and through the wanderings in the Sinai desert, the Israelites would introduce a new social order. The bitter experience in Egyptian bondage would necessarily force the ancient Israelites to declare for all time that social injustice is evil. At the Sinaitic moment of absolute moral truth, the Israelites received a code of ethical commandments that established a Divine standard for social behavior, revolutionary at the time. It held: "You shall not render an unfair decision; do not favor the poor or show deference to the rich; judge your neighbor fairly" (*Leviticus* 19:15). Why? "...I am the Lord your God who freed you from the land of Egypt" (*Leviticus* 19:36).

Moses, as undisputed leader of the Jewish social revolution, had proven himself worthy of institutionalizing a national identity based on social justice and equality, because of his meritorious behavior before and during his flight from Egypt.

The narrative at the outset of the book of *Exodus* is concise. Moses is supervising the work of the Israelites when he sees an Egyptian overlord beating one of them. Moses becomes enraged. The text gives no indication as to where this righteous indignation comes from. But his rage is so powerful that Moses kills the Egyptian. Not a day passes, and Moses sees two Israelites engaged in a bitter quarrel. Equally outraged as the day before, he intervenes, only to discover that his act of the day before is known to all. Fearing for his life, he flees to the land of Midian. There he encounters some shepherds harassing daughters of the Midianite priest Jethro. Moses' sense of moral justice is once again aroused, and he drives the shepherds off.

It is only after these events that Moses is called to the "burning bush" (*Exodus* 3:2) where he is called upon to accept the mantle of leadership, for he had intuitively demonstrated the most important characteristic of a leader — the commitment to social justice. But the story indicates that Moses was a reluctant leader. Whatever faith God may have had in him was not reflected in his own confidence to lead the Israelites. Returning to Egypt to plead on behalf of his people was no easy task, particularly because he was a "hit and run" suspect. He also knew that Pharaoh was not restrained by Amnesty International or the Human Rights Division of America's State Department.

The most compelling reason that Moses was hesitant, apart from his inarticulate manner of speech, caused by his stuttering, was that he had grave doubts about his own moral integrity. As one examines the story further, a glaring challenge arises. The text leaves out one crucial area of concern, and it is the one area that is most relevant for modern day Israel. Moses acted appropriately when a non-Jew abused a Jew (the Egyptian beating an Israelite); when a Jew abused another Jew (the violent quarrel that broke out between two Israelites); and when a non-Jew abused a non-Jew (when the Midianite women were intimidated by passing shepherds). The text does not include any reading of a Jew abusing a non-Jew. Did Moses encounter such a possibility and not act? It is impossible to know. But that possibility may help to explain his reluctance to assume the leadership of the revolution.

The maltreatment of a non-Jew is definitively proscribed in the biblical commandment that stems directly from the experience in Egypt: "When a stranger resides with you in your land, you shall not wrong him. The stranger who resides with you shall be to you as one of your citizens; you shall love him as yourself, for you were strangers in the land of Egypt. I am the Lord your God" (*Leviticus* 19:33-34). The Divine appendage exalts the text in such a manner that for Jews the sanctity of human life and respect for human dignity of all are the highest values within the Jewish moral heritage. This theme is so central to Passover that Jews are commanded to recite: "In every generation, one is obligated to see himself as if he (himself) personally went out of Egypt" (*Passover Haggadah*).

This moral sensitivity toward others shaped the thoughts of the founders of the modern state of Israel. In his *Jewish State*, Theodor Herzl viewed Zionism not only as the ideological trigger to bring Jews to their ancient homeland, but also as an ideal "whose ultimate aspiration must realize spiritual and moral wholenesss." He gave added force to this hope when he wrote in *Altneuland* (*Old-New Land*), a book that describes what Israel will be like twenty years after its establishment: "The state will be dependent on the principles of democracy, technological advancements and equal rights for the inhabitants of the land (Arabs)." Israel's first president, Chaim Weizmann, wrote in his Diaries: "I am certain that the world will judge the Jewish state by what it will do with its Arab minority, just as the Jewish people will be judged by what we do or fail to do in this state."

And herein lies the ultimate contradiction between how Israel was commanded to behave at the initial stage of its formation as a people and how centuries later it fails to carry out the Sinaitic Divine mandate to be a "holy nation," dedicated to the principles of respect, social justice and equality. How would Moses have reacted to administrative detention, collective punishment, forced expulsion, confiscation of property, month-long curfews, school closings, continued harassment, humiliation and abuse?

How is it possible that after breaking the bonds of slavery, brought about by the abuse of power, modern day Israel should invoke its power to place strictures on the freedoms of another people? If Israel is afraid that the Palestinians are becoming "too numerous" as Pharaoh was fearful that the Israelites were becoming "too numerous," then let them enjoy the freedom of their national deliverance — for theirs and Israel's sake. If not, any continued attempt to deny human rights, by accident or design, will eventually "drown Israel in a sea" of moral bankruptcy.

Only once does the *Passover Haggadah* mention the name of Moses. The implication here is that a Jew should understand that deliverance from slavery to freedom was executed by the hand of God. Yet in Israel today, regarding compromise in the territories, the most ardent "rejectionists" come from the religious right. They have erred in their interpretation of the Divine social themes of equality and social justice that characterized the dramatic beginnings of the Jewish people. More so, they inserted themselves as God's spokespersons, assuming the role of Moses, without his understanding and execution of God's Will as handed down at the beginning of collective Jewish time.

And so, Israel lives in blissful ambiguity. Its theological and historical roots say one thing, but its actions today project something quite opposite. "Upon three things the world rests: upon justice, upon truth and upon peace. And the three are one. When justice is done, truth prevails and peace is established" (*Ta'anit* 4:2, *Megilla* 3:5).

Because of such a lofty ideal, God called upon Moses to lead the Israelites out of Slavery, to show the world for all future generations that Israel's freedom would guarantee the freedom of others and adorn Israel with peace. Any peace (including peace of mind) is a stabilizing factor in the national psyche of a people. Israel can attain such stability when it harmonizes its past with its present.

The Nature of Independence[1]

Israel's Independence Day is a little more than a fifty-year old Holiday, extremely new in Jewish terms. While religious longing for a "return to Zion" has always been part of Jewish liturgy, the advent of the Jews' actual return to their ancestral homeland has yet to be formally canonized in their prayers. Within Orthodox circles there has been much controversy as to the manner in which traditional Judaism should relate to the establishment of a basically secular state. There are those who reject the Jewish state's sovereignty because it was founded, not by the will of God, but by the act of mortals. Still others reject the notion that the "promised land" should adhere to civil laws and not Torah laws.

For this segment of the Orthodox world, it is impossible to invest the liturgy with any changes that would acknowledge the reality of a Jewish state. More dramatically, there are those elements in Orthodoxy that refuse to celebrate Israel Independence Day in any form whatsoever. There are other elements within Orthodoxy which recognize that Israel needed to be forged by the Jewish people, whatever their religious orientation. These same people would hold that the present state is a preparatory stage for an eventual messianic state. Therefore, they find no difficulty in adding elements of the traditional rituals to the religious significance of the Jewish people's return to Israel. They add the *Hallel*[2] prayers to the morning service, thereby elevating Independence Day to the level of the three pilgrimage Holidays of Sukkot, Passover and Shavuot. Yet apart from this addition, even the more moderate elements in Orthodoxy have yet to establish a set religious tradition for the celebration of the modern day "miracle" of the state of Israel.

Yet in today's political climate, with the continued frantic race by both major political parties in Israel to woo the religious parties to their side, perhaps it would be better not to strain to inject Independence Day with any measure of religious content. The ultra-Orthodox Shas party is pressing for "observant" observance of secular Holidays. And here is one of the great ironies as well as

---

1. Partially excerpted from the author's book *Israel on Broadway; America: Off-Broadway — Jews in the New Millennium*, pages 221-224, Gefen Publishing House, 1998.
2. Group of *Psalms* recited in synagogue during Sukkot, Chanukah, Passover, Shavuot and Rosh Chodesh (the new moon or new month).

contradictions of Israeli society. Ultra-Orthodox Jews, who do not send their children to serve in the army, demand that the secular public, which does send its children to serve in the army, "cover its head with a hat and to recite a *Mishnaic*[1] passage or *Psalm* when the siren is sounded for one minute on Holocaust and Memorial Day" (*Ha'Aretz*, December 29, 1999). Such a demand is a "fig leaf" for the fact that many ultra-Orthodox Jews in Israel do not stand in reverence when the sirens are sounded. Not to stand in prayerful reverence as a religious Jew when the memorial siren is heard throughout the land, but to demand that secular Jews do so is like complaining to a waiter that the food is terrible and the portions are too small! This is a real expression of schizophrenic behavior.

As pointed out earlier, the conflict between religion and state, so prominent in Israel because of the unholy alliance between religion and politics, needs not be fueled with an infusion of religious symbols. As it is, national symbols like the Wall, the Israeli flag, and even Jerusalem have been institutionalized with such religious rhetoric, that those who relate to these symbols in historical or cultural terms are seen as impostors.

On one Independence Day, like so many other Israelis, I had an Israeli flag waving from my car. It was next to my bumper sticker calling for "Peace Now." A car pulled up next to me, also sporting an Israeli flag, but with a "religious" bumper sticker, "I trust in God." The driver rolled down his window and told me that it was sacrilegious to display an Israeli flag next to a "Peace Now" slogan.

The religious language of today's Israel has become emotionally charged. Religious concepts that might be chosen in order to add to the sanctity of Independence Day could very well take on a political meaning that could lead to dire consequences. Religious concepts like "Messiah," "redemption" and "promised land" are all politically loaded. They are absolute terms that have little concern for "realpolitik" or compromise.

---

1. From the word *Mishnah*, which is the codification of Jewish law compiled by Judah HaNasi around 200 CE. It contains the basis for Oral law, traditionally given to Moses at Mount Sinai and handed down by word of mouth, side by side with the Written Law (Torah), from generation to generation. The Mishnah is divided into six parts (orders), each one being divided into tractates, and each tractate divided into sections, which in turn contain paragraphs — also called Mishnayot.

Israel's first prime minister, David Ben Gurion, often used religious terminology to lend support to the needs of the modern state. In a play on the Talmudic concept, "concerning three things one should die, lest he perform them — idolatry, incest and murder"(*Babylonian Talmud, Sanhedrin* 74a), Ben Gurion added his own "three things." He said: "concerning freedom of Jewish immigration, the right to build up our land, and the political independence of the Jewish people in its land." But even Ben Gurion's seemingly innocuous application of an important religious paradigm can have its dangers. Once religion is called upon to set absolute standards of behavior, as opposed to guidelines for human interchange, then regretful actions can result. Suppose the independent state of Israel turns out to be racist in practice, or pursues a foreign policy that would extend its borders to match the biblical borders of ancient Israel? Should Jews feel so religiously bound that they would willingly die to defend such a Jewish state? Does not such an attitude give a contradictory message?

One needs to be extremely cautious when contemplating the religious significance of the establishment of any nation-state. Often a cozy relationship that exists between religion and state leads to extremism. The Jewish religious tradition in the Diaspora had as one of its themes the return to Israel "from the four corners of the world." It does not follow from this that the establishment of the Jewish state necessarily means that the Jewish religious tradition is the sole raison d'etre for its sovereign being or the singular prop by which to govern that state.

In fact, it may even be unwise to have any permeation of Independence Day celebrations with ceremonies whose dominant mood is one of religious somberness. The conclusion of Memorial Day for Fallen Soldiers serves as the opening ceremony for Independence Day. It is comforting to many to see Israel's chief rabbis and army cantors intone mournful Jewish prayers. But one must be careful that such religious overtones do not exclude the secular Jewish population, and most significantly the Israeli non-Jewish population, which comprises almost twenty percent of the total citizenry. It can be discriminatory when a ceremony of a national Holiday finds its religious expression in Jewish terms only, thus leaving out Druse, Bedouins and Christians who have fought and died for Israel. Religious beliefs (essentially a private matter) can take on state-like proportions, and can breed exclusivity. Such exclusivity can beget intolerance; intolerance can beget prejudice; prejudice can beget hatred; and hatred can beget murder.

The role that Jewish Holidays, especially national ones as opposed to religious ones, plays in Israeli society must be approached delicately. Israel's independence should be "dependent" on religious influence but "independent" of religious control. Any enlightened society should be governed by religious persuasion and not by religious coercion. Given the political passions that abound in Israel today, when virtually all the internal political violence has come from the religious right — Goldstein, Amir, the Jewish Underground and the late Rabbi Meir Kahana's Kach — it would be best if Israel shed Independence Day of any religious content.

Israel's Independence Day, like all Jewish Holidays, is essentially an expression of the ultimate victory of the Jews over their enemies, of freedom over enslavement. All Jewish Holidays in Israel must never contradict this singular most important lesson.

PART TWO
THE MICRO

or

"You say potato, I say pot*ahto*"

INTRODUCTION II

I am a news aficionado. I cannot get enough of it. Viewing the nightly news is a ritual in my house. Phones are lifted off their hooks so that nothing, absolutely nothing can disturb my concentration. I walk the streets with a transistor to my ear. But my real "habit" is the print media. I cannot eat a meal or ride the bus without a newspaper in hand. I am sure that the epithet on my grave will read: "He had a 'subscription for life' to the *International Herald Tribune*."

But I am not alone. All Israelis are news fanatics. Every hour on the hour, public buses blare out the news on their radios. Work places come to a stop when the hourly news reports are on. No head of a company, no Supreme Court justice, no owner of a local kiosk or grocery store can begin his or her day without a glance at the headlines. For such a small country it is mind-boggling that there are so many daily newspapers. In addition to the Hebrew papers, there are a dozen or so papers in foreign languages. Like me, Israelis seem never to satisfy their "daily fix." For example, as I write these lines, the hot topic in Israel is the rise to power in Austria of the extreme right-winger Joerg Haider. It is not so much that I believe everything that is written about Haider, but rather that I believe that he is all that I should be reading about.

The reason for the Israeli obsession with the news is that daily life in Israel brings continual surprises. Israelis never know what to expect when they turn on the radio or read the headlines in the morning. One day, they wake up to the dramatic news that the two hundred Jews and Israelis who were hijacked to Entebbe, Uganda, by Palestinian terrorists have been miraculously released by a daring Israeli military operation. Another dawn ushers in the word that an Iraqi nuclear reactor has been bombed. Almost any wake-up call could be accompanied by the great news that the Israeli army whisked 14,000 Ethiopians out of war-torn Addis Ababa, or the tragic news that fifteen early morning shoppers at an open market were blown up by terrorists. For the most part,

Israelis stay so glued to the media because they are fearful. They suffer from a "what next" syndrome.

Yet with all the dramatic and emotionally laden events that strike Israel far too frequently, most days are filled with more mundane occurrences. The trouble is that Israelis have difficulty distinguishing between the dramatic and the unimportant. Benjamin Netanyahu's extra-marital shenanigans, as titillating as they might be, are not worthy of the same amount of attention as peace negotiations with Israel's Arab neighbors. Jerusalem mayor Ehud Olmert's smoking of a Cuban cigar on the Sabbath is not worthy of a headline larger than the one reporting on Israel's air attacks on terrorist bases in Lebanon.

Yet Israelis know that if they concentrated only on the "heavy" issues and events that so dominate and overwhelm the country, they would literally go crazy. They come too fast and furiously. So they divert their attention by dallying in lighter, yet intriguing matters. This might be defined as calculated schizophrenic behavior: Let me swallow "sugar and spice and everything nice" rather than swallow the "bitter pill" of wars, terrorism or anti-Semitism.

The rhythm of daily life in Israel is such that one can readily be distracted from the major events. The reason for this phenomenon is that daily encounters in Israel can be extremely frustrating as well as all engrossing. Because Israelis are continually faced with life and death situations, they tend to be quite high strung, and so blow many simple interactions out of proportion. In the classic American film, *Network*, the TV newscaster screams into the camera: "I'm mad as hell and I'm not going to take it anymore!" That is precisely how Israelis feel. They seem often to be "mad as hell." And who can blame them? They bear such monumental responsibilities that they justifiably feel that in a pause between dramatic events, they should experience a little peace and quiet.

But in a quasi-schizophrenic fashion, they thwart any tranquility they seek by often parading around with a "chip on their shoulder."

The other day I was short-changed the shekel equivalent of two-and-a-half dollars in a bakery. When I mentioned this to the salesperson, he immediately accused me of being mistaken, and reluctantly did an accounting of the money in his cash register against the receipts printed. After waiting for fifteen minutes, he slapped ten shekels on the counter, heaving a resentful grunt that I was right. After retrieving my money, I said: "I believe you forgot something." Stunned, he replied that he had returned my money. To which I retorted: "You forgot, 'I am sorry. I apologize.'"

Erich Segal wrote in his sappy novel, *Love Story*: "Love is never having to say I am sorry." Wrong! Love is always having to say you are sorry. If not, hurt goes unnoticed and unattended. Again this points to a real contradiction in Israeli behavior. Inevitably that same "angry" salesperson at that bakery will take an IOU of a perfect stranger who, after buying some baked goods, will discover that he does not have enough money to pay for his purchases. Two Israeli strangers can find themselves locked in a most acrimonious argument over virtually nothing, and then wind up in a cafe sharing army stories as if they had been best friends. An American Jewish teenager participating on a high school program in Israel was scheduled to visit a long lost family relative over the Sabbath. Having difficulty locating the family, she finally spoke to someone. After a brief conversation, they both discovered that they were not related. But the Israeli invited the girl for the weekend in any case.

Israelis are in turn argumentative, self-righteous, omniscient, braggarts, opinionated, aggressive **and** gracious, unselfish, warm, generous, trusting and committed. Their psychological frame of mind finds their "holy place" split between two sanctuaries — one of time and one of space. They occupy a space that is fraught with anxiety and fear, a space where paranoia is real. But they also dwell in a time that is devoid of high drama, a time where paranoia is imagined. It is difficult for Israelis to distinguish between these two worlds.

When Benjamin Netanyahu admitted to his extramarital affair on television, claiming that his "political enemies" were out to destroy him just as Israel's enemies were out to destroy the Jewish state, one knew that not only was he engaging in hyperbole, but also shifting responsibility completely. He confused what was real and what was imagined. And while Israelis recognized the basic immorality of his behavior, the religious guardians of the Jewish people's moral character would urge their ultra-Orthodox constituency to vote for Netanyahu because "he is good for the Jews." This was not just confusion, but outright contradiction.

Every day life in Israel brings with it these types of contradictions. They almost seem endemic to Israeli society. It is the reason that Israelis have perfected the art of "intense conversation," or as some outside observer might describe it, "controlled hysteria." As one looks at the routine of daily life in Israel, one cannot help but notice that the left hand does one thing and the right hand does the other (often the left hand has no idea what the right hand is doing). It is similar to the story of the client who hired a one-armed lawyer to argue his case. The client was asked why he hired a one-armed lawyer' since the litigation did not involve anything even remotely related to the lawyer's particular handicap or any sort of personal injury claim? He responded: "I am sick and tired of lawyers who say 'on the one hand this, and on the other hand that.'"

On the one hand, because of all the wars that have devastated Israel since its establishment, life is extremely precious. On the other hand, the number of deaths on the roads due to aggressive and careless driving is staggering. On the one hand the Bat Sheva Dance Company is forbidden to perform an artistic piece because it is considered sexually perverted by the Orthodox community, yet on the other hand, a transsexual represents Israel in the Eurovision International Song Festival. On the one hand the Jewish people are often referred to as "the people of the Book," yet on the other hand, teachers (of books) are some of the lowest paid professionals in the country. On the one hand, Israel's hostilities have produced so many handicapped war veterans, yet on the other hand facilities for the handicaped are woefully inadequate. The list of contradictions could go on and on.

The following vignettes and essays will hopefully provide the reader with new insights into the everyday machinations of Israeli life — the frustrating ambiguities and the entertaining conflicts. While these contradictions do not indicate a full-blown case of "schizophrenia," they certainly produce schizophrenic peculiarities. The primary reason Israelis turn minor issues into major crises is because they suffer from an exaggerated sense of self-importance. And when someone is so absorbed with one's own sense of self, it will prompt all sorts of neurotic behavior. It is like the story of the mosquito, who, doing the back stroke on New York's Hudson River, in order to spread its wings, yells out: "Pull the drawbridge, I'm coming through!"

Such is the case with the vast majority of Israelis. The theatrical production of their collective lives plays itself out in the simple one act drama of their daily private lives. The inability to separate between the two finds Israelis often incapable of just floating with ease on their back. They are forever worried that they won't get through the day without having to shriek for help. And so they dwell simultaneously in the macro and in the micro world, never quite distinguishing which behavior is the appropriate for each world.

CHAPTER 8

SEX AND THE MARRIED POLITICIAN

Bibi Versus Billy

There is little question that money, power and sex often go hand in hand. Top selling writers like Danielle Steele and Jackie Collins make their money off this sure-fire triple formula. Unfortunately in this day and age, art imitates reality. When US president Bill Clinton was in the throes of his impeachment trial because of his illicit affair with Ms. Monica Lewinksy, a number of prominent Republicans suddenly came forward in one long sexual confessional.

Congress' chairman of the Impeachment Committee, Henry Hyde, admitted to an affair, as did congressional Representative Bob Livingston, who then chose to retract his candidacy for Speaker of the House. Former Speaker of the House, the self-righteous Newt Gingrich, the leader of a return to moral rectitude, is presently being sued because of his long-standing affair.

Israel's own Benjamin Netanyahu, colloquially known as "Bibi," publicly admitted to having an affair. He was just following in the footsteps of Israel's late legendary figure, that one-eyed general, Moshe Dayan. When Israel's first prime minister, David Ben Gurion, was challenged in his cabinet by one of his Orthodox ministers that a fellow cabinet member was "fooling around" out of wedlock, Ben Gurion replied: "Tell me who it is, and I will poke out his other eye!"

When it comes to sex, many political leaders just cannot help but run a parallel course of political drive and sexual drive. That the latter might destroy the former does not seem sufficient to put the brakes on presidential or prime ministerial sexual antics. Clearly when one works against what he or she knows rationally to be in his or her own self-interest, then that person must be diagnosed as morally, and possibly emotionally, unbalanced. So the question remains: Can someone who is decidedly emotionally unstable because of an inability to control his or her sexual urges, even at one's own expense, be charged with the ultimate responsibility of running a country? The logical answer should be "no," but the practical result is less definitive. Perhaps it is just a given fact that anyone who would want to be president or prime minister must be "crazy" in the first place, so any sort of morally aberrant behavior makes sense. Who the hell knows the answer? Maybe it is a good thing that our political leaders "screw" around, otherwise they would "screw" us!

Take Israel's national soccer team. A match with Denmark's national team took place in Israel. It was part of the pre-Olympic qualifying games. Israel was routed by a score of 5-0. It was considered a national humiliation. And then came the shocking news that some of the players on the Israeli team had spent the evening before the big game with call-girls. A commission was set up to investigate the affair. Could it be that having sexual relations before a game might be injurious to a player's performance? On the proverbial other hand, could being sexually active actually enhance one's performance? Should a married player sign a contract that either forbids or insists that he have intercourse with his wife prior to a game? Only the commission of inquiry will determine this. It probably will never occur to anyone that the reason Israel was so roundly beaten was because its team was dreadful and the Danish team was excellent.

Ah, but one can miss the point! Should an Israeli soccer player engage in such lurid behavior, irrespective of whether he is playing a game the next day or any day? No! Because that player represents Israel, and Israelis expect more from their national leaders, be they soccer stars or prime ministers. So why do they do it? And who really cares? And here virtually every society expresses schizophrenic tendencies on the matter of their leaders' sexual infidelities. On the one hand, people say that it is a matter of his or her private life, yet on the other hand, they cannot resist the temptation to read every shred of information that appears in the papers. Israelis, who, at the same time are stoic and emotional, private and back-slapping, more than other people, seem to possess at the same time the need to know and the desire not to know.

On the matter of Bibi Netanyahu's affair, it is particularly complicated because when he was elected prime minister, it was primarily due to the voting strength of the ultra-Orthodox community, which went out on a limb with the message: "Netanyahu is good for the Jews." Leaving aside the racial innuendo that such a slogan implies, there is a clear contradiction here. How can a devout religious faction, which demands a strict interpretation of Jewish laws, support a man who publicly admits to violating one of the most crucial laws, one of the Ten Commandments, "Thou shalt not commit adultery?" Politics do indeed make strange bedfellows. These same ultra-Orthodox Jews would sit in Netanyahu's coalition government. Is this a case of schizophrenic behavior or simple hypocrisy? In Israel's case, it is difficult to judge who is more contradictory, its leaders or its average citizen.

Bibi's Boo-Boo

Benjamin Netanyahu (Bibi) was accused of running an American-style campaign in his bid to become prime minister as well as in his attempt to run the country. Now there is nothing inherently wrong with the US system of elections, except for the length of the presidential campaign and its all-too-public exposure of its candidates and their families. The redeeming worth of the system is that nothing is decided behind closed doors or by party hacks. Instead the American people play an active role in choosing their contestants for president.

Yet Bibi, in his attempt to emulate the American model, upped the ante considerably with the admission of his affair, rivaling the likes of Gary Hart, Ted Kennedy, Bill Clinton, et. al. From the moment Netanyahu revealed his extra-marital escapade, the enduring political question has been asked, particularly since his short reign in power was such an abysmal failure: Is there any correlation between the behavior of a politician in his or her home and his or her behavior in the market place? The question assumes that one's private life has an influence on one's public life. A cursory look at the background of some of the world's most famous political leaders might just prove the opposite.

Franklin Delano Roosevelt is generally considered a great leader. Eleanor was not the eternal love of his life. Dwight D. Eisenhower was an extremely successful general in World War II. The pictures of him in his jeep riding around Europe showcased a woman other than his wife Mamie. The Reverend Martin

Luther King Jr. led an overly exuberant love life. This did not impair his ability to advance the cause of the African-American. The list could go on and on. From Thomas Jefferson to John F. Kennedy, a political leader's achievements and/or failures seemed to bear no relation to his or her private dealings.

In Jewish terms, two of the greatest leaders were those who established Israel's First Kingdom. There is not a politician today who could hold a candle to King David's moral gymnastics. Not only did he have a steamy relationship with Bathsheba, but, in order to satisfy his lasciviousness, he also ordered her husband to be sent to battle, where he was sure to be killed (*II Samuel* 11:14-17). His rule has been acknowledged as one of incredible magnitude, only to be matched by that of his son Solomon, who was known to have many wives. Both David and Solomon were considered great moral leaders.

This in no way should be interpreted as an endorsement of Bibi's or Billy's behavior. Ideally, one would like to view any political leader as a paragon of virtue. But, unfortunately, morality in the political sphere is not part of realpolitik. Were it so, Israel would never have had dealings with South Africa during the latter's apartheid era, the US would sever relations with China because of its continued human rights violations, the Western world would have put a stop to Russia's brutal conquest of Chechnya, and the industrial nations would share their wealth and resources with the poverty-stricken countries of the Third World.

Yet the jury is still out as to whether a politician's personal affairs have any bearing on his or her public dealings. In Bibi Netanyahu's case, it would seem that his creative ability to make up a lie faster than he could acknowledge the truth, and not being able to distinguish between the two, affected his term of office, as well as his relationship with his own government ministers, with foreign leaders and eventually with the citizens. Remarkably, Bill Clinton was able to continue his reign and retain great public support for continuation in his position.

As for Bibi, it is clear that his distasteful exploitation of his affair, demonstrated in his public waving of the "hidden" tape of his peccadillo, would lead to further cynical exploitations, often without shame. Such is the case, in this following example, of his relationship to Israel's gay and lesbian community.

During Netanyahu's term of office, he "came out of the closet." He advised the World Congress of Gay, Lesbian and Bisexual Jewish Organizations that the Palestinian Authority has no use for their kind (*Ha'Aretz*, April 6, 1999). His assumption was that anyone who would belong to such an organization must be "politically left," and therefore would lend support to the Palestinian cause. Yet he could not say this. He needed a "politically correct" cover. Saying Bibi Netanyahu is politically correct is the best example of an oxymoron. Under the guise of his great concern for the rights of Jewish gays and lesbians, he felt the "moral" need to apprise the world of the alleged negative Palestinian attitude toward those who have an alternative sexual orientation to the homophobic norm, as articulated by a senior member of the Palestinian Authority.

What was interesting about his sudden outburst of moral outrage was that it was just that — sudden. And as usual, terribly calculating. Like so many, he portrayed his own prejudice by assuming that the gay, lesbian and bisexual community is politically monolithic. His syllogistic reasoning holds that if an American Jewish male loves another American Jewish male, then that male would necessarily identify with the Palestinian cause. According to this warped logic, one should also determine that such an American gay should in actuality relate only to Palestinian males. Netanyahu's creative form of diplomacy was an affront to both the gay and lesbian community **and** the Palestinian people.

What about some of the coalition partners, not only in Netanyahu's government, but the present and previous ones? In a moment of righteous indignation, Netanyahu did not think to tell the World Congress of Jewish Gays, Lesbians and Bisexuals about the views of the ultra-Orthodox parties, Shas and Degel HaTorah, toward homosexuals. Unlike the Palestinian Authority, which one would suspect does hold various views regarding gays and lesbians, the ultra-Orthodox world has a one-dimensional attitude toward homosexuals. As defined in the Torah, homosexuality is considered an abomination, worthy of no less than being stoned to death. Indeed it was surprising that those same rabbis who declared that "Netanyahu is good for the Jews" did not lambaste him for this breach of Torah. Only if there were a hint of schizophrenic understandings of the Jewish tradition, could one be "good for the Jews" and homosexuals at the same time. But politicians in Israel, including ultra-Orthodox ones, have little difficulty in speaking out of both sides of their mouths.

Then again, one can use the example of Israel's president, Ezer Weizman, who managed in one sentence to insult both gays and the Jewish tradition, when he referred to King David as "one big faigele" (Yiddish slang for "fairy," indicating someone who is extremely effeminate and possibly gay). Bibi conveniently failed to mention this little fact to the World Congress of Jewish Gays and Lesbians. Yet here one encounters another contradiction. Israel is a very homophobic society, but the laws handed down by its Supreme Court are some of the most liberal in the Western World when it comes to insuring the basic rights of gays and lesbians.

But none of this is comparable to the contradictions that have plagued Mr. Netanyahu. His ridicule of so many people in Israel, culminating in the public humiliation of his own wife when he told the world of his affair, would make him the last person to come to the defense of the gay and lesbian community. More than that, relating the whole issue of gay and lesbian rights to issues affecting Palestinians is laughable. Bibi was right, there is a comparison to be made between gays and lesbians and Palestinians. All have their human rights trampled.

It is cruel to use the gay and lesbian community as a pawn in a political game in order to score points to further discredit the Palestinian Authority. Sadly, there is enough within Palestinian behavior and its often lame enforcement of the principles of democracy that guarantees it own disdain, so why the need to abuse the sensibilities of gays and lesbians who are always so unfairly abused?

All of this points to one thing: Bibi's wayward ways clouded his mental equilibrium. It could be that this was not the case with his clone, Bill Clinton, because Clinton's ego is stronger. But the following scenario of what Mr. Clinton might do after he concludes his second term in office might shed some light on "Billy Boy's" behavior. As for Bibi, the voters decided to send him back into the closet.

Bill Clinton for Prime Minister of Israel

Under Israel's Law of Return, any Jew is entitled to immediate citizenship upon moving to the Jewish state (except those with a criminal record). The law was and is an absolutely necessity, given the historical reality of the Holocaust and the continued role that anti-Semitism plays in too many countries around the world. Over the years, the law was expanded, becoming more inclusive. For example, the cultural Holocaust that erased much of Jewish identity in the former Soviet Union brought about a situation whereby any person who could trace his or her Jewish ancestry back to one of his grandparents, would also be entitled to immediate Israeli citizenship.

Similarly, if a non-Jew was married to a Jew, the non-Jewish spouse would also be granted citizenship upon immigration to Israel. Certainly, thousands of Russian Jewish immigrant families who have arrived in the country over the last number of years are mixed-marriage couples. Only at some later date, when any issue of "personal status" comes to the fore, will the "Jewishness" of that person be questioned, but not his or her "Israeliness."

So against this background, there is a solution for Bill Clinton to have his legacy as a great leader engraved in the public mind, instead of the image of a sex-starved boy scout who could not resist the physical lure of a pretty (or not so pretty) girl scout. More importantly for Israelis, the rehabilitation of Bill Clinton could be the best thing for the Jewish state.

Bill Clinton should not follow his wife to New York. Instead he should leave her. Indeed, had I earlier thought about what I am about to write, I might have saved Mr. Clinton from himself, and saved his family, his country and the world the embarrassment of his highly publicized and juicy impeachment process. Everyone knows that his relationship with Hillary is a sham. After he divorces his wife, he should call Monica and propose marriage to her. Unable to handle all the publicity, Monica and Bill decide to escape. Being Jewish, Monica applies to Israel for citizenship under the Law of Return. Bill comes along as her spouse and gains citizenship as well. Being the political animal that he is, he opts to run for prime minister of the Jewish state.

He would get the vote of hundreds of thousands of Israelis. Whenever he came to Israel, he was swarmed with genuine admiration and appreciation. He knows how to connect, dwarfing both recent Israeli poor carbon copies of his style of presidency, i.e., Netanyahu and Ehud Barak. As for his roving eye, it would in no way influence the electorate or, for that matter, Israeli legislators. After all, one of the things that Israelis can be proud of is that until Benjamin Netanyahu came on the scene, with his public parading of his wife Sarah, no one knew who the spouse of any of Israel's politicians was. Indeed, after watching Hillary and Chelsea Clinton and Tipper Gore dragged out into the public domain ad nauseam, it is sheer relief not to be able to identify Shulamit Shamir (Yitzhak Shamir's wife) or Sonia Peres (Shimon Peres' wife). Israel is one of the few nations in the democratic world that has honored this separation between the public's right to know and the individual's right to privacy.

As for Clinton's penchant for looking directly into the camera's eye and lying, that is no problem, for lying has become a virtual staple of the Israeli body politic. Sexual promiscuity? As noted, while Bibi is somewhat of a match for Clinton, if we can have the real thing, why settle for a poor imitation?

Clinton has a proven record of achievement. He could do for Israelis what he has done for America: encourage economic growth and stability, lower inflation to infinitesimal numbers and reduce unemployment to a few percentage points. He would appoint to key positions in government individuals from all sectors of society. He would set education and health as his top priorities. At present none of these praiseworthy achievements are part of the Israeli scene. In fact the opposite is the case: unemployment is high, inflation is above average and economic growth is stagnant. Partisan appointments still dominate the political stage and education and health issues are on the back burner.

In the international arena, having brokered agreements in Northern Ireland, Bosnia and the initial agreement between Israel and the Palestinians, he would have a vested interest in bringing the Oslo Accords, the Cairo Agreement, the Wye Memorandum of Agreement and the Sharm El Sheikh Agreement to their fulfillment. Having initiated the negotiations between Israel and Syria, he would be driven to see them to fruition. While applying his diplomatic skills to the Syrian front, he could teach the Hizboullah in Lebanon a lesson, Iraqi-style. Having already made a "state visit" to Gaza, he would have no trouble in admitting what everyone knows, that there not only will be a Palestinian state, but also that there is one already — with Jerusalem as its capital in the Holy City, which is today divided de facto.

He would bring back our global friends whom we have managed to alienate over the years. He would even be able to travel to the United States and successfully argue before his presidential successor for increased financial and political support. Having dealt with the hostility of many in the Republican-controlled Congress, he still managed to work with its members to ultimately implement a fairly progressive legislative agenda. Building on that experience, through his charm and public appeal, he would be able to convince recalcitrant Knesset members to see the good of a cause rather than the parochial needs of a particular constituency. Because of his natural tendency to be race-creed-color-religion blind, he would embrace the notion of an open and pluralistic society.

In short, Israel needs a competent rogue. Being dishonest or unfaithful is an irrelevancy. Just take a look at Israel's recent president, Ezer Weizman and the present and immediate past prime ministers, all investigated by the police for wrong-doings.

What distinguishes Bill from Bibi is that, despite the insanity of Clinton's behavior, Clinton could differentiate between delusion and reality, whereas Netanyahu confused the two. Clinton knew that he could not "screw" the nation and get away with it. Netanyahu believed that he could "screw" everyone, and no one would catch onto him.

"Who is a hero? He who conquers his will" (*Sayings of the Fathers* 4:1). Neither Bill Clinton nor Benjamin Netanyahu was capable of conquering his will. When caught with their "pants down," they chose to lash out at others. The reason that Bill Clinton would make a good candidate for prime minister of Israel is that his behavior is stereotypical of the average Israeli politicians' reactions, especially Bibi Netanyahu, to contradictory events of their own making. Israel as a nation is dominated by a history of survival. Having an identifiable enemy is a psychological necessity, not a political one. In Israel, the personal becomes the political.

Such was the case with Bill Clinton, as evidenced by the words of his wounded wife in response to those who attacked her husband for his affair with Monica Lewinsky, a White House intern. She, and he, conjured up the enemy, blaming a "right-wing conspiracy." Netanayhu, waving a video cassette before the television cameras of his affair, blamed "unknown gangsters" who were out to destroy his political career. The fact that Clinton and Netanyahu were not able to substantiate their claims was unimportant in their eyes.

When neither of these men are in their "right mind," their "left mind" gets crowded with all sorts of distortions. Clinton eventually recovered, probably because he got some sound religious and spiritual guidance as well as psychological treatment. Netanyahu sought no help, but clung to the Nixonian philosophy that his enemies were out to get him, not recognizing that his real enemy was within. But who can blame him for his Pavlovian reaction? It is the same with virtually all Israeli leaders. Arye Deri is not guilty of his crimes, it is the secular Ashkenazi establishment that is out to destroy him (see *Chapter 3*, "Baseless Hatred — the Deri Case, Part II," page 70). Arik Sharon, found guilty by a national board of inquiry of deceiving the government during the Lebanon War, points the finger at the left-wingers who always hated him. (The fact that the national board of inquiry was appointed by his own government did not deter him from going on the counter-attack.) The list could go on ad infinitum.

Just as earlier contended in this book that religion should be kept out of politics, so too should sex. Their mixture is like "fire and water." The two cannot exist together. They go to war with each other, and in Israel's case, such a war splits the person in two. Because Israelis live such a pressure-cooker existence, the last thing they need is a divided personality leading a country that is already divided. "A man without self-control is like a city stormed and its walls shattered" (*Proverbs* 25:28). Israel needs someone with moral grounding to guide it through the thicket of the Middle East's delicate terrain. Less than that will see Israelis both shattered and stormed, pulled in too many directions for their collective personality to sustain.

CHAPTER 9

HELL ON WHEELS

You're Driving Me Crazy

Life in Israel is very tenuous. When one considers the wars of survival that Israel has fought and the terrorism that strikes the country, one would naturally assume that the protection of life would be the highest concern of the nation and of the individual. When faced with the possibility of danger in the civilian world, one would draw the conclusion that the value of life would be the single most precious commodity. Therefore, it would make perfect sense that Israelis would be the most cautious of drivers, and that safety on the roads would be a top priority. But the opposite is the case. When Israelis get behind the wheel of a car, it is as if they are driving a tank, bulldozing over hostile terrain, with every other driver being a designated enemy. Proportionately to the number of people who drive cars in the country, as compared to any other country in the world, Israel has the highest rate of deaths in traffic accidents.

There is little question that the Israeli who packs his or her children off lovingly to school is not the same mad individual who then jumps into the driver's seat. The Israeli at home and the Israeli in a car are two different personalities. One is inviting and the other is aggressive. It is safe (or unsafe) to say that in this one area, an Israeli definitively displays all the symptoms of one who suffers from a "split personality." As aforementioned, given the fact that Israelis risk their lives on the open field of battle, it makes little sense that they fail to be cautious on the open road. Instead, the tensions of daily life somehow take over the Israeli psyche and they become virtual "raving maniacs," speeding recklessly on the open highway. And so, the "split-personality" syndrome, as it relates to driving, is further complicated when an Israeli's rational thought process is overwhelmed by his or her emotional state of mind. The carnage that occurs daily on Israeli roads, primarily due to carelessness, points to a real "sickness," more devastating than virtually any other consequence stemming from an unstable personality.

For the first few years that I lived in Israel I refused to buy a car, because I was fearful for my survival. But I finally broke down and bought the first of many used cars. Then, one day, I made the fateful decision to buy a new car. Until that time, I never owned a car produced in the same decade I lived. So I looked at my budget and went car hunting. This adventure will perhaps give the reader an insight into the Israeli attitude toward the automobile. Neither the car nor its potential buyer is treated with any respect by the salesperson.

The first thing I realized is that in Jerusalem, where I live, there is no competition in the car business. There is one dealer for each make of car. The person who owns the dealership is also the one who owns the repair shops that are the only places, which honor the official warranty. The customer is stuck. He or she has to put up with whatever sales pitch there is — or is not. And one must keep in mind that the cost of buying a car in Israel is virtually twice the cost of buying a car anywhere else in the world because of the tax and custom charges.

Having fond memories of my first car in Israel, a two-cylinder Citroen, I headed for the Citroen outlet. (At one time I owned two small Citroens. My father used to tease me that his Oldsmobile had twice the cylinder power of my two cars together.) As I walked around the showroom, not a single salesperson offered to help. Frustrated, I finally interrupted a salesperson: "I am most interested in this Citroen and I have the exact amount money to purchase it in advance." The reply was a terse one: "Don't expect a discount." With that sort of pleasant largesse, I walked out.

I went next door to the Fiat dealer. The new Tempra cost $25,000. I circled the car more times than a bride circles a groom at a Jewish wedding. No salesperson budged. I finally went over to the woman behind the sales desk. As cigarette smoke spewed forth from her nostrils, she took five phone calls, accepted a sandwich from a co-worker, and almost shattered my eardrums as she yelled across the room to another unattended customer to stop opening and closing the trunk of one of the floor models. God forbid the prospective buyer should inspect the car before shelling out a life's savings on it. One should note here that an Israeli driver carries out all the same activities that this car salesperson did — driving while smoking a cigarette, eating a sandwich and talking on a cell phone. No wonder accidents occur with such frequency.

I then went to look over a Spanish car, the Seat. There a salesperson actually got out of the chair, trying to sell me the Cordova, the "bad girl" of the Seat line of cars. But comparing the rear-end of the Cordova to the posterior of a woman, as was done in the advertisements for this car, offended my sensibilities. So I left the place behind!

Test drive a car? One must get down on his knees and plead to execute such an outlandish request. I went into the Toyota, Mazda, Ford, Daewoo, Suzuki, Mitsubishi, Hyundai, Honda, Skoda, Opel, Lada, Volkswagon, Renault, Nissan, Daihatsu, Rover and Subaru car dealerships; never once did a salesperson offer me help unsolicited. I even tried General Motors, thinking that an American company would extend courteous customer service.

This all points to an incredible smugness on the part of virtually anyone who supplies services in the country. One could ascribe this "I don't give a damn" attitude to the leftover vestiges of a socialist society. If everyone is paid equally, and in many cases pitifully, and if everyone is guaranteed tenure, then there will be a less than ambitious work ethic. While this makes sense in the public sphere, it makes little sense in the private sector. Here one would expect the free market competition to dictate behavior. Since there is no real competition in the car selling business, Israeli salespeople, who probably drive in a crazy manner, drive the automobile customer crazy as well!

So what to do? I ride a bicycle, but it would be rather difficult to pack my family of six on my mountain bike. I could put the names of different cars in a hat, and blindly pick one name out. I could take a personal route and buy a Czechoslovakian Skoda station-wagon, just because of its brand name — the "Forman." Or I could adopt the Maimonidean approach to "negative theology,"[1] and choose the car company whose salesperson is the least reprehensible.

And that is exactly what I did. Yet the story does not end here. In Israel, one must pay for a car almost all in advance. Having a prepaid check from an American bank, I paid for the car, and then some, up front — a risky proposition. The dealer has all my money and I have no leverage. Never mind that I shelled out a fortune, I am now at the mercy of the car dealer. The tension sets in. When does the car arrive? Will it arrive? A whole month passes by until it gets to the Holy City. I am ecstatic. Of course, it would be too much to expect that the car would be

---

1. See *Introduction*, page 11, footnote 2. Maimonides held that the way to know God was to define what He was not. This was classified as "negative theology."

spanking clean or that there would be more than a drop of gas in it. But I was so thrilled to get the car that I simply overlooked the absence of these most basic services. What the hell, it will serve as the first lesson before taking my new car on the Israeli roads: to overlook the most basic aspects of driving — courteousness, respect and defensiveness.

Anyway, I should be happy. I finally have a new car, but I am still disquieted. Why? The saga is not over. I am still waiting to receive money back from my overpayment.

A Losing Battle

Israel's roads are becoming more crowded every day and the traffic is becoming more overwhelming. Many Israelis, fleeing an overcrowded city life, have moved to one of the many new suburbs that have cropped up in the country over the last decade. If one does not leave for the office before seven in the morning, he or she can expect to spend at least one hour in the car before arriving at work. This testifies to the further Americanization of Israel. The reasons for this unbearable situation are manifold: too many cars, too few roads into and around the city, new neighborhoods, roads continually under construction, confusing traffic signs, lack of truck routes and separate bus lanes, a non-existent train system, illegal parking, narrow streets and, of course, the selfish behavior of the Israeli driver.

Since the Japanese market broke away from the Arab boycott in the Eighties, it has flooded the country with Mitsubishis and Toyotas. As Israelis become upwardly mobile, many mimic their American counterparts and insist on owning two cars. There is no concept in the country of car-pooling. While it is difficult to monitor car-pooling in the city, it should be relatively easy to supervise those who come into and go out of the city from the cities' bedroom communities. In many countries there is a fine for driving alone during rush hours. Alternately, there are special fast lanes for those who participate in car pools.

Then there is the matter of road improvements and repairs. Road improvements become obsolete as soon as they are completed because of the increase of cars on the roads and the influx of new residents to the cities' new neighborhoods. In addition, Israeli roads suffer from a unique phenomenon: the transportation on trucks of tanks, artillery and half-track troop carriers. Yet even with all this, it is difficult to understand why so many of the same roads seem to be continually in a state of repair.

Ah, but there is a reason. The city managers parcel out contracts to their favorite companies. A contractor for the telephone company opens up the street to lay down the phone lines, and then closes it. Another contractor is hired to open the street again so that the sewer system can be installed. No sooner is the pavement restored when yet another contractor opens it up to put in the electrical wiring. And so on.

Driving by a basketball or soccer arena, which, when built, did not provide for sufficient parking, is an ordeal. Israelis are incredibly creative. In fact, they may have invented the concept of quadruple parking. They even set up their own median strip of parked cars in the middle of the road. Simply put, Israel's traffic jams are turning into a carbon copy of the traffic jams on the George Washington Bridge and the Lincoln Tunnel during rush hour. Add to this the rudeness and complete lack of consideration on the part of the Israeli driver and one can well understand why driving in Israel is frustrating and exasperating. It can turn a usually calm and retiring person into a raging bull. The personality shift is as great as a shift from fifth gear to reverse! It is the stuff of what makes a person have a complete mental breakdown.

I never thought I could identify with a movie anti-hero. But actor Michael Douglas, the star of the film *Falling Down,* has become a sympathetic figure to me. His violent outbursts, and the shooting spree he went on, after being caught in a traffic jam almost parallel my own emotional state on any given morning that I drive through the streets of Jerusalem on my way to work. By the end of my trip to work, my even temper evaporates. I breathe fire from my nostrils and steam streams forth from my naval. I tell myself to remain calm but only undeleted expletives trip off my tongue. I have become a schizophrenic monster, controlled on the inside and maniacal on the outside.

As I walk to my car, which is parked on one of Jerusalem's narrow suburban streets, I must literally hug the walls of the road as the cars come racing down it as if they were entered in the Indianapolis 500. Somehow, without my heart attacking me, I get into my car and pull onto the main drag. I am no more than two minutes on the road when the cars in front of me come to a screeching halt. A bus driver has pulled one of his usual ploys with his accordion bus. He has stopped in the middle of the road to let passengers on and off, rather than take a few extra seconds to pull over to the indented part of the road set aside for bus stops.

As I continue on my way, I once again slam on my brakes. The cab driver in front of me has identified a potential passenger on the opposite side of the street. Rather than wait to make an illegal U-turn at the light a few yards ahead, he chooses to make his illegal U-turn right in the middle of the road. I stop at the next light. But before proceeding when it flashes green, as any Israeli driver knows, I must wait a few seconds (maybe even minutes) before stepping on the accelerator, so that the opposing cars can finish running the red light.

I am ready to continue on my way when I notice an incredibly long line of traffic. How could I be so dumb? It is the street cleaner and the garbage truck plotting their busy schedule to coincide with rush hour traffic. I finally break through and head toward my daughter's school to drop her off. There is a line of fifteen cars waiting to make a left-hand turn. Since the green arrow holds its color long enough for only one-and-a-half cars to make the turn, I prepare myself for a half-hour wait. I finally make the light to cruise down the narrow street where the school is located. Cars are parked everywhere. Parents are dropping their kids off in the middle of the street. There are no crosswalks, no road bumps to slow cars down, and no policemen. In addition, there is constant building going on that allows for cement trucks, tractors and cranes to further congest the area. It came as no surprise when a little girl was hit by a car.

I return to the main road (the light is not working now) and head back toward work. At the next light, there is a huge back up. Yet, as I approach the intersection, I am relieved that my light is green, but I cannot move. Why? All the cars turning at the intersection to head toward a highway leading out of the city clog the intersection, causing a gridlock. I begin to feel Michael Douglas getting the better of me. All the cars begin their weaving and tailgating, accompanied by a cacophony of horn blowing, finger gesturing and name calling. I now lurch forward in my car, hitting every red light. I guess it would be too much to ask that traffic lights be synchronized. I then cross over from this eight-lane speedway which suddenly turns into a narrow two-way street. As I edge on at a tortoise pace, I have to avoid grazing the illegally parked delivery trucks in front of the vegetable and flower stores.

I creep up to another crowded intersection where a hundred arteries lead into one massive blood clot. Cars are streaming in from all directions. I have to traverse five lanes in order to have the privilege of making a right-hand turn on a street now enjoying its second year of repairs. But I breathe a sigh of relief, as I am now in the final stretch.

I turn onto the street where my office is located, when I get stuck behind an avalanche of tourist buses in front of the new Hilton Hotel. One would have hoped that the Hilton would worry about a parking lot for buses, but that apparently is too much of an optimistic thought. Further delaying my arrival at work are the police barriers, protecting the visiting US Secretary of State and slowing traffic to a crawl.

At last the logjam is broken, and I almost reach my destination, when suddenly two drivers on opposite sides of the street meet by chance after a millennium of separation and begin an intense conversation. But finally, after quickly jumping out of their cars for an exuberant bear hug, they go on their way, and I, exhausted and fuming, pull into my parking lot, relieved that I finally made it to work. I get out of my car and head toward my office. I nod at the security guard, say hello to the receptionist and run up the stairs to my office. A sign is on the front door: "Office Closed." I look at my watch. It is 5 P.M. Time to return home!

Driving by Numbers

Because of the psychological trauma that driving in Israel has caused me, I now walk to and from work each day. Every day I pass one of the busiest intersections in the city of Jerusalem. After witnessing some unusual occurrences, I decided to place myself there for two hours during the morning rush of traffic and jot down my observations. I counted approximately 130 cars passing every five minutes, and had the opportunity to witness the behavior of 3,120 drivers.

My first jottings included a record 32 gridlocks. Those turning off the main road were in such a rush to make the light that they stopped their cars in the middle of the intersection so that on-coming traffic could not enjoy the green light.

In Israel, the law is clear that one can use the horn only to avoid a potential accident. I counted no less than 563 horn blasts over the two hours — not one blast initiated to prevent an accident. One may think that I am stretching the point by claiming it is in the area of horn blowing that Israelis truly display their schizophrenic tendencies. But a close examination of the quality of the horn blowing by Israelis will lend support to this thesis. My observances definitively indicate that the Israeli driver possesses a multitude of "honk" personalities. There is the driver who "sits on the horn" so that it sounds like a "t'kiah g'dola," the one long *shofar*[1] blast at the end of Yom Kippur. There is the staccato horn blower who sounds like a stuttering tuba player. There is the "faster than a speeding bullet" horn blower. He is the one who, well before the light turns green and whose car is fifth in line at the light, is already honking his horn — thus making Israel the only country in the world where "the speed of sound is faster than the speed of light!"

Whenever a driver has to turn left, he encounters a crosswalk with a blinking light, indicating that pedestrians have the right of way. Of the hundreds of cars that turned left, only six slowed down to check if someone might be crossing the street. On 12 occasions, drivers screeched to a halt to avoid hurling a pedestrian over the Dome of the Rock into the Dead Sea. In such cases, a honk on the horn would have been useful as well as legal. Each time the driver screamed at the pedestrian even though the latter had the right of way.

I also observed the exhaust factor. Not my exhaustion, rather the cars' exhaustion. There must be no emission standards in the country. The filthy smoke that streams forth from cars, trucks and especially buses (352 in all) was horrendous — poisoning the city environment. Speaking of ecological issues, 26 people threw trash from their cars, ranging from nut seeds to ashtrays full of cigarettes to plain old paper products. I counted 16 people who cast huge balls of throaty phlegm out their car window. Two joggers went sliding across the pavement on this less than appetizing human emission. (This was matched by 19 dogs, walked by their owners, relieving themselves on the sidewalk. Not a single dog-walker sported a "pooper-scooper." Here the pedestrians were a little more cautious because a dog leaves evidence of his presence that is far more prominent than that of someone's spit!)

113 people ran red lights. 26 drivers made illegal U-turns. I lost count of how many cars were speeding. 18 people had a bus door close in their face. Two people actually got caught in the door itself. 19 buses stopped substantially away from the bus stop. 58 people crossed the street illegally. Two drivers killed a cat, the first one wounding it and the second one killing it. 13 (a purely coincidental number) ran over the now very dead cat until a teenage boy shoveled it up.

Four people got out of their cars, holding up traffic, to argue some mundane point as to who was to blame for not letting someone traverse a lane. 67 people cut in from the left lane to make a right turn, while 83 people cut in from the right lane to make a left turn. (I hope that this is a reflection of a change in their political leanings.)

---

1. A ram's horn, which according to Jewish tradition was taken from the ram sacrificed in place of Isaac and passed on from Abraham to Moses, *(Genesis* 22). Even as it was sounded at Mount Sinai, so too it is sounded during Rosh HaShana and Yom Kippur.

31 learners irritated seasoned drivers, no doubt making up for a large percentage of those 563 horn honks. 17 drivers made creative gestures with their fingers. 22 people rolled down their windows to shout some obscenity at another driver or pedestrian. 37 people shook their fist at what seemed to be a slow or indecisive driver. Eight drivers squished their faces agonizingly, and five drivers brandished their thumb and forefinger in the shape of pistol. One figure saw 42 drivers with their cellular phones glued to their ears. How does one dial a number, apply the car brakes, activate the windshield wipers, smoke a cigarette, blast the horn and shift all at the same time? Some people had a speaker-phone in their car. If not, then at least 19 adults were talking to an imaginary friend. (My fantasy has always been that while stopped at a red light, I would lift up my cell phone, turn to the guy in the car next to me and say: "It's for you!")

I saw 23 people riding bicycles. Only three wore helmets. Two cyclists were actually talking on a cell-phone. Six parked cars were side-swiped. In each case the offending driver did not stop to see the damage caused or leave a note. I took down their license plate and left a note on the parked cars. Three drivers smashed into the cars in front of them. Incredibly, every one of these rear-enders blamed the driver of the car in front of them for stopping on too short a notice. 141 drivers tailgated, and a whopping 643 drivers failed to signal when turning. 44 school children darted between moving cars rushing to catch their bus, thus taking literally their parents urging "to go play in traffic."

What does my experience tell me? Nothing that most of us did not know already. An Israeli behind the wheel is indeed "schizophrenic," in that he poses a homicidal **and** suicidal threat at the same time. (Incidentally, I entered the number "0" only once the entire time. It was the number of policemen present at one of the busiest intersections in the world.)

Not the _Gallup_ Poll, but the _Gallop_ Poll

Before every Israeli election, surveys come out on an hourly basis. Some are objective, others are commissioned by a particular party. Given the failures of the predictions by the professional pollsters in the last few Israeli elections, one would be wise not to place too much stock in these hypothetical poll-takers.

I have developed a new brand of poll reading. I have it down to a science, and I can safely predict who will win any given prime ministerial race and which party will win the most

Knesset seats. My system is a particularly mobile one. In fact, it is so fast and seemingly reckless at times that one has to be extremely sure-sighted to keep up with it. Just like the time when I placed myself at that crowded intersection to gain a better insight into the Israeli psyche based on his driving habits, I did the same thing to measure the voting patterns of the general population.

The beauty of my system is that anyone can duplicate it. It can be done while walking or driving or riding the bus, or even gazing out of a house window. To put it into a Jewish context, one can conduct this survey "when you sit down in your house and when you walk on your way, when you lie down (possibly) and when you rise up" (*Deuteronomy* 6:7). The further beauty of this system is that you need not interact with other human beings to receive accurate results. No painstaking phone surveys are necessary. After all, with phone surveys, people can change their views as soon as they hang up. I guarantee that under my system, once someone has determined that he will vote a certain way, he will "stick" to it.

Growing up in the Sixties in America, we wore our political views on our bodies. Our clothes, especially our T-shirts, gave away our ideological leanings, not only with general slogans such as, "Make Love, Not War," but also with hard-core political expressions like, "Hey, Hey, LBJ, how many kids did you kill today?" A person who waved a placard with the latter rhyme was a sure bet to vote for Eugene McCarthy. If you had a bumper sticker that read: "America, Love it or Leave it," chances are you were going to vote for Richard Nixon.

And so, with this bit of historical time-frame as my backdrop, I will now reveal the incredible, yet basically simple system of poll taking: "Not the Gallup Poll, but the Gallop Poll." That's right. One has to **gallop** around Israel in order to predict the outcome of any Israeli election.

This is how it should be done. Instead of observing Israeli drivers at one busy intersection of one city, expand the lookout posts. One can observe Israeli voters by standing at a number of busy intersections throughout the country. Throw in a few development towns, kibbutzim, Arab villages (Druse and Bedouin included) and settlements (West Bank and the Golan). If one devotes considerable time to this effort, he can complete the survey in a two-week period at the most.

Check out the bumper stickers of the cars that pass by. Simultaneously, check out the brand of car that sports a particular bumper sticker. This is the only somewhat tricky part of the survey, but is critical to guarantee accuracy. Not all cars will have bumper stickers. But if one can figure out how many cars display which stickers, then one can guess the voting tendency of the same brand of non-stickered cars.

If Israeli drivers can display schizophrenic tendencies as indicated in the above section, well so can their cars. For example, Mitsubishi vans divide themselves almost equally into two contending political camps. The Mitsubishi has a "split chassis," so to speak. The owners either veer to the far left or the far right of the political spectrum. One sees stickers plastered on the back of these vans that read either "Hebron, Now and Forever" or "Peace Now with Syria." For fine-tuning, one must look at the additional bumper stickers. If the "Hebron" sticker also has the "The People with the Golan" next to it, then his vote will go to the right. Without this additive, the vote moves to the National Religious party.[1] If the "Peace Now" sticker has a "Goodbye, Friend"[2] sticker alongside it, the vote strays toward the Labor party;[3] without it, *Meretz*.[4]

Families who own Volvo station wagons, particularly older models, will vote for the ultra-Orthodox parties, because these Jewish voters have extremely large families and therefore need an ample size car like the Volvo station wagon. One must double the number of voters in this category because the ultra-Orthodox fly over in droves from Brooklyn to vote in a state they do not recognize. Owners of BMWs — 1971-1980 models — will invariably vote Likud,[5] as will owners of old Chryslers. This is because the Likud, being out of power for so many years, suffered from an inferiority complex, and the purchase of either a BMW or a Chrysler is seen as a status symbol.

The Arab parties have a lock on older Peugeot station wagons, because the French were always partial to their plight and the car could double as a transporter of goods to different places in the country. Former Russian refusenik,[6] Natan Sharansky, can count on the Skoda and Lada vote (a Czechoslovakian car and a Russian car). Ultra-Orthodox Sephardi sympathizers (or Shas voters) usually are found driving Isuzu "Na…Na…Nach…Nachman"[7] easy rider pick-up trucks. Many of these voters are blue-collar workers employed in construction and have a mystical bent to their religious views. The yuppie Mazda van clearly falls into the Labor party's lap as does the Volkswagon Beetle. Both, for different reasons, are generally owned by the upwardly mobile elements of society, which is the case with Labor

---

1. A right-wing Orthodox political party.
2. The slogan that Bill Clinton coined when he eulogized Yitzhak Rabin shortly after he was murdered.
3. The largest political party in Israel, originally professing a socialist agenda.
4. A left-wing party.
5. The second largest political party in Israel, right leaning.
6. Refers to those Jews of the former Soviet Union who refused to withdraw their application to immigrate to Israel and refused to temper their protests. They were oftentimes arrested, as was the case with Mr. Sharansky.
7. Rabbi Nachman of Bratslav, a small town in the Ukraine, is considered a spiritual and almost mystical Orthodox leader.

voters. The Renault also goes to Labor, because former party head Shimon Peres speaks a more sophisticated French than does *Gesher*[1] party leader David Levy, who garners the vote of the more plebian Citroen owners. As for the Subaru line, until the middle 1990s, one could count on their voting for the Likud party's candidate for prime minister, while the newer Imprezia, Grand Leone and Legacy model drivers tend toward the Labor party candidate. Labor voters are simply wealthier than Likud voters.

The parties that do not favor return of any territory get the tractor vote, as most of these people are settlers who claim to work the land. In the last elections, the Third Way party, whose platform called for the retention of the Golan Heights, got the Susita vote. The Susita, the only car ever manufactured in Israel, is now defunct. Since the Third Way party did not get enough votes to be elected to the Knesset, it is clear that Susita owners voted for it. The Daewoo reveals the only undecided voter. The car is too new on the Israeli market to give one an indication of how its owners would vote.

Motorcycles vote left, while motor scooters vote right, canceling each other out. American cars find their wealthy owners already abroad for a vacation during election time. Bicyclists, an iconoclastic lot by nature, will cast their votes for the more esoteric parties like the one that opposes a national income tax. Cab drivers, no matter what cars they drive, will vote for their very own Taxi party. Fiat voters never make it to the voting booth. Their cars are always in the shop.

Now, to predict election results, all one has to do is to figure out what bumper stickers go with which cars, and then go to the Registry of Motor Vehicles to find out how many cars of each make and model are on the road. Then average out the cars with bumper stickers proportionally to the number of cars of each make and model. It is so simple that one does not even have to employ the usual "margin of error."

According to this new format for polling, the results of any election will be clear, a forgone conclusion, an absolute reality. After predicting election results based on this infallible system, there will be no surprises. There will not be the usual split response on the part of the Israeli, who tells the pollster one thing and then upon entering the voting booth, says something else. The system does not allow for inconsistencies or contradictions. What you see is what you get. Perhaps this is the best cure-all for the schizophrenic voter. Plaster a sticker on someone's forehead that tells the world for whom he or she will vote. That individual may vote otherwise, but those who come into contact with that person will be

---

1. A moderate political party whose platform is primarily based on social issues.

convinced that the voter would never parade around with such a declarative statement of his or her voting preference if he or she were not completely "single-minded!"

Til' Death Do Us Part

In order to survive on the roads in Israel, one must maintain a sense of humor. This is true in most areas of life in Israel. Yet, the sad truth is that the catastrophic number of car accidents in Israel, so many resulting in deaths, is no laughing matter. There have been more deaths caused by traffic accidents in Israel than there have been deaths in all of the wars.

Before I was born, my 12 year-old sister was killed in a traffic accident. The year was 1939. For my parents, not a day went by that they did not think about her. Losing a child is the most painful of human experiences (See *Chapter 7*, page 155). Her death was useless, a waste of a human life. It was unfair and cruel.

Virtually every day, one hears of a fatal car wreck on Israeli roads. Yet it seems that almost every public and governmental outcry against this senseless carnage is met with more of the same. Nothing anyone does puts a halt to this terrible plague haunting Israeli existence. Truth to tell — nothing is done to try to stop it, except for the outcry. After a particularly tragic week, there is always an urgent rush of political activity on the "traffic front." But the deaths still continue. Words are cheap. Measures taken by the authorities to contain the situation are half-hearted. One gets the impression that the authorities responsible for road safety are more interested in public relations than they are in measures to reduce the outlandish amount of traffic fatalities. One is reminded of the steps taken to protect children on school trips after a rash of terrorist incidents in public places. A 65 year-old man, carrying an ineffective Czech M-1 rifle, is supposed to protect a class of third graders. It is ludicrous. Yet if anything should happen, the Ministry of Education could boast that the group had an armed guard.

Such is the case with traffic safety. After an especially calamitous week, police are put on the roads for a few days, and then disappear. There is talk of immediate prosecution of traffic violators, but most traffic citations take more than a year to process. This most certainly is the case with hidden cameras. Apparently it takes the Israeli bureaucracy a lifetime (or a life) to develop the film. Also many of Israel's highways, which desperately need widening, are subject to political considerations. A right-wing government diverts monies originally budgeted for the improvement of the road infrastructure to the building of settlements in the territories. Such a mercurial approach to matters of vital importance is all too typical of the state.

There has to be a drastic change in society regarding any and all aberrations of the traffic laws. People have to be reprimanded and/or punished appropriately for their actions. Too many Israeli drivers are "getting away with murder." On the roads, the national character is a selfish one. Each driver has to be the first in everything: the first to cause gridlock, the first to pass on the right, the first not to let someone into the line of traffic from a side street and the first to honk a horn at the person who is not traveling the speed limit. Israelis seem to adhere only to the first part of Hillel's great statement: "If I am not for myself, who will be for me?" But Israeli drivers should consider the second part: "If I am only for myself, what am I" (*Saying of the Fathers*, 1:14).

Israel needs a "declaration of war" on traffic accidents. There must be a mobilization of forces. Setting up more government committees or increasing fines is too cosmetic an approach. If the police are strapped for manpower, then soldiers should be trained to help out. There are many soldiers in marginal positions in the army who could well be utilized to combat the present insanity on the roads.

Anyone caught speeding, tailgating, weaving in and out, running red lights and stop signs should have his license suspended on the spot. Anyone involved in a traffic accident that causes injury or death should have a criminal file opened up against him, and should stand trial. Guilt or innocence would be determined like any criminal case. Since so many accidents involve commercial vehicles — taxis, trucks and buses — not only should the traffic offenders have their licenses revoked, but also their vehicles should be impounded; and the owner of the cab companies, trucking concerns and bus cooperatives should penalized.

Israel is in crisis. The deaths on the roads are a national tragedy, and sh be treated on a national level, as a national emergency. Television should broadcast the funerals of those killed. Details of the accidents should invade the comfort of one's living room. Government ministers should attend the funerals and visit the homes of those in mourning. The president and the prime minister should formally address the country. If they cannot find the time to do this, then the hundreds of families who have lost loved ones through senseless traffic accidents must "take to the streets" to protest, to make the whole subject part of the national consciousness. Perhaps their suffering can tame the selfish Israeli driver who takes his life and others' lives so callously into his hands. Those who have experienced the tragedy of a life taken in vain should take matters into their own hands before "death do us part."

In order to effectively erase this dreadful scourge and prevent a spread of this terrible disease, which has caused the double-edged sword of national suicide and homicide, there can be no division of opinion, only unanimity of thought and action.

e
he
be

ould

CHAPTER 10

THE PEOPLE OF THE BOOK

A Brief Background

The Jewish people are often referred to as the "People of the Book (Torah)." This stems from the biblical account of their historical development. Further, the Torah has served not only as a documentation of the historical progression of the Jews, but also as a spiritual, moral and ritual guide-book for their Divine faith, their religious practices and their ethical behavior. The Torah has been interpreted over the years and incorporated into a vast wealth of written commentary that serves to maintain and perpetuate Judaism and Jewish life. Jews are supposed to "live by the Book".

Because Jewish literature is so vast and all encompassing, as a people, Jews always put a great emphasis on learning. When ghettoized, the Jews stressed Jewish learning. The study of Jewish texts became a primary goal within the Jewish community. The learned individual, not the wealthiest or the oldest, was the most respected. As Jews integrated into the modern world, they extended this historical mandate and ingrained passion for learning to general areas of education. As a result, the number of Jews who have occupied high positions in many academic fields is totally out of proportion to their numerical strength on the world scene.

This concern for excellence in education should be an integral part of the political ethic of the Jewish nation-state. Indeed, Israelis are highly educated. There is virtually no illiteracy in Israel. This is a tribute to the state when one considers the number of immigrants it absorbed in its relatively short history and under what difficult circumstances this was done. To work with generally undereducated people from the Atlas Mountains of Morocco and the desert regions of Yemen, during a time when Israel was setting up its new state — all the while waging a war against eight Arab armies — and help them become literate was a truly remarkable feat.

As Israel grew as a state, it was pressured with the immediate needs of building a defense establishment to protect it from the continual aggression of an Arab world determined to destroy it. Also, the fledgling state, short of many natural resources, had to set the economy as one of its primary concerns. Social services and educational institutions, once the defining priorities of the Jewish people, were placed on a back burner.

Yet while Israel is a highly educated country, there has been a worrisome backsliding over the last number of years. This is complicated by a tripartite school system that includes a state secular school system, a state religious school system and a state sponsored independent school system (ultra-Orthodox). In addition there are variations of each school system that also add to the country's educational quilt.

Open schools, non-Orthodox religious schools (TALI),[1] kibbutz schools, youth villages, with their emphasis on agriculture, and military schools add to the creative potpourri of Jewish education in the State of Israel. Often it is difficult to set unified standards because the demands of each school system are so different.

The establishment of separate schools for the two predominant sectors of Israeli society, Orthodox (modern) and secular, was the political price that Israel's first prime minister, David Ben Gurion, had to pay to the *Mizrachi*[2] in order that he and his socialist coalition parties could establish a majority government. In retrospect, it is difficult to judge whether this division would prove necessary, because the two worlds would eventually go their separate ideological and educational ways, or whether the two-fold system contributed to the split in the nation based on secular and religious readings of the country's needs.

A third educational stream, that of the independent ultra-Orthodox school

---

1. A relatively new school system that, while under the auspices of the secular department of the Ministry of Education, was established by Jewish immigrants from North America. TALI is an acronym for "Jewish enrichment studies." It serves those Israelis who are interested in an education that includes religious studies, but in a manner that is persuasive, open and egalitarian.
2. A religious Zionist movement. Established in 1902, it amalgamated with its labor wing, forming the National Religious Party. It has participated in virtually every government as one of the coalition partners. It maintains a variety of cultural, religious, economic and educational institutions.

system, which is basically divided into several sub-systems, including the relatively new Ma'ayan educational system of the ultra-Orthodox Shas Sephardi party, adds to the educational maze in the country. Because one's educational training ultimately affects one's ideological outlook, each school system projects a different personality within the Israeli populace. An individual graduate of one particular school is likely to display a very one-dimensional and single-minded world-view. Therefore collectively, as one people, at best the image that is portrayed is one that is highly diversified. At worst, the picture that is drawn is one of a greatly split people, representing many sides of the same coin.

The Soaring Cost of "Free Education"

At the end of each month, I have an overdraft in my bank account of approximately $2,000. This overdraft has steadily grown over the years. I was always baffled as to why I had more days left at the end of the month than dollars. Did I suffer from a deficient education in the field of mathematics whereby I am now incapable of balancing my checkbook? But lo and behold, after years of being puzzled by this predicament, I finally figured it out — **free high school education**!

That's right. Until now, for the academic school year, on an average, I have spent on "compulsory free" education close to $4,000. There are times when the fee goes up — when I have to shell out an additional sum of money for the right of my children to take their matriculation examinations. And there are additional increases with each new academic year, which include registration fees. My estimate is that the final cost in one year for exposing my four children to Israel's version of free education will be about $6,000 (one does get a discount for each additional child in the school system).

I have broken this figure down in the hope of understanding what costs so much. After all, I pay taxes that I assume go partly to support the Education Ministry. I know that my taxes cannot include teachers' salaries. My wife is a teacher, and given the paltry remuneration she receives for full-time work, it does not play a role in my "school" overdraft.

I pay registration fees, school supply fees, Parent's Association fees and guard fees that amount to $850. Schools do not supply books, and so a family must purchase them for $600. I assiduously save my kids' books for reuse, but for some unknown reason, the reading lists change from year to year, thus denying me savings. I pay for enrichment programs, specialty programs, plays, performances, museum visits and ceremonies a total of $2,300. School trips and a week of voluntary work at a kibbutz or an army base amount to $1,600. (The rationale to pay for my kid to be afforded the privilege of working at a kibbutz or army base somehow has always escaped me.) Add another $650 for graduation examinations, and I reach the grand total of $6,000.

I would be more sympathetic to these out-of-pocket expenses if I felt that there was a decent educational exchange for them. However, the monies demanded of me do not go toward those areas that contribute to top-flight studies: increased teachers' salaries, better libraries, intramural sports, clubs (debating, drama, art, music, etc.), remedial aid and creative programming. Rather, upon inquiry, I am told that my payments are for the security guard who never seems to be on duty when I drop my children off at school; for the substitute teacher who never shows up when the regular teacher is on army reserve duty; for the "heating" in the winter that leaves my children shivering in class and wearing coats and half-gloves; or for the stencil machine that forces my children to read their assignments as if they were written in invisible ink.

While there are a number of new schools in the country, the physical state of too many schools is dreadful. In fact there have been a number of fatal accidents at schools because they did not satisfy the minimum safety requirements set up by the Ministry of Education. Where does money go if not to guarantee that the school my child attends will at least not have a ceiling that will collapse or a gas tank that will blow up?

My greatest fear is that my expenses are not over. My children are good students, but with the incredible competition to be accepted into the few universities in the country (count them on one hand plus a forefinger), they may have to pursue their studies in the far more expensive colleges that have recently cropped up or go abroad. I dread to think what my checkbook will look like then.

Something is wrong. A society can best be judged by the value it places on education, social welfare and health care. Because, as noted, these priorities are rather low on Israel's national agenda, the burden falls upon the individual to subsidize the tax system so that he can guarantee minimal standards of service and attention. But there is a financial breaking point even for the most caring person, as well as the inequality in educational opportunity that such a system creates. The economically deprived elements in society can never afford these fees, which should be covered by taxes.

Israel's children are its future. In educating them, Israelis place their trust in the state, as is the case with any nation. The reason that Israeli law makes schooling compulsory is that the state also believes education is one of the Jewish people's highest values. But when parents are asked to pay for compulsory free schooling, beyond their tax allotment, it means that the state is abusing that trust, diverting public funds to other priorities that may very well be of dubious worth. Like any citizen in any country, Israelis want to know how their tax dollars are being spent. Certainly that is the question an Israeli asks when seeing the five-year seventy million dollar subsidy that the Israeli government has promised to give to "Birthright" in order to bring a college student from Beverly Hills to Israel for free (See *Chapter 6*, "Israel as the Jewish People's Birthright," pages 142-149).

Israel's national poet laureate, Haim Nachman Bialik wrote: "A school is the workshop of the nation's soul." The budgetary agenda of a nation reflects that nation's values. Israel's investment in education is the best down-payment it can make to guarantee the preservation of the soul of the Jewish state.

School Overload: A Factory Approach to Education

As stated in the introduction to this chapter, Israelis are highly educated. The scholarship and research that takes place in the country is truly impressive, especially if one takes into consideration the size of Israel. In the fields of math and sciences, as well as in technology (particularly in the area of hi-tech studies), Israelis are among the leaders in the world. Also in the field of the arts and humanities, Israelis have distinguished themselves. Yet Israelis should not rest on their academic laurels. Not always is cognition translated into healthy decisions.

One of the first personal liturgical petitions, which a Jew prays three times a day, touches upon the relationship between knowledge and practicality. "You favor 'Adam' with knowledge, and teach to human beings understanding. Share with us a portion of Your knowledge, understanding and insight (common sense). Blessed are You, Lord, Who graces us with knowledge" (*Prayer book*). **Knowledge** has to be internalized for **understanding** to take place. But both cognition and comprehension need the additive of **common sense**, which is often the product of one's personality. This prayer presents the well-rounded individual as the model of an educated person.

It is here that one sometimes witnesses a gap between what Israelis know and understand, and what they do. Their knowledge may be a mile wide, but their practical application of that knowledge may be an inch deep. In judging an individual, one must not only look at that person's wealth of knowledge, but also at his or her strength of character, breadth of experience and measure of commitment.

Here is a list of the courses that my child takes at her high school: Math, Geometry, Biology, Chemistry, Talmud, Bible, Literature, Grammar, English, Arabic, History, Geography, Civics, Liturgy, Education and Physical Education. Yes, count them. Sixteen different disciplines. Of course, each one is sub-divided. For example, English includes grammar, composition and literature; Bible and Talmud naturally include all the commentaries. In short, my kid has to be a virtual logistics genius in order to figure out not only what her weekly academic schedule is, but what and where her next class will be.

As the marking period comes to its conclusion, the teachers go into their usual end of the term panic, and set a test schedule that would break the intellectual will of Stephen Hawkins. In a week's span, my daughter will be tested in Literature, Math, Biology, Geography and Chemistry. She will have to submit papers in Bible, English and Talmud. She will also have quizzes in Arabic and grammar. All this is in addition to her regular assignments with which she has to contend.

She returns from school after three in the afternoon. She barely has time to sit down, before she is off and running to outside activities. More often than not, these extra-curricular activities are far more significant than what goes on at her school.

Like many kids her age, my daughter is active in a youth movement and in one creative activity, jazz dance lessons. Her youth movement has her serve as a counselor for younger kids once a week and participate in a leadership-training program once every other week. Her dance-troupe meets twice a week and has numerous performances. Each performance requires additional hours of practice. As a parent, I do not want to deny her these interests. And, since her high school does not offer her such possibilities, it is only natural that she goes elsewhere for this necessary enrichment. (Also my daughter's school has an uncanny way of scheduling a test for the day after she and her friends return from a weekend youth movement trip. This is difficult to comprehend since she belongs to a youth movement that is officially sponsored by her school.)

So what happens is that she needs to burn the midnight oil in order to complete her homework. Add to this the fact that "zero hour" exists in Israel's high schools, which forces my daughter (and me) to get up before dawn to get ready for school. Those disadvantaged students who live in an outlying suburb may just as well stay up all night, because the interval of time between going to bed after they finish their homework and getting up in the morning is infinitesimal.

While teachers work a five-day school week, our children have to contend with a six-day school week. A child needs to unwind every so often. When every evening, except Friday evening, is a school night, this need can never be met. "Table for Five" is a high school kid's favorite TV show. Add to this a couple of other teenage shows, and surely the desire for a child to watch three TV shows a week is not unreasonable. God forbid she would want to see the news!

Overburdened with additional tests, quizzes and papers, it is little wonder that she is sick, exhausted or angry at a system that seems factory-like. And the situation will only get more intense, as she begins her matriculation schedule when she will need to regurgitate years of material. And she sadly knows, should she want to attend one of Israel's universities, she will be judged exclusively by the mathematical combination of her matriculation test results and her psychometric examination scores. Such a system discourages a child from participating in those extra and co-curricula activities that are so important for human development and growth.

I am reminded of the time that I returned from a sabbatical in the United States. My oldest daughter, then in the ninth grade, had to take a standardized test prior to her continuation in high school. A few months after the test, my daughter and I were invited to a meeting with the school counselor, where we discussed the results of the test, or better yet, where my daughter was told what she should do with the rest of her life.

The counselor was surprised that she did so well in the English, but only fair in Hebrew. Of course, having grown up in an English-speaking home (and having spent one year in an American school), would make her English accomplishments understandable. The year's absence explained her performance in Hebrew-related subjects. She did quite well in the math and sciences. And so the conclusion was that she might want to consider transferring to a vocational school, although we were reassured that she would be capable of doing passing work in a strictly academic setting. She was advised, however, that should she opt for an academic tract, she should lean heavily on the math and sciences.

At that suggestion, my daughter and I burst into hysterics. She barely tolerates math and science, and never performed particularly well in those subjects. When asked what we found so humorous, my reply was a simple one: "This is a great test if one does not take into account the personality of the individual taking the test!" Years later, my daughter finished her academic high school with above average grades, and with high scores in her psychometric exams.

Yet with all this (and despite the dire predictions of her ninth grade school counselor), educationally her personality is still a secondary consideration. After the army, my daughter decided to apply to the Hebrew University in Jerusalem. Nowhere in the application process was there any room for a personal recommendation and/or interview. She was interested in sociology and Jewish studies. As far as the university was concerned, it mattered little that she was a social worker in the army, that she volunteered at a hospital for physically disabled children or that she attended a religious school. What mattered was not who she was, but rather the combined output of her matriculation exam and her psychometric tests.

Israeli education has a tendency to judge a student exclusively by objective criteria: his performance on this test or that matriculation examination. The "grade" becomes the sum total of an individual's capability and worth. Under such a system, the goal is to "teach the material" rather than to "teach the child." But many kids do not perform well on standardized tests, yet their work ethic is such that they manage to do quite well in school. One should not deny that these tests may be an indicator of either potential growth or stagnation; however the negative influences far outweigh the positive ones. (In many countries these standardized tests are being phased out because of the prejudicial nature of the tests. Wisely, Israel is also considering canceling its matriculation examination program.) The same tests are administered to all layers of a population without regard for economic, social, cultural or ethnic backgrounds. Once taken, the results can stigmatize a child.

An overly objective, and thus oftentimes callous, reading of test results can be devastating to one's self-confidence. It tears away at one's motivation, and puts undue pressure on the individual. A bright child with undiagnosed dyslexia might be rendered an idiot; a child with an unnoticed attention span deficit would be considered a failure; and a child two years out of the country might be labeled a moron. And of course, a child who comes from a disadvantaged family may score poorly on such a test, but with the proper encouragement and tutorial aid might succeed quite satisfactorily in school. Dry test results simply lead to a self-fulfilling prophecy whereby kids from problematic social backgrounds would be doomed to failure. Given that there is so much working against children in a difficult home environment, schools should not exacerbate an already problematic family structure.

A child's personality, history, interests, character traits, life experiences, everyday performances, hobbies, inter-personal relationships, psychology, family background and social environment should fashion the criteria for judging children. Children should be treated as human beings, rather than as a statistic resulting from an out-dated prejudicial evaluative process. Educationally, Israel's school system has become antiquated, and as a result it stresses grades more than creativity; performance more than values. It is a bureaucratic maze that leaves little time for the child to think, play, develop and yes, relax once in a while, so at a later date that same child will be able to join an Israeli adult community, which perhaps is too tense and intense for its own good.

A "dry" academic approach to learning bypasses a value-oriented approach to learning, that which shapes the very nature of a society. Given the steady erosion of moral leadership in the country, the rise in verbal and physical violence and the increase in self-protectionism (selfishness), it is vital that Israel cease using schizophrenic methods to educate its children. It must learn to educate the **whole** person, not all his **individual** parts.

Israel must overhaul its educational system so teachers teach children and not courses. This is particularly important as the high school in Israel also serves a unique and vital purpose: to help students reach a mental place in their lives where they will be ready to serve in the army. (Upon graduation from high school, virtually all Israelis must serve between two to three years in the army. The exception is those from the ultra-Orthodox community.) This is particularly important because Israel has been faced lately with what has been termed, "a motivation factor." A number of surveys report how many high school graduates sign up for elite fighting units, how many make a career out of the army and how many report for reserve duty. According to all the surveys the numbers have taken a slow, but steady, downward slide.

One reason was the Lebanon War. The war caused great dissension. For many Israelis it seemed the war was waged for a political ideology that had no clear consensus among the general populace. Israel's long presence in Lebanon, with the almost daily deaths of young Israeli soldiers reported, added to the unwillingness of Israelis to serve in Lebanon. Once the government decided to withdraw from Lebanon, even citing a specific date for withdrawal, there was naturally a sharp decrease in the motivation to serve there. No one wanted to be the last casualty in an obviously lost cause. Added to this were the many protest groups against Israel's involvment in South Lebanon, not just the "Four Mothers against the War,"[1] but also officers, including those in Yesh G'vul (see *Chapter 3*, page 84, footnote 1) who refused to serve in Lebanon.

A second reason was the Intifada. The army was turned into a police force. Chasing rock-throwers in the nooks and crannies of Palestinian villages was humiliating. Trying to maintain order over two million hostile Arabs was untenable. After the initial troop withdrawals from much of the West Bank and the Gaza Strip, it became extremely dangerous for many soldiers to guard Jewish settlements that numbered only a few people. Few soldiers were motivated to protect a handful of "fanatic" settlers in the heart of the Gaza Strip or a half-a-dozen yeshiva students at Joseph's tomb in Palestinian Nablus.

In addition, it would be misleading not to include sociological developments in Israeli society that also influence the motivation of young people to serve in the army. The world has grown smaller, and young Israelis are witnesses to freedoms of other Western societies. They too, at a young age, want to begin their university life, travel the world and start earning a living. Additionally, cynicism has set in regarding national commitment, especially when so many in the ultra-Orthodox community do not serve in the army, thereby not fulfilling any type of national service. Also when young Israelis see too many of their

---

1. An a-political group of mothers of soldiers who served in Lebanon who protested Israel's continued presence there.

political leaders, those who would decide on whether to send them into war, getting away with every manner of dishonest behavior, they are not inclined to put themselves out for their country, let alone risk their lives. When increasing numbers of high school graduates seem to succeed in avoiding mandatory army duty for the flimsiest of reasons, the average teenager who willingly enters the army sees himself as a "sucker."

Despite these reasons, and even in light of the increasing number of young Israelis who either avoid army service or go in without much enthusiasm, the vast majority of young Israelis serve with distinction, accepting the responsibility with equanimity. To reach those who are truly lacking in motivation, it is incumbent on those in the political echelon to institute policies that have a national consensus, and it is also essential for those in the educational sphere to help their students express their feelings in a creative and open manner. This can only be done when each student is treated with respect.

There is a natural affinity between teacher and student in Israel because they have in common similar experiences, especially in regard to the army. A generation gap between these two populations is virtually non-existent and often there is an aura of informality between them. Yet at that sensitive stage in a young Israeli's life, when faced with life and death situations, a student should not be burdened with highly pressured matriculation examinations. A decade ago, maybe one could get away with ignoring the emotional and psychological needs of a student, but in view of Lebanon, the Intifada and an open world community, this is no longer feasible or desirable. No one in Israel wants to see a "Vietnam Syndrome" develop, which caused soldiers who returned from America's war in Southeast Asia to become psychologically dysfunctional. With the majority of young people serving in the army, Israel needs not only sane soldiers, but also whole persons who will make the transition from army life to civilian life with maturity and stability.

"Three Strikes, You're Out"

A little more than thirty years ago, in 1968, students around the world set off massive protests. In France, Germany, England, Canada, South America and the

United States, mass protests took place to highlight the injustices prominent in each society and the many abuses perpetrated the world over. This international "student movement" bypassed Israel's student population. It was understandable. Coming off the Six-Day War, Israelis simply wanted to return to a normal and unpressured routine, which even then was difficult, as the war was followed by two years of the "War of Attrition," and then the Yom Kippur War in 1973.

Because of their two to three year stint in the army, immediately following graduation from high school, Israelis begin their university studies later than their counterparts around the world. Many have to support themselves and have little time for political activity. It also should be noted that most events, fads and trends that occur elsewhere in the Western world usually reach Israel a decade later. With the advent of cable TV and computers, the time lapse has been reduced, but in the Sixties Israeli students did not have the advantage of "instant replays."

Another important factor in understanding the student protests of the Sixties, and later protests in places such as Tienanman Square (Beijing) and Indonesia, was that they all were "other-directed." Students expressed concerns of social and political worth: equal rights, human rights, nuclear disarmament, environmental balance, economic justice, etc. In Israel, when the student population finally rose in protest, striking their classes, it was not for the greater good of society, but rather for a parochial concern — reducing the cost of tuition. While they went on strike, they mouthed the universal student phrases of creating a "social revolution," but even here it was directed toward volunteering in various areas of Israeli life so as to receive credits toward their tuition. One must not discount the incredible sacrifice Israeli students make for their country by giving so much time to the army, even doing reserve duty during their university studies. They truly are willing to risk their lives. It is precisely because of this sacrifice that one would expect the student population in Israel to take the lead in fashioning a socially progressive and egalitarian society for which they put their lives on the line.

Yet one rarely sees students participate in protest rallies as a defined student population. One rarely encounters a student contingent protesting police brutality that has been unleashed not only against them, but also against Peace

Now demonstrators, Women in Green demonstrators,[1] Israeli Arabs, ultra-Orthodox Jews or Palestinians. Where are the students when it comes to holding a "street theatre" to protest prejudicial treatment of Ethiopians, a march through the major cities to call attention to the 500,000 Israelis living below the poverty line, or lying down before bulldozers to prevent another Palestinian home from being demolished? More telling, why were there so few students at the forefront of the protests against remaining in Lebanon, considering that so many of them were affected by Israel's prolonged stay there?

In short, it was to be expected that all the student strikes in favor of lower tuition costs would eventually fold. Without a cause beyond themselves, ultimately the students realize that staying out of school hurts them more than it hurts the country. If they fight for someone else's rights, they continue the battle until the wrongs are addressed (i.e., until Sukharno was sent packing, or until African-Americans were registered to vote, or until America pulled out of Vietnam).

It is too bad that so many student protests in Israel fail, especially since their cause is just. Given the fact that Israeli students spend so many years in the army, they should be able to get a free education. Indeed, Israel should adopt an open-admission policy.

Israeli secular students must be entitled to the same educational advantages that Yeshiva boys, who do not serve in the army, are entitled — at the taxpayer's expense (ironically including taxes of the students themselves). The "People of the Book" should not turn higher education into an elitist possibility. Yet if students want to achieve their own rights, they first must act on behalf of others. Only then will they succeed in staying the course.

Every one in Israel knows on what side of the women's issue former Knesset member, education minister, and founder of the political party Meretz, Shulamit Aloni, stands, just as they know the viewpoints of her successor, Yossi Sarid. Both built their political careers championing the underdog. In Ms. Aloni's case,

---

1. A woman's organization with right-wing leanings that opposes the return of West Bank territories to the Palestinians and the return of the Golan Heights to Syria.

she seemed to be ahead of her time in promoting the indivisible concept of gender equality.

Whenever there was discrimination against women, she and her party were at the forefront to rectify it. When the "Women at the Wall"[1] were denied their minyan, she spoke of the universality of the Wall for all Jews. When women are relegated to a secondary role in matters of personal status,[2] she went after the religious establishment. When women were used as sex objects in advertising, she vigorously campaigned against such crass exploitation. All those who believe in the equality of the sexes were ecstatic when she became the minister of education during Yitzhak Rabin's term as prime minister. It was expected that she would continue in her tenacious struggle to attain full equality for women.

Indeed, her crusade for religious pluralism was partly predicated on her abhorrence of the separation of the sexes that is so endemic to the Orthodox world. Because of the power of Orthodoxy within Israel's body politic, she felt any halachic belittling of women would only serve to institutionalize a condescending attitude toward the female of the species in all areas of Israeli society. Shulamit Aloni, who represented the Israeli female in virtually every international women's forum, gave Jewish women around the globe a sense of pride. More significantly, her defense of Jewish women pushed her to greater universal heights, as she became the defender of all those who suffered discrimination — racial minorities, the poor, the homeless, gays and lesbians, non-Orthodox religious Jews, Palestinians. She bequeathed this legacy to those in her party who came after her, and for the most part, Meretz has remained true to this ideological charge.

And then came one of the many teachers' strikes, and suddenly Aloni and her party's image became tarnished. The teaching profession in Israel is a female profession, as is the social service field (social workers) and the health service field (nurses). It is not possible for a teacher (woman) to support a family on the meager remuneration given her. But why should it be any different when in Israel a man is considered the "breadwinner" and the principle authority in the family structure? For example, dependents are taxed on a

---

1. An ad hoc group of observant Jewish women who want equal access to the Wall.
2. A reference to issues of divorce, marriage, inheritance, conversion, etc., which are adjudicated by the religious (Orthodox) establishment in Israel.

husband's salary and not on the wife's. Property jointly owned is first registered in the husband's name. Matters of inheritance or divorce give priority to a husband's demands. Therefore, it is no accident that teachers' salaries are embarrassing low. After all, teachers are mostly women. If the teaching profession were dominated by men, the story would be quite different.

The teachers, nurses and social workers seem to be frequently on strike. The entire female population should stage a massive protest, which would include those who have not achieved political parity, those who have been denied managerial positions, and those who are subject to harassment. The insulting salary that teachers earn is indicative of an overall humiliation that women suffer. This tragic fact returns us to Ms. Aloni, the "woman's woman," and her party successors. Because of their access to political power, they have come down on the wrong side of every teachers' strike. They always seem to defend management, a male institution. Instead, they should be joining in the strikes, handing in their cabinet resignations to protest a societal world-view that discriminates against women.

If political leaders like Shulamit Aloni and Yossi Sarid do not join the picket lines when the teachers go on strike, they will forfeit their roles as the defenders not only of women, but also of all those who are downtrodden in the country. This is what the teachers' strikes are all about — the abuse of the underclass, of which the teachers, as women, are but one element.

A Brief Conclusion

There is a basic faith in the effectiveness of schooling and its influence on a nation's culture and beliefs. The hopes for Israel's educational goals ran very high because the State Education Law of 1953 was based on: "values of Jewish culture and the achievement of science, of love of the homeland, and loyalty to the Jewish state and the Jewish people, on practice in agricultural work and in handicraft, on pioneering training, and on striving for a society built on freedom, equality, tolerance, mutual assistance, and a love of mankind."

In his book, *Israeli Democracy-The Middle of the Journey,* Professor Daniel Shimshoni writes: "There is a widespread faith in the effectiveness of schooling and in the influence of teaching on culture and beliefs. Since the early days of the *Yishuv*[1] schools have been expected to transmit Hebrew culture. The schools are asked to preserve Jewish values in a secular world and to help close the distance between Jews in Israel and those in the Diaspora. More intellectual depth and understanding of Zionism, of Judaism, of the Bible, of the Talmud, of Jewish history, and of the Diaspora communities could, it is hoped, bring Israeli children into the stream of Jewish culture and experience. Against this goal are marshaled the dominant culture of the secular Western world; the rejection of the exile in many Zionist ideas; the desire to build a new Jew, and the political and cultural separatism of Orthodoxy... Emphasis on achievement and with it the seeking of equality of opportunity, or at least the universal attainment of minimum standards, has become of much greater concern than left or right ideology."[2]

Over the years, something has gone awry. Like in too many aspects of Israeli life, there is a substantial gap between the ideal and the reality. Israel wants to go in one direction but often winds up going in the opposite one; or it gets to a fork in the road and chooses to follow both paths. Students, teachers and politicians straddle both sides of the fence. Secular schools promote an ideological world-view that competes with the theological world-view of the Orthodox schools. All the while, the ultra-Orthodox schools pull a growing segment of the population in a more ecstatic, almost other-worldly direction creating a "brief encounter of a third kind."

Can Israel's educational system thus be defined as clinically ill? It would seem that the deep divisions within the Israeli school system is the stuff of a real schizophrenic approach to learning and nurturing. It is not as if there are variations on one theme, or as if there is one overall guiding philosophy of education in the country, with different routes to reach the same destination. There are competing philosophies. Harmonizing these different philosophies requires a team of highly trained specialists. They will have to sift through the multitude of educational options in order to return to the original goal of Jewish education in Israel as defined in the State Education Law of 1953: "striving for a society built on freedom, equality, tolerance, mutual assistance, and a love of mankind."

---

1. Reference to the Jewish entity in Palestine during the pre-state years.
2. *Israeli Democracy — The Middle of the Journey,* Daniel Shimoni, Free Press, 1982, pages 321-322.

CHAPTER 11

ISRAEL: THE WORLD'S SCAPEGPOAT

To Feel Good, Fault the Jews

Not only does Israel suffer from schizophrenic tendencies, but it also arouses schizophrenic reactions. As an illness, "schizophrenia" does not include a will to be malicious. The result of schizophrenic behavior may be such that the "schizophrenic individual" may act in a malicious manner. This certainly is not intentional, but rather a byproduct of the illness. Within the international arena, Israel occupies a very strange position. It still garners great support and sympathy, not only because it came into existence on the heels of the Holocaust, but also because it built a model democratic society in the midst of a regional panorama that includes feudal states, religious sheikdoms, dictatorships, monarchies and military-run nations.

It is only natural, as Israel would develop and grow, that the initial idealism on which it was founded would become more difficult to maintain as the reality of running a country set in. As Israel enters into its second half century, it is clear that the country did not live up to the utopian ideals it set for itself and that the world expected of it. Israel may indeed have yearned for the "impossible dream," harkening back to God's demand for Jewish people to become "a holy nation." As difficult as it is, Israel should disregard the double standards that the world applies to it, because it basically asked to be judged by a single standard, one based on a prophetic vision of social justice and equality. As for the nations of the world, they should first balance themselves on the same moral scale on which they weigh Israel. While disappointments abound, any objective analysis would determine, that given the harsh realities Israel faces, it dwarfs many Western countries in its openness, creativity and willingness to sacrifice for the sake of creating a better Middle East, first and foremost for itself, and then for its Arab neighbors.

It is not only that other countries express their disappointment in Israel, but also Diaspora Jews do. Here there is a real case of schizophrenic judgments. Israel is supposed to become the "surrogate" for the Diaspora Jew. This type of Diaspora Jew is best referred to as the "vicarious Jew," as opposed to the "alimony Jew." The "alimony Jew" says: "I'll pay for it just so I don't have to live with it!" The "vicarious Jew" says numerous things: "Better you than me; you should do it better than me; you do it instead of me!" Diaspora Jews are not only disappointed, but are appalled when their Israeli "co-religionist" travels on the Sabbath to eat in a restaurant. Israelis are expected to be "religious," in order to compensate for their New York Jewish cousins' traveling on Rosh Hashana while eating a ham and cheese sandwich with their non-converted Sufi spouse.

Next to the Unites States, the largest concentration of international media is in Israel. The obvious reason that Middle East reporting is centered in Jerusalem or Tel Aviv is that it would never receive in the Arab countries the freedom it enjoys in Israel. Because virtually every Israeli action comes under an international microscope, there is always something about Israel that is reported in the world press. There is a media obsession with Israel. The obsession is so total that it should be classified as "OCD," an obsessive-compulsive disorder. The hypocrisy of focusing on Israel's every little foible, while often ignoring serious faults of others, is a sure sign of psychological illness. With such a media obsession, it is always challenging for an Israeli to travel abroad because he may immediately be attacked for what is happening in his country.

I was not very eager to go on one of my brief trips to the United States, because it came on the heels of the universal uproar over Israel's deportation of 415 Palestinians to Lebanon. They were suspected of being involved in or carrying out terrorist acts. I did not look forward to turning on American TV news or reading American newspapers, where the issue would be the focus of all international reportage. But to my surprise, the furor had died down and no longer dominated the attention of the news media. But no more than two days had passed when other items on Israel appeared. None of them struck me as being in any way newsworthy.

One item detailed the controversy surrounding the candidacy of Rabbi Yisrael Lau for the position of one of the Chief Rabbis of Israel. The news item highlighted rumored vignettes of his alleged womanizing (none of which was true). Another article dealt with Professor Uzi Even's quasi-dismissal from the army following his disclosure that he was a homosexual.

On the scale of world events, these two items did not warrant any news coverage. They may have been good human-interest stories, but only for a local community, not for the international one. So why the media obsession with Israel? The truth may be that it is not so much an obsession with Israel as it is a fixation on the Jewish people. Obviously, since the largest concentration of Jews can be found in Israel, it is the most accessible target for focusing on Jews and, more significantly, on Jewish behavior. In a Judeo-Christian world, Jewish "moral" actions in Israel often become the yardstick to measure one's own ethical conduct.

A non-Jew does not want to be judged by Jewish behavior. Therefore, it is incumbent upon the world community to monitor Jewish behavior and condemn it if necessary, in order to protect its sense of moral and religious self-righteousness. Those who condemn another's actions feel they are elevating their own standard of behavior. Every time Israel is roundly criticized, other nations feel a sense of superiority. This sense of superiority is necessary because the behavior of other countries in so many parts of the world is a legitimate subject for harsh judgment. If Israel deports 415 Palestinians or kills rioters in the territories, then capital punishment for a murder/rapist in Texas or the shooting death of some protesting students in Indonesia is relatively not so bad.

If America has been less than enlightened regarding homosexuals serving in the US armed forces (despite President Clinton's promises that things would be different), then the *Washington Post* is called upon to point out that Israel's treatment of Professor Even and other gays in the Israeli army is far more severe, even if this contention is a blatant falsehood. If Bill Clinton was a bit wayward in his relationships, then the *New York Times* feels a need to address the alleged sexual trysts of Israel's chief rabbi, as unfounded and ludicrous as the reportage may be. In short, a country's media can excuse, if not justify, its own shortcomings by doing a little comparative shopping at the Jewish mall, Israel.

If Jews, who purport to be a "kingdom of priests," fail, then a little backsliding on the part of other peoples is understandable, even acceptable. And if the world focuses on Israel ad nauseam, it is bound to uncover a myriad of foibles, weaknesses and immoral actions on the part of the Jewish people. What country, under far less pressurized circumstances, could undergo the microscopic examination under which Israel is placed and not come up with its own foibles, weaknesses and immoral actions? Syria's media and its highest government officials routinely direct the most inflammatory rhetoric at Israel, often accusing it of being a "Nazi" state. Yet when Israel's foreign minister gives a heated speech threatening the Arabs for real attacks that have killed Israelis, he is condemned in a manner that far outstrips the condemnation directed at Arab countries for far worse statements. The response is that Israel is not expected to behave "that way." No such expectations are extended to the Syrians, even if their vitriolic anti-Semitism results in terrorists attacks against Israelis or katyusha rockets ripping through a town in the north of Israel.

Jewish frailty has always made the world feel good. Indeed, Israel has committed some acts of which it should be ashamed. Yet they are not that shameful when compared to what is done in the rest of the world (although Israel should not draw comfort from this sad fact). Since the Jewish people has been at the center of world controversy from time immemorial, their behavior, as acted out in the modern state of Israel, becomes the focal point of the international community's mouthpiece — the world media. It is unfair, obsessive, prejudiced, and possibly even anti-Semitic.

Accentuate the Positive

Often there is a direct link between public relations and public policy. The public relations fallout for some of Israel's political decisions can be devastating. Given the double standards applied to Israel, the country's leaders should be particularly sensitive as to how its policy decisions are translated into the world's perception of the Jewish state. Some cases in point were mentioned above: Israel's deportation of 415 Palestinians, the inflamed rhetoric of its foreign minister. Also some of the more blatant human rights violations in the territories seriously compromised Israel's international standing as a progressive democratic state. Other political realities that have tarnished Israel's image include the distasteful specter of coalition horse-trading with over eager ultra-Orthodox parties, the lack of religious pluralism, and the absence of accountability on the part of political leaders, many of whom have been and are currently being investigated for alleged criminal shenanigans.

For these reasons and more, coupled with the aforementioned obsession with Israel that puts it through "media hell," Israel takes a public relations beating. News of any sort of oppression, military excesses or political corruption always captures the headlines. Bad news is newsworthy. Good news, even if it reflects the true character of a nation or a people, rarely qualifies for even a footnote in either the electronic or print media. It is here that Israel suffers unfairly. A negative public image flows easily from negative events. The converse is not the case. A positive public posture for enlightened policies requires a public relations effort, something that is sorely lacking in Israel.

It is difficult to understand Israel's failure in this area. Israel's paranoia is very real. It is held accountable in ways that the rest of the world is not. The United Nation passes its infamous resolution that "Zionism equals Racism" (only repealed years later), ignoring real racism that existed and still exists in so many other countries. While not justifying in any way Israel's treatment of the Palestinians during the height of the Intifada, in comparison to America's treatment of its African-Americans citizens, Israel looks quite good. (It was not until 1964 and 1965 that African-American were granted full rights.) Yet, much of the world really does not like Israel, some in a most visceral manner. So Israel has to work hard to stress the positives that are so much a part of the country.

Israel is the opposite of some of the world's perception of it. It is not an extreme occupying and colonial nation. It is far more democratic than many other countries in the free world. Given the hostilities to which it is subjected, it merits kudos for remaining such an open society. For example, what other nation would tolerate a delegation from another country, with which it is technically at war, to call for its destruction from its own capital? One might fault Israel's government for having allowed some Libyans such a public forum. Indeed it does smack of real schizophrenic tendencies to tolerate such a contradiction. Still it was not stupidity that prompted Israel to host a Libyan economic delegation, but rather a desire (perhaps naive) to seek a dialogue that might lead to peace. This reality should he turned into a public relations coup.

Almost daily, one hears that the "greatest and most free" country in the world, the United States, has implemented capital punishment. Israel has no capital punishment (except for Nazis war criminals). Terrorists can kill twenty-one schoolchildren on a class trip, murder travelers on public buses and stab Israelis to death at random, and the severest sentence they can receive is life imprisonment. What an incredible testimony to a humane society! Why does not the world judge Israel according to this noble policy?

Communists sit in the Knesset, some of whom identify with Israel's sworn enemies. Israel recognizes "spousal" rights of homosexual and lesbian couples. The list of enlightened practices is never-ending. While Western Europe, as well as America, clamps down on immigration, Israel continues to open its doors, not only to Jews (including black ones), but also to Moslem Bosnians; and in the past to Vietnamese boat people. And of course the ultimate expression of Israel's openness was the transfer of all of Sinai back to Egypt for a peace treaty, its complete withdrawal from Lebanon, its basic agreement to transfer the vast majority of the territories to the Palestinians, and a clear willingness to do the same on the Syrian front. No other country in the world, attacked as mercilessly as Israel has been, would have taken such risks. Why did, for example, Egypt garner more public relations credits than Israel? The world is still awaiting the United States to return land stolen from Native Americans.

Israel must go on the offensive. It may choose not to alter some public policies even if it means negative public exposure. But it must put into operation a public relations apparatus that will rid the world of the notion that Israel is a repressive society. There are some Israeli policies that unfortunately reinforce this view. But for the most part, Israel can take pride in its expression of freedom and progressiveness. In this area, Israel must coordinate its actions with its image. It must help the nations of the world see it through a clear lens, not a cloudy one that produces distorted images.

It must also guarantee that the nations of the world judge it by the same criteria by which they judge others. Finally, Israel must rid the nations of the world of its schizophrenic reportage of the country. No longer should the nations of the world accuse Israel of what they consider wrongful actions, while allowing other countries the luxury of getting away with similar misdeeds — misdeeds for which Israeli is so readily condemned.

CHAPTER 12

A COLLAGE

Life's Frustrations

confessions of an israeli red sox fan

I dreamed I had died and gone to heaven. I am certain that I experienced the "Olam HaBa" (the world to come). There can be no other explanation.

On one Sunday evening, in my suburban Jerusalem home, I sat glued to the TV set — first watching my hometown Boston Celtics play the Utah Jazz on one channel, and at the game's conclusion, the same cherished team face the Philadelphia 76er's on another channel. All the while, I was chomping on M&Ms, washed down by a Miller Lite — neither brought to me via a care package from America, but purchased at my local grocery store. From the time I moved to Israel almost thirty years ago, I had lived through a seemingly endless drought of "true-blooded" American sports. So who would have believed that this would be my new reality? Israel is truly the land of miracles.

After that Celtic double-header, I went to bed feeling like a zombie, as I had sat mesmerized in front to the "idiot box" for hours, just like the good ole' days when I lived in the States. But like "a pig in mud" — whoops, I mean like "a kneidelach in chicken soup" — I could not have been happier. I had been fully sated… **almost**.

When visitors from the States used to ask me: "What do you miss about America?" I could present them with a perpetual list of nostalgic items: frozen juices, fast food, Saran Wrap, a telephone, Reeboks, and of course, American sports. It seemed only natural to list the physical things I missed, and not to mention more esoteric remembrances like good manners, courteous driving or representative government. So while my "spiritual" list is still never-ending, my "material" list has been substantially reduced to include only one item: **American baseball**!

It hits me every time springtime rolls around. It is at this time of year that I usually become forlorn, questioning my Zionist commitment. Even an Antoine Walker "dunk" cannot lift me out of the doldrums. Why? Because in the spring, Pedro Martinez takes the mound.

Yes, during baseball spring, my heart begins its nostalgic palpitations. My stomach craves not a Hillel sandwich,[1] but a Kenmore Square knockwurst with sauerkraut. True, Israel can satisfy my gastronomical needs with its local brand of hotdogs, sour cabbage and mustard (even relish is now available). But baseball? It does not seem to be in the cards.

But we all know that, for a Boston fan, the absence of American baseball coverage in Israel may be a saving grace. I happened to be in the States on sabbatical during two fateful years. The first one was when Bucky Dent of the hated New York Yankees smashed that three-run homer to beat the Red Sox in the playoff game at the end of the season. The second sabbatical caught me suffering through that little grounder that slipped between Bill Buckner's legs, causing the Red Sox's ignominious defeat at the hands of the New York Mets in the 1986 World Series. How my heart did not attack me on those two occasions is beyond me. That should have taught me: Never leave Israel!

So whenever the baseball season gets underway, I remain in Israel, a dedicated Boston fan, longing for the excitement of Nomar Garciaparra hitting the ball off the "Green Monster," yet having to settle for Paul Pierce dribbling the length of the parquet floor, popping a "turn-around jumper" as the final buzzer sounds (hopefully).

That being the case, I guess I will open the freezer; take out some Ben & Jerry's ice cream, topped with hot fudge; reach for a Dr. Brown Root Beer, potato sticks and a fluffernutter (courtesy of Israel's new 24-hours-a-day supermarkets); settle into a comfortable chair in front of the "boob tube" and get absolutely sick, as I "root, root, root for the home team," reluctantly coming to grips with this sad fact: Israel TV's Sunday evening orgy of Celtic basketball will be the closest I will ever come to realizing the perfect aliya!

theatre of the absurd: an aliya play in three acts

ACT I

(Interior Ministry, Jerusalem. A retired couple, having recently made aliya, after a four-hour wait meets with a ministry clerk. The subject — verification of the couple's Jewishness.)

Clerk: *(Addressing the woman)* It is clear that you are Jewish because I see that your son married in Israel in a ceremony that was registered both with the

---

1. A sandwich of contrasting tastes: two pieces of Matzah (unleavened bread) filled with sweet apples, raisins and wine and hot horseradish. It is eaten at the Passover Seder meal.

Ministry of the Interior and the Ministry of Religion.[1] *(Turning to the man)* Now, what proof do you have that you are Jewish?

Man: My papers are in order. I was born in Austria and I submitted my birth certificate to the aliya emissary in the United States that I was born into the Israelite community in Vienna. I also have my entrance certificate into the Jewish Theological Seminary of Vienna.

Clerk: Not good enough. What were your parents' names?

Man: *(Bemused)* Reb (rabbi) Avraham Yitzhak and Sarah Rachel. By the way my children live in Israel.

Clerk: How nice. Doesn't provide proof.

Man: *(Exasperated)* I left Vienna a month before the *Anschluss*.[2] Here is my Jewish wedding certificate.

Clerk: Doesn't look like an official *Ketuba*[3] to me.

Man: *(Desperate)* Here look at this roster of rabbis; I just happen to have it with me. There, that's my name. It says rabbi before my name.

Clerk: Okay, you're in. Welcome to the Jewish state!

ACT II

(Ben Gurion Airport. A family of five has just arrived in Israel on aliya. New immigrants to Israel receive certain "rights," like exemption from custom and taxes on electrical appliances and cars. They are entitled to reduced interest rates on mortgages or rent subsidies from the government. The father approaches passport control after a four-hour wait.)

Clerk: *(Looking quizzically at the passport)* What is this all about?

Father: I have come to Israel quite a bit over the last ten years. I was the director of Jewish college programs in America.

Clerk: It seems that you have come to Israel one too many times.

Father: *(Puzzled)* I led Jewish college students here to encourage them to make aliya.

---

1. According to Jewish law, a child is Jewish if the mother is Jewish.
2. The invasion of Austria by Nazi Germany in 1938.
3. A Jewish marriage contract.

Clerk: You should have thought better of doing that if you yourself wanted to move here.

Father: *(Incredulous)* What seems to be the problem? *(Meanwhile, the family is getting impatient and cranky.)*

Clerk: Well, there is a direct correlation between new immigrant status and immigrant rights. See, what...

Father: *(Cutting the clerk off in mid-sentence — apparently he has acclimated quicker to Israeli society than he cold have ever imagined)* Let me see your supervisor. *(People behind him start screaming as well — at him.)*

(Suddenly two border policemen appear, and take him into an adjacent room, placing the rest of the family in a separate waiting room.)

Child: *(Turning to his mother)* We make aliya, and they arrest Dad? *(The two younger children burst into tears.)*

Mother: I was never big on making aliya.

Supervisor: Don't think for one minute that you are going to get rights.

Father: Are you referring to mortgage rights or just plain old human rights?

Supervisor: Your passports indicates that you have been in Israel so many times as a tourist that you have gone over the allotted time period that is allowed for rights.

Father: I already explained that over the last number of years I brought Jewish college students from the United States to Israel to learn about it, in the hope that they might consider to move here one day. I am an active Zionist, and now I have decided to make aliya.

Supervisor: It's not that simple. Welcome to the Jewish state!

ACT III

(A soldier, a new immigrant from the United States, just finished a special two-and-a-half month army training course in the Negev. According to the Israeli law, he must get written permission from the army to leave the country to visit his father who is quite ill. When he was assigned to this course, he was removed from his regular army unit, and had yet to be transferred to a permanent unit. He goes to his commanding officer at the training base.)

Soldier: *(After a four-hour wait)* I need a pass to go abroad. Until I am assigned to a permanent unit, I was told to get permission from you to leave the country.

Officer: We are only a temporary base, you will have to go to the central command offices at the national army headquarters.

Soldier: But I was there, and they told me to come here.

Officer: Sorry. Try to go the army office in your local city.

Soldier: I did that as well, and I was told to come back here.

Officer: And I have told you that I am not authorized to give you a pass to go abroad.

Soldier: Can you shortcut the system, and transfer me to any unit?

(The soldier receives a referral to another unit, a supply base near his home, just outside of Tel Aviv.)

Soldier: I have been assigned to your unit. Here are my transfer orders. I need a pass to go abroad to visit my sick father.

Officer: I don't want you if you're going abroad. You can't help me.

Soldier: But I'm only going for two weeks. Here is my ticket to prove it.

Officer: Doesn't mean a thing. Maybe you'll stay longer. Maybe you'll move away from Israel for good. You wouldn't be the first to try to pull something like that. Here, take this transfer referral to another a unit. Maybe they can help you.

Soldier: *(Arrives at new base with the referral order in hand)* I have been transferred to your base. But I cannot start my reserve duty for a couple of weeks because I must visit my Dad who is in the States, and is seriously ill.

Officer: Not on my watch. I ain't takin' anyone just to release him.

(After being transferred to five other units, none of which will take him because no one wants someone who immediately requests a pass to go abroad, the soldier returns to the original base. He learns his lesson. He leaves the country illegally on his American passport.[1] Two weeks later he returns to Israel, arriving at passport control at Ben Gurion Airport, and shows the clerk his American passport.)

Clerk: Welcome to the Jewish state. Wait a minute. The computer shows

---

1. Israeli citizens are permitted to hold on to one foreign passport, issued by a "friendly country."

something wrong. You're an Israeli. You should be entering Israel on an Israeli passport.

(At this point, what happens to the father in ACT II, happens to the soldier.)

EPILOGUE

This play is true. The names of the characters have been withheld to protect their privacy. Amazingly, all the actors are still living in Israel. They discovered that Israelis like immigration, it is just immigrants with whom they have difficulty. The gap between the idea and reality is very wide.

---

i can't get no satisfaction

Everyone can list a number of things that absolutely sends him into fits of apoplexy. In my family, one of the things that drives us nuts is the manner in which our clothes dryer seems to consume socks. We are always left with an abundance of solo ones. Also, in most countries, one turns on a faucet and out comes hot water. In my house, I have to make certain that the electric boiler, the gas system and the solar heater all function in a state of harmonious goodwill in order to guarantee that luke-warm water will spill forth into the kitchen sink. Yet the most frustrating aspect of my household is reflected in my total incomprehension as to why, if someone in Cyprus flushes the toilet, I am left shivering in my shower under a trickle of luke-warm water.

The irritations in my private domain that haunt my family's tranquility and stability are not of public concern. However, the particular peculiarities of my Jerusalem home are easily dwarfed by the universal frustrations of Jerusalem's streets.

I admit that I am not much of a dog lover. Ever since our darling Scottish terrier, Timmy, bit my nose when I was in the third grade, I have never held the canine species in the highest esteem. But there was one good thing about Timmy, he always managed to find obscure hiding places to relieve himself. I wish Jerusalem dogs would be as discreet. Instead, what did I witness on a Jerusalem road? My youngest daughter sliding down the entire street to my house at fifty kilometers an hour. What was the cause of her newly acquired agility? You guessed it. Take a walk on a busy street in Israel's capital and you have to be more careful than when dodging land mines in South Lebanon. Driving by the Hilton Hotel, I heard a tourist scream: "Oh shit!" And he meant it — literally. I jog quite frequently and it is rather tiresome to treat each jogging adventure as if I were competing in a high hurdle race. In one of the most beautiful and enchanting places in the world, a person should not have to keep his eyes glued to the ground.

Israel, more than most countries, is truly made up of so many little irritations. Take for example my bank. Just consider these banking hours:

Sunday: Closed all day
Monday & Thursday: 8:30-1:00, 4:00-6:00
Tuesday: 8:30-1:30
Wednesday: 8:30-12:30
Friday: 8:30-12:00
Saturday: Closed

One needs to have a photographic memory to retain all this information. But the real challenge is once one gets inside the bank and waits in line to execute a transaction. The transaction is a relatively simple one, one done all the time. But now the bank teller looks at the customer's request as if it were totally new. "What? You want to change a hundred shekel note for two fifty shekel notes?" Of course, one has to wait in line for quite some time to actually get to the teller. That is because the line is always twice as long as the waiting customer expects. Israel has invented the "invisible line." Just as one approaches the teller, someone invariably butts in and says: "Oh, I was here." It turns out that "here" means that the "buttmeister" claimed a place in line and then went off to tend to one hundred and one other financial matters.

It is impossible not to catch a cold waiting in one's turn because the person standing next in line is literally breathing down one's neck. Israelis suffer from a severe pyschological disorder called, "Gapitis" — fear of gaps. If one studies the elements of "Gapitis," a study known as "Gapology," one discovers that this sickness has reached epidemic proportions in Israel, affecting all areas of society. This fear of gaps translates itself into "tailgating," where such a passion for physical intimacy often winds up in fatal car accidents (see *Chapter Nine*, pages 192-206).

smoke gets in your eyes

My father smoked three packs of cigarettes a day — unfiltered Camels — until he suffered a heart attack at the age of sixty. In the late 1940s and '50s, there was little awareness of the evils of nicotine. Our meals always had a halo of smoke hovering over them. Driving in the car in the winter, when all the windows were closed, was frightening, not only because of the stifling stench, but also because the smoke caused a film of fog in the car that made it virtually impossible for my father to see where he was driving.

The constant smell of smoke offended me so greatly that I never took so much as a puff of a cigarette. Classmates of mine at university were absolutely shocked that I never succumbed to the social pressures of trying marijuana, let alone inhaling it. In this one area, I am grateful to my father because, given the fact that I was a "hippie" and political radical, without this aversion to smoke, I would have wound up in a methadone clinic.

When I arrived in Israel almost thirty years ago, I was appalled at the amount of smoking taking place. Everywhere I turned, someone was blowing smoke in my face — on the buses, in the movie theatres, in the supermarkets and at work.

Today, one rarely encounters smoking on buses. While it is virtually impossible to locate the movie snack bar during intermission due to the layers of smoke that fill the lobby, in the theatre itself, smoking is non-existent. Supermarkets and banks are also better, though not foolproof. Of course what is amazing is that below the "No Smoking" sign one might encounter an ashtray. If this does not fit into a general definition of "schizophrenia," it most certainly serves as a perfect example of a mixed message. Such contradictions exist at restaurants as well, where non-smoking tables still have ashtrays on them. A case in point is Israel's Supreme Court. There are "No Smoking" signs everywhere with ashtrays directly underneath them. Try to explain the "judicial" logic in this. Perhaps the High Court is simply accustomed to the fact that even if there are signs banning one from smoking, few will obey the order. So if one is going to violate the law anyway, why not make it easier for the person? For the most part, in too many public places, Israelis simply ignore the "No Smoking" signs.

Israel has a law that bans smoking in public buildings and government institutions. In addition, restaurants must designate "smoking" and "non-smoking" areas. The law was almost not passed because at the time, the late

Yitzhak Rabin, in addition to being prime minister, also held the Health Ministry portfolio. As a smoker, he refused to sign the law because he felt it would have been hypocritical. The then president of the Supreme Court, Meir Shamgar, should have hauled him into court for his refusal to enact the law. Alas, Shamgar was also a smoker.

But if one really wants to experience smoking at its "hazardous best," then step into any one of Israel's many malls. They are a smoker's haven. There simply is no limitation on smoking in the enclosed non-fresh air environment. It almost seems that all of the nicotine addicts in the country visit the malls to smoke away "to their hearts' content" (or rather discontent). There is an interesting phenomenon at Israel's malls. Individual stores have not been determined as smoking areas de jure, but de facto that seems to be the case. Out of the one hundred odd stores at any given mall, surveys have indicated that no less than seventy-five of them employ salespeople who smoke — in the stores. One would think that if the law does not stretch to one's private business, at least economic considerations would provide enough of a restraining influence on store owners so they would not permit smoking. Apparently, nicotine addiction is so great that self-interest plays no role.

"boker tov, (good morning) eliyahu" or: "hello!" (emphasis on the last syllable)

Israel's past State Comptroller, Judge Miriam Ben Porat, revealed in March, 2000, that between 1988-1992, there were **"severe violations"** by the Israel's Secret Service in interrogations of Palestinian prisoners. During the entire period of the Intifada, human rights groups such as B'Tzelem, Rabbis for Human Rights, The Committee against Torture, and writers from virtually every major Israeli paper were coming out with daily reports of the excessive use of torture. But the State Comptroller's report, eight years late, made it "official." Now one could "legitimately" register shock and outrage. "Boker Tov, Judge Porat. Hel<u>lo</u>!"

This reminds one of the same bewilderment recorded in Israel when Judge Zawabi, as part of the Shamgar Commission on the Baruch Goldstein massacre, suddenly discovered that some Jewish settlers actually terrorized Palestinians. Anyone with a surface knowledge of what happens in the territories has witnessed vigilante settler groups shooting holes in water tanks on top of Palestinian homes, midnight raids into Palestinian villages where windows of houses were smashed, uprooting of olive trees and random beatings of Palestinians. Was not "respected" Jewish settler Moshe Levinger convicted for the shooting death of a young Arab shopkeeper and then raised on his shoulders as a hero when he entered and exited his four-month jail term? "Boker Tov, Judges Zawabi and Shamgar. Hel<u>lo</u>!"

It is the same with Lebanon. Ariel Sharon had the audacity to pontificate and insist that Israel should get out of Lebanon. Any simple soldier who went into the Lebanon War at its outset knew that the whole adventure was one grand mistake. Eighteen years after Sharon led Israel into the fiasco, eighteen years after so many deaths, wounded, missing and nights in shelters, he informs the world that Israel should unilaterally withdraw. "Boker Tov, Mr. Sharon. Hel<u>lo</u>!"

One reads that the Dimona Nuclear Reactor is old and unsafe. As if the smell of the toxic waste being dumped all over the northern Negev is not enough of a warning that a disaster like Chernobyl is around the corner. And when the disaster does occur, a national committee of inquiry, headed by an esteemed general, retired supreme court judge and a prominent scientific academic, will be established to inform the Israeli public that there were not enough safeguards established to prevent the reactor from leaking its radioactive poison. "Boker Tov, Israel. Hel<u>lo</u>!"

Former secret service directors like Ya'acov Perry, as well as Moshe Levinger, a host of other Jewish settlers (particularly some of their spiritual guardians who praise Goldstein's actions) and Ariel Sharon — should all stand trial. They have all committed **"severe violations,"** not only of their professional duties, but also of the moral values of the Jewish people. That is the only way to avoid more "I told you so" situations.

Because Israel is such a small country, because Israelis find it virtually impossible to keep a secret, because Israelis are generally so well informed about what happens in their country, there is no such phenomenon as learning something after the fact. All these "after the fact" committees never contradict what Israelis already know. However, what is contradictory is to set up these committees in the first place, or one should say, in the last place. Sadly, if a

Chernobyl does happen in Dimona, Israelis may not have the luxury to say: "Boker Tov, Eliyahu. He<u>llo</u>!"

❖ ❖ ❖

One could go on and on about life's frustrations in Israel; e.g., only being able to get a credit at a store if an item is returned because there are no cash refunds or visa cancellations tolerated; diet Coke that costs fifty cents more than regular Coke; guards at the malls who stand in silent bewilderment as cars block the emergency lanes (God forbid, should there be a terrorist attack, no ambulance would be able to approach the many gates of the malls); being unable to add the tip on a credit card.

Does any of this matter? Absolutely, because these little frustrations wreak havoc with one's equilibrium. For example, that smoker at the mall demonstrates a total lack of respect for the well-being of others. Such a lack of concern must not become paradigmatic of Israeli society so that there is a general disregard for rules, norms and laws in the country (which unfortunately seems to be the case on the political level). Death on the roads, buses and factories polluting the environment, economic imbalances, and a host of other aberrations are all a result of a lack of respect for one another.

Israel has too many good things "going for it" to turn it into an irritating place to live. There are enough serious challenges in Israel as it is, so no one needs to be bothered with "minor sores." They must not fester into something more intense. Yet reality would hold that Israel's annoyances are often blown out of proportion as Israelis themselves tend to be overly excitable. And so, these frustrations drive Israelis crazy. Instead of being unified by the country's spiritual center, the Wall, Israelis are being driven up it!

Life's Inconsistencies

it's 9:00 a.m., do you now where your children are

I walked into my local bank to carry out a routine financial transaction. Shuffling my papers and reading some bank statements, I sat behind a desk waiting for a bank clerk to appear. When I looked up, the banker was sitting in front of me — wearing pigtails and sporting a huge toothless grin.

It is August in Israel. Kids are finished with their summer camps and programs, and they, like the rest of the country, are on vacation. Israel has a "concentrated vacation" time a few times during the calendar year: during the eight days of Sukkot, the seven days of Passover and the entire month of August. Heaven help one and all should there be an emergency any one of these times, and that poor soldier from the above play would have to get a visa because he had to go through a European country on his way to America. The poor guy would undergo a bureaucratic hassle far outstripping that which he went through with the army, because he would find the Ministry of Interior closed during these periods. But for those Israelis who still must report to work, they have to come up with a creative solution as to what to do with their precious little ones. So... they bring them to their place of employment.

It seems at times as if the entire kindergarten population is running the country: checking out food at the local supermarket, selling sandals in the shoe stores, dispensing drugs in pharmacies and processing bank dealings.

So for those who are stuck at work in August, they drag their kids with them. Everyone suffers under this system: the boss, the parent/employee, co-workers, the client and most significantly, the child. The kid usually brings along crayons and a book. That sums up the creative forms of entertainment that occupy the kid at the office. After a very short time, the "kvetch factor" (fidgeting and complaining) takes hold. The parent with a clenched mouth and very controlled smile tries to humor and then calm the child. When this does not work, the kid is placed at the word processor, where the child proceeds to destroy the keyboard with the dripping chocolate from the ice cream cone bought for the little tot to stem the constant flow of repetitive verbiage, like: (*read with increasing volume and whining*) "I'm starving... I'm starving... I'm starving!" This happens after the kid, banging on the computer, has succeeded in scrambling the entire stock market readings of the bank for which the parent works.

One day in August, I called a municipal office to inquire about my water bill, only to be treated to this response: "My Daddy isn't here. He went to make pee-pee." Serves me right. After all, I did ask about something to do with water!

In such a kid-oriented society, it is amazing that Israel's wonderful child-care centers fold up in August. In most enlightened countries, the issue of child-care is dealt with in the framework of the work place. The institution worries about the needs of the family. If one wants efficiency at a job, a more pleasant and conducive work environment and an appreciative cadre of employees, then care must be taken of the workers' children.

The inconsistency here is all too plain to see. Israel's pre-school and early elementary school education is superb. It is open, creative, bonding and loving. And while the home may provide the same sort of warm environment that is created in these pre-schools and early elementary schools, neither the home nor the schools are available to these young kids for almost three months out of the year. Three-quarters of the year, there is full time attention and excitement for a child, and one-fourth of the time, for those who accompany their parents to their work, there is boredom. The solution does not call for a balance, but rather completion. No less of an institution than Israel's Supreme Court can serve as an example of efficiency and caring. For the month of August, the Court hosts two separate play-groups for its workers' children. The employees pay a reduced price. In setting up this mini-camp, the Court shows itself to be an institution with a human face.

Most people care a great deal about others caring for them and showing respect. Genuine appreciation can go a long way. Serving the needs of a working parent — particularly the children — is the best way to guarantee a decent work ethic and a sane adult society.

Life's Absurdities

yitzhak rabin: the film — by oliver stone

The night that Yitzhak Rabin was assassinated, my father called from Dallas, Texas, in order to console me. He then asked if I was still planning to visit him during the Thanksgiving holiday. I replied that I would be arriving in Dallas on November 22. For a moment, my heart stopped.

What a coincidence. To inadvertently plan to fly to Dallas on the anniversary of the day President John F. Kennedy was assassinated, and to mention that date to my father the same day Rabin was murdered!

It is five years since Rabin's tragic death. With the daily revelations about the General Security Services' (GSS) involvement in a host of areas surrounding Rabin's death, there seem to be many more chilling coincidences pertaining to those events than those that still haunt Kennedy's assassination. While there is no match yet for the numerous books and articles that came out about Kennedy's assassination, Israel has produced enough independent material that calls into question the "lone killer" theory concerning Rabin.

Yet some of the theories are so fanciful that one should not be surprised if American playwright/director, Oliver Stone, would produce a film about the assassination of Rabin to rival his acclaimed movie on the assassination of JFK. It is quite possible that Israel could provide Stone with more believable and suspenseful material than he ever possessed when he made the film on JFK's death.

Stone would have a field day with Israel's equivalent of the FBI, the GSS. Stone might fashion a script based on intelligence information that suggests that the GSS plotted Rabin's assassination. Avishai Raviv,[1] who served as a GSS mole, was to carry out the assassination. Raviv was once a member of ultra-rightist Rabbi Meir Kahana's party. (Kahana himself was rumored to have been on the FBI dole). But why would the GSS want to kill Rabin?

Former Generals Ariel Sharon and Raphael Eitan, sworn cold warriors, strongly opposed the Oslo agreements. Once Oslo II was signed, and the first stages of withdrawal from the West Bank and the Gaza Strip were implemented, they could no longer restrain themselves. Possessing strong ties with the GSS because of their military background, they easily convinced this secretive branch of government to unleash its fury. (In addition they could exact revenge for the Labor Party instigated Kahan Commission that censured both of them for their "deceptive" during the Lebanon War.) The only way to stop the peace process was to "knock off" its leader. A cover was needed, so the GSS infiltrated

---

1. He was a Secret Service Agent provocateur. His exact role in Rabin's assassination is shrouded in mystery.

extreme right-wing religious movements in order to make it look like that they were the ones who carried out the assassination. The GSS would even go so far as to create its own right-wing organization, AYAL, that would cajole other right-wing movements to become more radicalized. Raviv was to be the instigator.

But something went awry. Stone would imply that there were competing forces within the government that wanted Rabin dead. Just as the JFK movie had the FBI and the CIA at each other's throats, so might Stone pit the GSS against the Mossad, Israel's CIA (not yet implicated in the whole mess). Stone might even hint that Shimon Peres, the foreign minister at the time, played the same role in Rabin's assassination that he suggested Lyndon Johnson played in JFK's assassination.

Peres felt that Rabin was moving too slowly in the peace process. He told the Mossad to recruit Baruch Goldstein, the killer of the twenty-nine Moslem worshippers in Hebron. Peres hoped that Goldstein's act would prompt an immediate reaction on the part of Moslem fundamentalists, like Hamas. He was right. Suicide bombings took on a new intensity. Peres was convinced that such a cycle of violence would swing people to the view that Israel would have to accelerate its evacuation of the territories. But the bombings backfired. Rabin, playing into President Weizman's public urgings to slow down the peace process, suspended the talks temporarily. When Weizman came out against the Oslo II agreements, Peres feared that Rabin would further capitulate to the president.

So Peres told the Mossad to recruit right-wing activists from a supposedly repeted institution — Bar Ilan University — to assassinate Rabin. Yigal Amir, a law student, rumored to have once worked at the Israel embassy in Russia, was recruited. (Shades of Lee Harvey Oswald[1]). Peres reasoned that Rabin's murder would create a groundswell of popular support for the peace process, not only on the Palestinian front, but also on the Syrian/Lebanese axis.

Simply put, the Mossad's underground cell got to Rabin before the GSS's underground cell got to him. Amir beat Raviv. Not that it mattered, because both sides, though working at cross-purposes, thought they got what they

---

1. JFK's assassin.

wanted. But with the Israeli penchant to talk too damn much, and point the finger at the other guy, everyone ran for cover (up).

Enter the Shamgar Commission of Inquiry. Stone would have a grand time comparing the Shamgar Commission to the Warren Commission of Inquiry into the death of JFK. For certain, one of Stone's leading actors would be the former president of Israel's Supreme Court, Meir Shamgar. As far as a Stone quasi-fictional/documentary film is concerned, it would make perfect sense that Shamgar be chosen to head the inquiry. Like Chief Justice Earl Warren, Shamgar is a distinguished and highly respected personality. Who better to so innocently serve as a perfect foil for a judicial cover-up? But Stone could point to Shamgar's suspect performance as the head of the National Commission of Inquiry into the murder of Palestinians by Baruch Godlstein, where Jewish settlers barely received a "slap on the wrist" for their provocative and often violent actions against local Palestinians.

Meanwhile, as more information was leaked to the public, Benjamin Netanyahu, would be chosen to run for prime minister on a "reform" ticket. Promising to follow in Rabin's footsteps, but more cautiously, he was elected. The right-wing in the country would now not only be rehabilitated, but also absolved of any blame in the Rabin assassination. This would be crucial because much of the verbal hatred directed at Rabin was laid at Netanyahu's doorstep, and rightfully so as his rhetoric too often crossed the lines of a "fighting opposition." But with ideas taking hold in the public mind that Shimon Peres may have had a hand in the whole sordid affair, Netanyahu and the "right" would be let off the hook.

Israel does not need Oliver Stone to make a fantasy-like film of Rabin's death. Rabin's tragic end has been turned into a sick game of intrigue, some parts of it being sadly true and others grossly exaggerated. But as much as it is trying, the right cannot so readily use these ruses as an excuse to suddenly absolve itself for its extreme and vitriolic rhetoric. Benjamin Netanyahu's presence and behavior at that fateful demonstration in downtown Jerusalem, where a picture of Rabin in a SS uniform was burned, was inexcusable, no matter who created that sign.

After all, Netanyahu's tone at that rally, and at others, helped set the stage for the hatred that stalked Rabin for months prior to his assassination.

What is the ultimate tragedy in all this? So many Israelis, who could not contain their mourning, who could not be consoled, who continue to visit Rabin's grave, are being robbed of their deep sadness at the loss of a truly great statesman, by all sorts of implausible theories and absolute absurdities.

Life's Hypocrisies

a human rights hoax

The right-wing Women in Green organization made an appeal to liberal human rights groups to participate in a demonstration to free Shmuel Cytryn, who was being held in jail under administrative detention. Cytryn was arrested following the assassination of Yitzhak Rabin because of his alleged extreme views. The Women in Green felt that human rights groups, which tend to be left leaning, have always opposed administrative detention as it relates to Palestinians, and so should stand up for a Jewish settler who is similarly held in custody.

One should understand why administrative detention is so objectionable. It is used to arrest individuals who the security arm of the government feels are a threat to the state. The minimal period of internment is six months, with the possibility of an automatic and indefinite extension. The individual is not accused of any specific violation of the law. The normal due processes of law do not accompany the arrest, other than the application of a British Mandate law from 1917 that allowed for administrative detention. (It is ironic that Israel should employ the very method of arrest that it so opposed during the Mandate era.) As a result, in such arrests, no one knows what goes on behind the cells' closed doors. Often those held under administrative detention suffer emotional, if not physical, abuse. Because of the nature of the arrest, it is difficult to uncover what happens to the prisoner. Often an element of collective punishment accompanies administrative detention. A host of other settlers were arrested with Cytryn. (Guilt by association should have no place in an enlightened society.)

So Cytryn, along with the other settlers, sat in jail, without a formal charge having been made against him and without the possibility of any sort of trial. Lacking any judicial procedure, it is unfair to claim that he was a threat to the state. What is a threat to the state is the anti-democratic act of administrative detention.

So why did human rights activists who rail against administrative detention of Palestinians not join in the demonstration to free Shmuel Cytryn? Despite the fact that the request came from the Women in Green, that should not have, a priori, prevented human rights supporters from lending their support. Silent when hundreds of Palestinians were detained under administrative detention, suddenly these right-wing women's consciences are pricked when Jews are held in jail. It is hypocritical of right-wing organizations to expect those in the liberal camp to come to their defense as proof of their evenhandedness, even as they exempt themselves from such a balance.

But even this should not deter human rights activists from defending any individual whose human rights have been violated. But just prior to the demonstration, a number of posters appeared sporting pictures of more than a dozen Jewish settlers who were either being held under administrative detention or were defined as "political prisoners." Shmuel Cytryn's portrait was prominently displayed on the poster. Just below his picture was another protrait, of Ami Popper, who indiscriminately opened fire on Palestinians waiting at an intersection in an Israeli town to be picked up for work, killing seven of them. Ami Popper was not arrested under the terms of administrative detention. He was tried in a court of law and convicted of multiple murders in that same court. He was not a victim of a "witch hunt." Did those who organized the demonstration in defense of Cytryn put up the poster of Popper next to his picture? It is hard to know, but it may not have been entirely coincidental.

Therefore, for human rights workers to have participated in a demonstration to free Shmuel Cytryn would have been a fraud. They felt they would be hiding behind a moral cloak of opposition to administrative detention to ultimately free the likes of Ami Popper. This would have been unacceptable and unconscionable. They refused to be drawn into what they perceived to be a deceptive web.

Shmuel Cytryn, like all kept in administrative detention, should have been charged appropriately or released immediately. But no one should expect human rights activists to participate in demonstrations where they sense convicted murders and administrative detainees are lumped together. This would undermine the legitimacy of protesting the application of administrative detention against any individual. Ultimately, it would harm the cause of opposing administrative detention in general.

Life's Contradictions

from the sublime to the ridiculous

Israel always seems to fluctuate between the mundane and the serious. Often Israelis paint their responses to people and events with broad strokes. There is little room for the gray areas in life. Either you are "for something" or you are "against something." Israelis seem to have a definitive opinion on virtually any and all subjects. When Israelis are asked directions, even if they do not have the foggiest idea where the place is, they will respond categorically. It is difficult to dislodge Israelis from their views on a particular subject. Preconceived notions become the mainstay of their outlook on life. Throw politics and religion into the mix, and the opinions become more extreme. When this polarity moves from the individual to the state, it fosters a bifurcation that can lead a country down many different and/or contradictory paths.

At the fifty-year celebration of the founding of the modern State of Israel, a gala affair took place. Present at the event were not only all of Israel's political, religious, social and intellectual leaders, but also leaders from around the world, including US Vice-President Al Gore. The program was almost cancelled because of a heated controversy over one of the acts. The Bat Sheva Dance Company, one of the most accomplished and internationally acclaimed dance troupes, had planned to perform an interpretive dance to a song from the Haggada of Passover. The Orthodox community felt that it was offensive because of both its message and its delivery. During the dance, each dancer takes off a layer of clothing. After negotiations that lasted right up to the opening curtain, the dance was scrapped. Not more than a few days later, Dana International, a transsexual who, representing Israel, won the Eurovision Song Festival, returned to Israel and was greeted warmly by the Orthodox minister of education.

In the last decade, Jerusalem has seen the ultra-Orthodox community grow at an incredible rate. As noted earlier, fifty-five percent of all first grade pupils in Jerusalem belong to ultra-Orthodox families. Half of the city council members are Orthodox. Yet despite this, the city never has been more open on the Sabbath. Restaurants in various parts of the city, including downtown, are open. Some movie theatres are open on Friday evenings as well as on Saturdays. Every time a street is closed on the Sabbath because the Orthodox community is unwilling to "truck with any moving violation," another cafe-bar opens up.

Israel's Supreme Court is the model of fairness, equality and enlightenment. When other institutions fail to maintain the principles of a free and democratic society, the High Court of Justice comes to the country's aid. Its rulings in so many areas have provided a necessary safeguard against some of the reactionary tendencies in the country one witnesses from time to time. While one may disagree with such highly charged emotional rulings as the ones handed down in the cases of Jon Demanjuk[1] and the Palestinian deportees, one cannot question the integrity and courage of the Court's decisions. Despite the extremely sensitive issues that have come before the Court, its judges have managed to steer clear of political and public pressures. But like every citizen in the country, even judges must abide by the rule of justice. No matter how legally erudite they may be, they too are human, as so aptly stated by the past chief justice of the Supreme Court, Meir Shamgar, when he concluded the case against Demanjuk with the words: "This was the proper course for judges who cannot examine the heart and mind, and therefore can only rely on what their eyes see and read. The matter is closed, but not complete. Absolute truth is not the prerogative of the human judge."

So wherein lies the contradiction? How can it be that Israel's Supreme

---

1. Demanjuk was charged with being "Ivan the Terrible" who was responsible for thousands of deaths during the Holocaust. His original conviction was overturned by Israel's Supreme Court because of "reasonable doubt."

Court, with such an impeccable reputation of integrity and decency, has never had as a permanent appointment an Israeli Arab judge (only recently was there a temporary assignment)? Israeli Arabs make up almost twenty percent of the population in Israel. While Israel's politicians may refuse to appoint an Israeli Arab as a minister or include Israeli Arab parties in the coalition, one would expect different behavior from judges who stand above political considerations.

As safeguarded in Israel's Declaration of Independence, the Supreme Court is duty bound to provide "complete equality of social and political rights to all its citizens, without regard to religion, race or gender." The appointment of judges from varied ethnic and religious backgrounds provides the Court with a necessary divergence of views that can only enhance its decisions. More so, it is impossible to believe that in Israel there are no Israeli Arabs qualified to sit on the High Court. Only a genuine commitment to equal representation of all sectors of society will motivate the necessary search for judges from all backgrounds.

So Israel's Supreme Court, which has proven itself committed to the principles of social justice and equality, has failed to meet its own standards by not appointing someone from the Israeli Arab sector a permanent Supreme Court judge.

It seems too easy in Israel to make the transition from the concrete to the esoteric, from the sublime to the ridiculous, back to the sublime and again back to the ridiculous. Kibbutzim, still espousing a philosophy of socialism, live as capitalists.

Castigating inflammatory rhetoric by Arab leaders against Israel, Israel's foreign minister screams hysterically from the Knesset rostrum: "If one Arab bullet is shot at one Israeli, Lebanon will go up in flames. It will be blood for blood, a child for a child." An Israeli prime ministerial candidate violates one of the Ten Commandments, "You shall not commit adultery," and is pronounced a person who is "good for the Jews." A salesperson treats a customer as a hostile buyer, the man who led Israel into Lebanon calls for unilateral withdrawal, gays and lesbians who are treated as pariahs in the general society and as "abominations" in the ultra-Orthodox world enjoy the most far-reaching and liberal laws that grant them full rights, and the Israeli government spends money for an American Jewish kid from Miami Beach to come to Israel for free while an Israeli Jewish kid from an underprivileged home cannot afford to go on a school trip. The list of contradictions is never-ending.

Life's Excitement

the wonder of israel

All countries experience life's frustrations, inconsistencies, absurdities, hypocrisies and contradictions. Israel does not have a monopoly on the ambiguities that life offers up. But Israel seems to embrace them with a passion and excitement that few other countries can emulate. The pendulum moves so furiously back and forth between ecstasy and depression, that it is impossible at any given moment to measure the mood of the country. No single emotion expresses at any one time what Israel is all about. Israelis live in perpetual uncertainty and with continual perplexity. They occupy a space and time somewhere between the raptures of heaven and the ravages of hell. "Bi-polarity" wins the day. Israelis walk out of their dark and depressing "sealed rooms" during the Persian Gulf War to the jubilant roar of jumbo jets lighting up the sky with 14,000 immigrants being flown to Israel from Ethiopia. The search for a more even-keeled and less emotionally charged life that brings with it calm stability may be in vain; and while Israelis may claim to want some calm in their lives, it is difficult to imagine a passive and/or uninvolved Israeli.

The frenzy of Israeli life is what makes the Israeli such an intriguing personality. It brings about rapid changes that just maybe what is needed to adjust to the complex realities of living in the Middle East. Yitzhak Rabin, the architect of Israel's "break their bones" policy in containing the Intifada finds himself shaking hands with Yasir Arafat, the architect of the Intifada. Was Rabin a closet "schizophrenic," intent on destroying his enemy while secretly harboring a wish to embrace him? Was Menachem Begin a clandescent "schizophrenic," waging war in Lebanon and at the same time standing in silent respect at a vigil against the war that was parked outside his residence? It is this sort of fragmentation of thought and action that not only makes life in Israel interesting, but just perhaps serves as a creative means to deal with the complexities of Israeli life.

In no other country is the excitement of contrasting emotions better experienced than in Israel. No sooner did Israel declare itself as an independent state than eight Arab armies tried to destroy it. At the beginning of June, 1967, it seemed as if Israel was on the brink of destruction, as once again the Arab world threatened to "drive the Jews into the sea." Then came the exhilarating victory of the Six Day War, which eventually came unraveled as the reality of ruling two million Palestinians set in. With great joy, Israel sent off its first significant delegation to the 1972 Olympics, only to sadly have its athletes return in coffins, after terrorists had slaughtered them in cold blood. On Yom Kippur in 1973, Syria and Egypt invaded Israel, driving across the temporary borders established in the Six Day War. But within days, fear turned to relief as Israel pushed on toward Cairo and Damascus. Is this what Israel wished for, to lord its power over the capitals of Egypt and Syria? And there he stood at the Knesset rostrum, only four years later, President Anwar Sadat of Egypt, stretching his hand out in peace, to be seized by the late prime minister of Israel, Menachem Begin, perceived as a sworn enemy of peace. The riddle of light and darkness continues.

All this drama is interspersed with the miracles of daily life in Israel: the absorption of two diverse immigrant populations at the tenuous incipient stages of the nation's statehood, the Jews of Europe and the Jews of North Africa; the resurgent identity of Soviet Jews in the early 1970s that brought almost one million of them to Israel's shores in a twenty-five year span; the airlift of a lost tribe of Jews from Ethiopia; the rescue of 210 hostages thousands of miles from Israel. Living with the intensity and precariousness of daily life, Israelis enter into flights of ecstasy over the seemingly most mundane events: a first-place finish at the Eurovision Song Contest, a bronze medal at the Olympics, a victory over the Russian basketball team.

Fear and hope, sadness and joy, shame and pride — antonyms of the Israeli collective being — fashion the country's national character. The drama of life in Israel produces contrasting emotions, which form the very essence of an exciting, yet multiple personality.

EPILOGUE

It is more than one hundred years since the establishment of modern Zionism. Its initial ideological expression found its practical fulfillment in aliya and settlement in an old-new land. In 1881, the first wave of immigrants arrived in Palestine, thus creating the new Yishuv (see *Chapter 10*, page 222, footnote 1). At the very outset, ideological conflicts marked their arrival. They were called the *Biluim*, which was a mnemonic for *"Beit Ya'acov l'chu v'nalcha"* ("O House of Jacob, let us get up and go"). However, the full quote, which a Jew recites before reading from the Torah, is: *"Beit Ya'acov l'chu v'nalcha **b'or Adonai**"* ("O House of Jacob, let us get up and go **in the light of the Lord**"). Secular immigrants excluded the theological underpinning of an obvious Divine command to move to the Land of Israel. Already at the outset of the new Jewish enterprise, a polarity was established.

Yet beyond this bifurcated beginning, the events that marked the pre-state years to the present have been so dramatic that they naturally have elicited multiple responses. The tragic devastation that the Holocaust wrought upon the Jewish people and the almost immediate joyous establishment of an independent Jewish state after two millennia should have been more than enough to stretch the emotional heartstrings of the Jew, collectively and individually. One needs an extremely stable psychological constitution to survive such incredible historical turmoil, to cope with such an emotionally laden transition from destruction to reconstruction, to go from the brink of death to the breath of a new life — all within the tiny span of only one blink of an eye.

Many of the political and social aspects of the early dreams of the first Zionists are a reality, but many are still elusive. The return to a national home was to be accompanied by a social and spiritual renaissance. The hope was that the founding of the modern state of Israel would go far toward the development of an *Am Segula*, a "chosen people" of unusual quality (see *Chapter 1*, page 23). Indeed, to many, a national home without this Divine concept was unacceptable. Only the forming of a unique society could make the Zionist adventure worthwhile. Yet to some, "normalization" would be enough. The Jews would finally have their own land, and be involved, like other nations, in the full spectrum of human life — for good and for bad. These two desires constantly confront each other, causing perpetual tension and conflict.

Israel's first prime minister, David Ben Gurion, expressed these two contrasting themes well: "Two basic aspirations underlie all our work in this country: to be a nation like all the nations, and to be different than all the nations..." Herein lies the schizophrenic wonderment of life in the Land of Israel. As Israelis move into the new millennium, they must maintain their desire to fulfill the Divine promise of becoming a "light unto the nations," even as they confront the modern realties of everyday existence. "The day is short, the task is great... It is not up to you to complete the work, but you are not free to desist from it..." (*Sayings of the Fathers*, 2:20-21).